# God's Missionary People

# God's Missionary People

**Rethinking the Purpose
of the Local Church**

## Charles Van Engen

*Foreword by Arthur F. Glasser*

**BAKER BOOK HOUSE**
Grand Rapids, Michigan 49516

Copyright © 1991 by Baker Books
a division of Baker Book House Company
P.O. Box 6287, Grand Rapids, MI 49516-6287

Second printing, October 1993

*Printed in the United States of America*

**Library of Congress Cataloguing-in-Publication Data**

Van Engen, Charles Edward
    God's missionary people: rethinking the purpose of the local church / Charles Van
Engen; foreword by Arthur F. Glasser
    p. cm.
    Includes bibliographical references and index.
    ISBN 0-8010-9311-2
    1. Mission of the church. 2. Church. 3. Missions. I. Title.
BV601.8.E54   1991

                                                            250—dc20
                                                            91-23586
                                                            CIP

to
hundreds of pastors and missionaries
from all six continents
whose love for, and commitment to,
the Church's call to be in mission in the world
has given me the energy and vision for this work.

# Contents

# *Figures*

# *Foreword*

I t is a tremendous privilege to be asked to write the foreword to this book, not unlike the experience of introducing a stranger to an audience that one knows desperately needs to hear what he has to say. I believe Charles Van Engen is uniquely qualified to shape the thinking of the emerging leadership of the Church. Although the future is crowded with imponderables, there are certainties that challenge the venturesome. He knows what these certainties are. Further, this book demonstrates his competence to lead the venturesome through the complex biblical and theological issues that are fundamental to the task God has given to his people.

Why am I so expansive about this book and its potential for worldwide significance and usefulness? In 1955 church missiologist and historian Kenneth Scott Latourette, then professor emeritus at Yale University, was asked to write the introduction to a book entitled *The Bridges of God*. Upon studying the manuscript he became quite solemn over his privilege. Here indeed was "a tract for the times." I can well imagine the sense of excitement that must have gripped him as he began to carry out his task. And what was his concluding statement? . . . "To the thoughtful reader this book will come like a breath of fresh air. . . . It is one of the most important books on missionary methods that has appeared in many years."

All those who have been in the vanguard of mission thinking and practice throughout the years since *The Bridges of God* first appeared will unhesitatingly agree with this judgment. Professor Latourette's commendation of Donald A. McGavran's initial contribution to missiological thought has stood the test of time. *The Bridges of God* became the most read missionary book in 1956, and the church growth movement was

11

impelled by its ideas to gather momentum. That movement has yet to run out of steam.

It is not presumptuous to expect that this initial study by Charles Van Engen will precipitate much discussion within the churches about themselves and their mission to the world. Imagine what would happen if each local congregation came to see itself as a local expression of "God's missionary people." Those of us who have studied his doctoral dissertation already look to him for guidance in our reflection on the true Church and her relation to the real world. My copy of *The Growth of the True Church* is heavily marked on each of its 517 pages. But now, with this more basic study of the role of the local congregation in the missionary purpose of God, we have something that Christians everywhere will undoubtedly find most helpful.

First, Charles Van Engen personally disclaims party association. Somehow, I have always found it a bit difficult to classify him. This is characteristic of the man. At all times he remains himself—unique, believing, critical, and always friendly. His heart is invariably with those who stand under the Word of God and are concerned to maintain experiential fellowship with Jesus Christ. Of course, he is deeply committed to historic, biblical Christianity, but he cannot be easily pigeonholed. Here is one who truly embodies that great affirmation of David: "I am a companion of all who fear you, of those who keep your precepts" (Ps. 119:63 NRSV).

As a result he is neither parochial in his churchmanship nor polemic in the manner in which he shares the results of his disciplined reflection. He is a member of the whole household of faith and reflects a breadth of reading that brings enrichment and balance to the themes he discusses. No segment of the Church will complain that its distinctives have not been given a careful hearing. Van Engen is willing to defend the faith, but he never descends to the level of either personal criticism or wholesale condemnation.

Second, although Van Engen has the privilege of being a "missionary kid" and has enjoyed long association with the Reformed tradition, he is not interested in extending without revision the European or North American distinctives of the Reformed Faith. He listens to the theologians in the two-thirds world. This means that his understanding of the continuing presence of Jesus Christ in the midst of his people obligates him to discern what "the Spirit is saying to the churches" today throughout the world. He recognizes the tragic presence of error which constantly challenges truth, but he is convinced that the Spirit continues to give relevant insights from Scripture to the faithful concerning their worship, their life, and their service. He recognizes that not all churches will develop precisely the same agendas, but he believes that each has something to contribute.

As a result, Van Engen bows to the essentiality of ecumenical encounter. You will be impressed by the wide range of authors he has consulted and whose books he encourages you to study. You will especially appreciate his effort to ascertain themes that particularly and comprehensively reflect the will of God for his people today. He refuses to concede that the only material worthy of study today comes from his or any other narrowly defined tradition. The best of us "sees as in a mirror, dimly" and "knows only in part" (1 Cor. 13:12, 13). For instance, he concedes that long before evangelicals were concerned about the poor, the oppressed, and those who live a marginal existence, other segments of the Church were seeking to address the theological implications of these realities. He has been willing to learn from them. I particularly like his constant willingness to recognize the contributions of others and to express his indebtedness to them.

Third, the author is no armchair strategist. The son of missionaries to Mexico, a bilingual, cross-cultural communicator of the Christian faith, he knows the folly of addressing complex church-mission problems in a detached, theoretical manner. This is what lends weight and authenticity to his theological reflection. Although he uses the insights of the behavioral scientists to clarify, he does not make the tragic mistake of some earlier church growth writings and depart from Scripture in the interest of "fierce pragmatism." As a result he endorses contextualization but condemns manipulation. He believes in theology from above, but he also reminds us to listen to those whose sensitivity to the human condition presses them to evaluate situations from below. Van Engen demonstrates, not rigid adherence to old methods and sacrosanct structures, but openness to the need to provide "at-homeness" for the churches in whatever culture they take root, emerge, and grow.

Fourth, this study is nothing less than a clear-eyed focus on the strangely neglected, even lost, key to all missiological reflection—the local church. When first approached to write this foreword, I thought of a noteworthy statement made in 1962 by Johannes Blauw, then secretary of the Netherlands Missionary Council. In 1960 Dr. Blauw had been commissioned by the Department of Missionary Studies, jointly run by the International Missionary Council and the World Council of Churches, to survey and appraise the work in biblical theology over the previous thirty years on the nature and necessity of the Church's mission to the world. The book he produced, *The Missionary Nature of the Church*, died an early death because of the massive shift in theological reflection then overtaking mainline churches. Inevitably, Blauw's work held little interest, although evangelicals were greatly helped by its biblical insights. Unfortunately, missiologists in Blauw's day had yet to explore what all this should mean to the local congregation.

Be that as it may, toward the end of his biblical review he made a singular affirmation: "There is no other Church than the Church sent into the world, and there is no other mission than that of the Church of Christ." Van Engen refers to this statement several times as he points out its significance. Whereas Blauw wants us to reflect on all that the Bible states about the role of the Church sent into the world by its Head, the Lord Jesus Christ, it is Van Engen who has taken up the challenge to relate this to the local congregation. That is what makes his book so timely.

Further, Van Engen has subjected himself to a careful review of the extensive missiological literature produced, largely since 1960, by those committed to the Church's historic, biblical faith. His review will convince you that the Spirit of God in our day has been raising up a new generation of missiologists. They are surfacing in all parts of the world and within diverse church traditions. And their concern is for the completion of the still unfinished task of world evangelization.

This book demands careful reading and critical study. Don't let tradition, vested interests, caution, or sheer inertia keep you from grappling with its massive themes. Then ask whether your understanding of the local congregation or your experience of its life, worship, and witness approximate the realities God intends should characterize the Church.

When I finished reading this book, I could not but say—almost out loud—"At last! Here is the book we've all been waiting for!" I believe you will say the same.

Arthur F. Glasser
dean emeritus
School of World Mission
Fuller Theological Seminary
Pasadena, California

# *Preface*

**T**he class roared with laughter. But the tall, solemn African pastor declared that he had not been joking: "Brother Chuck, you asked what is the least we would need to still have the Church? I am serious when I say all I need is a bell. I can walk out into the bush in my country, stand under a tree, begin ringing the bell, and the Church gathers."

A woman from Brazil was shaking her head in disagreement: "In my country we don't need a bell. All we need is people and the Bible. Both the Roman Catholic base ecclesial communities[1] and the small Prot-

---

1. Beginning in Brazil in the 1960s, and spreading throughout Latin America, groups of Roman Catholics began meeting in close-knit communities to reflect on the relation of Scripture to their socio-political and economic situation. Often meeting without the presence of a priest, these groups came to be known as "base ecclesial communities" (CEBs). They have had a tremendous impact on politics and the church in Latin America—especially as they became closely related to the development of Latin American Liberation Theology. Perhaps the best work on the subject is by an evangelical Protestant. See Guillermo Cook, *The Expectation of the Poor: Latin American Basic Ecclesial Communities in Protestant Perspective* (Maryknoll, N.Y.: Orbis, 1985). See also Cook, "The Protestant Predicament: From Base Ecclesial Community to Established Church: A Brazil Case Study" in *International Bulletin of Missionary Research* (July 1984): 98–102; Leonardo Boff, *Ecclesiogenesis: The Base Communities Reinvent the Church* (Maryknoll, N.Y.: Orbis, 1986); Samuel Escobar, "Base Church Communities: A Historical Perspective" in *Latin American Pastoral Issues*, 14.1 (June 1987): 24–33; J. B. Libanio, "Base Church Communities (CEBs) in Socio-Cultural Perspective" in *Latin American Pastoral Issues*, 14.1 (June 1987): 24–47; Rene Padilla, "A New Ecclesiology in Latin America" in *International Bulletin of Missionary Research*, 11.4 (Oct. 1987): 156–64; Valdir Steuernagel, "Base Ecclesial Communities: An Evangelical Reflection" in *World Evangelization* (May–June 1988): 17–18; John Welsh, "Comunidades Eclesiais de Bais: A New Way to be Church" in *America*, 154.5 (Feb. 8, 1986): 85–88.

estant congregations have something in common. They gather as the disciples of Jesus Christ to study Scripture, to reflect on its meaning for their lives, and to encourage each other to live out the implications of the gospel in their context. They know that where two or three are gathered together in Christ's name, he has promised to be in their midst" (Matt. 18:20).

The deep wisdom of the brother from Africa and the sister from Brazil brought back memories of my own involvement in rural evangelism in southern Mexico. Arriving in some remote town, we would ask permission of the town authorities to carry out a public evangelism event. Through the next few hours we set up a podium, connected a speaker system, a string of light bulbs, and a movie projector to a portable generator, and arranged some boards for benches. By the time the sun set the Church would be gathered, the Mexican pastor proclaimed the Word of God, a film presented the life of Christ, and inquirers were invited to accept Jesus Christ as Savior and become active members of his Church.

Almost all of my life I have been involved in some way with the Church, but especially during the last twenty years my involvement in theological education has compelled me to ask the deep and difficult questions about the purpose of the Church. And as I have lived, talked, walked, and worked with hundreds of pastors and missionaries, I have been increasingly impressed with the need to formulate the purpose of the Church, and particularly the purpose for which the local congregation exists.

Already I am drawing a line of distinction that will become increasingly important from this point on. There is the *church*, that congregation of believers in fellowship who seek God's purpose. There is also the *Church*, that body purchased with the blood of Jesus and called to be his people in the world. God's missionary people are called to be the Church in the church. We will definitely speak of churches but the purpose of the Church will dominate our interest.

Therefore we need to understand what the Church is. Lyle Schaller points out in "Marks of a Healthy Church"[2] that there are several approaches to our understanding, and he specifically mentions three: (1) the *Model Church Approach*—using certain congregations as examples or models for others; (2) the *Larger Sample Approach*—using statistical analyses and sociological studies to point out certain outstanding characteristics which might be desirable, and (3) the *Biblical Search Approach*—which takes into account the biblical examples, injunctions, and propositional truths about the Church.

2. *Parish Paper* (New York: RCA, 1983), 1.

This book works primarily within the third method. The strength of this approach is that it allows us to deal with certain given truths which have been instituted by Jesus Christ. We can be certain of our starting point, and we have a basis for judging what should or should not be included in the notion of *Church*. The strong norm within this approach gives us direction, impulse, motivation, and confidence which the other two approaches lack. At the same time, because this approach begins with ideal, theoretical, logical truths, it must constantly be put to the test of translation into real life; it must always remain in touch with the church as you and I know it. The meaning of the biblical-theological approach must always be held in dynamic, creative tension with Schaller's "model churches" and be compared for relevance with the findings of the "larger sample" approach.

Pastors, missionaries, mission executives and church planters all are involved in calling churches into existence. Ever since Henry Venn and Rufus Anderson[3] promoted the idea that mission organizations should develop self-supporting, self-propagating and self-governing congregations, the question has been with us as to the nature of the Church we are creating through these churches. Unfortunately, mission practitioners, mission executives, national and international church planters, and church growth specialists too seldom ask the difficult prior questions regarding the nature of the churches they are organizing. This book is meant to stimulate just such reflection. The more I have pursued this investigation the more convinced I have become that the Church is a marvelous, mysterious creation of God that takes concrete shape in the lives of the disciples of Jesus as they gather in local congregations and seek to contextualize the gospel in their time and place. My thesis is that as local congregations are built up to reach out in mission to the world, they will become in fact what they already are by faith: *God's missionary people.*

3. During the mid-1800s Venn served as general secretary of the Church Missionary Society of the Church of England and worked closely with Anderson, corresponding secretary of the American Board of Commissioners for Foreign Missions. Although Venn was an Anglican and Anderson a Congregationalist, they shared a common perspective on the ecclesiological goal of mission, which came to be known as the "Three-Self Formula." Under that formula mission churches should become self-supporting, self-propagating, and self-governing as quickly as possible. R. Pierce Beaver believed these two men to be "the two greatest Protestant missionary thinkers and administrators of the nineteenth century, whose influence lasted until the middle of the twentieth" (R. Pierce Beaver, *To Advance the Gospel: Selections from the Writings of Rufus Anderson* [Grand Rapids: Eerdmans, 1967], 5). See also Charles Van Engen, *The Growth of the True Church* (Amsterdam: Rodopi, 1981), 267–77; Bengt Sundkler, *The World of Mission* (Grand Rapids: Eerdmans, 1965), 41, and Harvie Conn, *Theological Perspectives on Church Growth* (Nutley, N.J.: Presbyterian and Reformed, 1976), 110.

I dedicate this work to the pastors and missionaries who lovingly sharpened my thinking with questions about the local church and then enthusiastically joined me in seeking substantive biblical and theological answers. I owe to them a debt of gratitude for their whole-hearted support and assistance with this project. The pastors, missionaries, and mission executives who have interacted with this material have also left their imprint on it.

I want to express my deepest gratitude to Fuller Theological Seminary for giving me a short sabbatical leave, during which I have been able to complete this manuscript. I thank God for my wife, Jean, and recognize with gratitude her labor of love in proofreading the manuscript. I praise God for my children, Amy, Anita, and Andrew, who have supported me and my work, while at the same time keeping me in touch with the most basic issues of the Christian life. Finally, I want to express my appreciation for Baker Book House and Reformed Bible College for sponsoring the 1989 Baker Lectures in Missions, which provided a forum from which to present some of this material.

My prayer is that this work will stimulate missionaries and pastors to reflect more deeply on the purpose for which their congregations exist, and the way in which their congregations can clearly and boldly demonstrate the good news of the gospel in their context.

Charles Van Engen
Pasadena, California
October 1990

# *Introduction*

I t was a day full of ambivalent feelings at the annual meeting of the American Society of Missiology. At breakfast some of us mulled over the announcement that about forty Roman Catholic parishes would be closed in Detroit, Michigan. On the way to the first presentation, a colleague enthusiastically described the growth of the church in Mainland China. His visit to a number of house churches there had brought about a deep transformation in his perspective of how the Church might live in the world.

Then came the first conference presentation on the base ecclesial community movement in Brazil, a renewal motivated by personal piety that we heard was wonderfully conscious of God's revelation in Scripture and painfully aware of the socioeconomic realities of the life of the masses. My thinking stretched by the nature, scope, and form of these dynamic grassroots communities of believers, I left that meeting exuberant and hopeful, full of new vision for what the Church could be in mission.

My next stop was to see a friend who pastored a church in that city. That evening we talked about the daily grind of his life. He explained how the church's life was organized around the traditional areas of worship, education, congregational care, and community outreach. He explained to me how insulated the congregation was from its surrounding transitional urban neighborhood. He complained that there was not enough time to administer all four arenas of the church's life; new staff were needed. Yet the members lacked commitment, so the church was in a financial bind. He felt all alone, managing the pressures of ministry and maintaining a deteriorating building.

19

I was abruptly brought back to earth; here was reality! Yet as I listened to my friend, I began to discern that he and his church had no integrated vision of what they were about. There was no cohesive understanding of their purpose or of how the congregation interacted with its environment. The extent of their concept of "mission" was that it meant money the church itself desperately needed was being sent away to support some missionaries, the denominational mission programs, and a daughter of the church who worked with a parachurch agency in Asia. As far as I could tell, although my friend had been in ministry for a number of years, he had never asked why the congregation he served existed, why it had been placed where it was, what its mission should be, or what the priority areas of its ministry ought to be in that context. My friend had been trained in a fine seminary—trained to maintain the members, keep the members happy, and be paid by the members. My heart ached for him, as it ached for the pastors in Mexico City, Nairobi, Caracas, and Seoul whose ministries seem to suffer from similar weaknesses.

Around the world one of the most neglected areas of missiological research has been ecclesiology. Rather than finding new avenues for creatively contextualizing the congregation so that it might represent the gospel, we have exported church polities, church forms, church structures, and church traditions, superimposing them on all the cultures we have encountered. Although we have become conscious of the relationship of gospel and culture, we have yet to understand how drastically we must rethink that relationship.

When I lay down to sleep that night I was more convinced than ever that some deep, searching, hard, bold questions must be asked about the nature and purpose of our congregations. And those questions must be asked in a way that would yield answers unique to the dynamics of each congregation. To develop a congregational missiology for the Church is no longer optional. Contrary to some predictions of the 1960s, local congregations are here to stay. But their quality of life is in jeopardy. They will either limp along struggling to maintain what they have, or they will rise to new life because they catch a vision of their unique purpose and mission within their individual context. This vision involves more than developing a philosophy of ministry—it impels action deeper than a call for better goal-setting and administration. Local congregations the world over will gain new life and vitality only as they understand the missiological purpose for which they alone exist, the unique culture, people, and needs of their context, and the missionary action through which they alone will discover their own nature as God's people in God's world.

The purpose of this book is to excite missionaries, mission executives, church planters, pastors, and leaders concerning their strategic role in building missionary congregations in the world. It calls leaders of local congregations to equip members to discover their nature, doing the hard task of setting priorities and goals . . . of developing strategies, personnel, and structures which participate in the work of the Holy Spirit. It demands that the Church become in fact what it is by faith.

This study includes observations made by those who, though representing different and often conflicting traditions, nevertheless display surprising agreement about the Church's missional purpose. Throughout this study we are involved in *teologia viatorum,* a theology-on-the-way. In our learning process we will consult many traditions, searching for a degree of consensus concerning the missionary nature of the Church. As we develop various themes we will not attempt to provide all the answers, nor suggest all the possible strategies, nor critique authors and traditions. Rather, our purposes are to introduce the reader to the rich goldmine of missionary theology of the Church, and to inspire the reader to take a closer look at the literature that can inform personal ministry and mission. We hope the reader will look further into the literature, consider the issues presented, and apply this crucial perspective of the Church to the local congregation. At the end of many sections of this book bibliographical notations offer helpful resources for study. My prayer is that this volume may in some small way contribute to the building of missionary congregations around the world.

# PART 1

# Local Churches

## *God's Missionary People*

# 1

# *A New Perspective of the Local Church*

I n 1980 I built a new house on the outskirts of Tapachula, a city on the semitropical, southernmost tip of Chiapas, Mexico. In front of the house I planted a small "framboyan" tree, about a foot tall. I cared for that tree: I watered it during dry season and trimmed it during rainy season; I shaped it; I sprinkled ant poison around it nearly every month to keep leaf-cutter ants away. And as the tree grew I had to fix the sidewalk because the roots pushed it up out of place. I spent countless hours caring for that tree, and it was worth it. After three years my tree was taller than the two-story house beside it, and its branches shaded the front yard, the living room, and my study. Its foliage turned the torrents of rain into a cooling mist. It provided a place to rest for many a passerby, and its bright orange blossoms fed a number of hummingbirds. The little sapling I planted was more like an overgrown weed. But I knew that out of the small seedling would emerge a tree.

Similarly, thousands of people plant little round bulbs in the fall, but they don't say they are planting small roots or little balls—they say they are planting tulips! People who plant don't look at what they see. They look forward to what will emerge.

The Church[1] of Jesus Christ is in many ways like a tree or a tulip. Around the world the Church has been planted small and weak and has grown to become a source of protection, of new life, and of increased health and nourishing spiritual food. For the first time in the history of humanity we find the Church spanning the globe, sheltering one-and-one-half billion people who in one way or another confess allegiance to Jesus Christ and call themselves Christian.[2] We are now at the beginning of a totally new era in the history of the world and of Christianity, a "global discipling era" characterized by "total global access to all peoples of the earth."[3] For the first time the Church is large and encompassing enough to be the missionary people of God. The opportunity exists for the one holy, universal, and apostolic community to witness to every tongue, tribe, and nation. And as local congregations are built up to reach out, they will emerge from their sapling stage to be their true nature, bearing fruit as missionary people.

In order for missionaries, church planters, and pastors to build missionary congregations, however, they must first gain a new vision of the Church in its local setting. The sapling already has its tree nature. It lacks maturity. This new perspective is extraordinarily exciting, for it sees in our nature all that Jesus Christ said we would become. Jesus expressed this perspective of emerging when he compared the Kingdom of heaven to a mustard seed and to leaven (Matt. 13:31, 33). In both similes the emphasis is not on what is but on what can be. We must recognize that the potential will not simply pop into existence; future maturity begins with present immaturity. Something becomes a catalytic trigger to change what is. The dough does not rise without that little touch of leaven. The mustard seed does not grow into a tree unless the seed is planted.

The Church derives its dynamism to emerge from its close association with the coming of the Kingdom of God. The impelling force of the Kingdom of God moves life from the "already" to the "not-yet" through the action of God in the power of the Holy Spirit. The Church is the spiritual body of Christ in the world. It can never be more fully complete than it is as the one holy catholic and apostolic people of God. Yet the Church *is* called to grow toward greater fulness in its nature. In this dialectic ten-

---

1. Throughout this work, the capitalized word *Church* will be used to mean the universal Church of Christ of all ages and in all places, and the lower-case words *church, congregation,* or *worshiping community* will be used to speak of those local groups of persons who gather on the basis of a common faith in Jesus Christ.

2. See David Barrett, *World Christian Encyclopedia* (Oxford: Oxford University Press, 1982); idem, "Silver and Gold Have I None: Church of the Poor or Church of the Rich?" *International Bulletin of Missionary Research,* 7.4 (Oct. 1983): 146–51.

3. See David Barrett, "Five Statistical Eras of Global Mission," *Missiology,* 12.1 (Jan. 1984): 33.

sion between what is and what is to become, the Church's position in the Kingdom infuses it with a unique quality to emerge as the mysterious creation of God, created not by human effort, but by Jesus Christ through the operation of the Spirit. Yet God's mysterious creation is in fact the spiritual body of Christ, and it grows as that body through the "equipping of the saints for the work of service, to the building up of the body of Christ" (Eph. 4:12, NASB). The Church, like a seed, already contains within itself the generative power necessary to become the plant of which it is seed. It will not become any other plant. But the seed's growth demands careful planting, watering, and care so that God may give the increase (1 Cor. 3:6). Karl Barth asked the key questions regarding this perspective of the emerging church: "How far does [the Church] correspond to its name? How far does it exist in a practical expression of its essence? How far is it in fact what it appears to be? How far does it fulfill the claim which it makes and the expectation which it arouses?"[4]

## The Relation of Mission and Church in Modern Missiology

During the last half century mission theorists, sociologists of religion, ecclesiologists, and mission practitioners have become increasingly aware of the urgent need for a new vision of local congregations as God's missionary people. The call for a new congregational missiology has come from at least three different directions. First, since the 1930s missiologists have called for a closer relationship between the concept of *mission* and the idea of *church*, focusing discussion on the missionary nature of the congregation. Second, sociologists of religion have recently begun to stress the strategic importance of the congregation. Third, modern ecclesiologists since Barth and Dietrich Bonhoeffer have called for a new way of envisioning the church, suggesting a new paradigm which has far-reaching missiological implications for the local congregation. These three arenas of thought converge in an urgent call to create a new perspective of the congregation as *God's missionary people in a local context*.

If we are to build missionary congregations in the world we must first carefully consider the relationship between Church and mission. The Church of Jesus Christ may find its fullest expression in relation to the world from within the Kingdom of God only if it lives out its nature as a missionary people. As Emil Brunner said, "The Church exists by mission as fire exists by burning."[5] And yet, the relationship of Church and mission has been the object of much discussion with little agreement during most of this century.

4. Karl Barth, *Church Dogmatics*, vol. 4:2, G. T. Thomson, trans. (Edinburgh: T and T Clark, 1958), 641.
5. Quoted in Michael Griffiths, *God's Forgetful Pilgrims: Recalling the Church to Its Reason for Being* (Grand Rapids: Eerdmans, 1975), 135.

Normally we do not assume that Church and mission are synonymous. We might define the Church as *the one, holy, universal and apostolic community of the disciples of Jesus Christ, gathered from all the families of the earth, around Word, sacrament, and common witness.* Further, we could define *mission* with Bishop Stephen Neill, as *"the intentional crossing of barriers from Church to non-church in word and deed for the sake of the proclamation of the Gospel."*[6] These two definitions demonstrate the difference between the two concepts, something Lesslie Newbigin highlighted:

> In the thinking of the vast majority of Christians, the words 'church' and 'mission' connote two different kinds of society. The one is conceived to be a society devoted to worship and the spiritual care and nurture of its members. . . . The other is conceived to be a society devoted to the propagation of the gospel, passing on its converts to the safe keeping of 'the church.' . . . It is taken for granted that the missionary obligation is one that has to be met AFTER the needs of the home have been fully met; that existing gains have to be thoroughly consolidated before we go further afield; that the world-wide church has to be built up with the same sort of prudent business enterprise.[7]

Thus our normal view of things tends to contrast church and mission somewhat as in figure 1.

Such a description may be a caricature; the fact remains that in the mind of many church members *church* and *mission* are seen as distinct and sometimes conflicting ideas. This has been especially true in Africa, Asia, and Latin America, where "mission" organizations too often operate quite apart from "church" structures. Such a radical distinction is disturbing because we also know that the two concepts should be closely interrelated, and it is precisely their interconnection that has been emphasized since at least the 1930s.

One of the most significant discussions of this matter occurred at the International Missionary Council (IMC) meeting in Tambaram, Madras, India, in 1938. At this meeting ecclesiological missiology was given its first major impetus. The record of this conference, *The World Mission of the Church,*[8] shows the delegates wrestling with the intimate relationship of church and mission.

The connection was emphasized again at the Willingen, Germany, conference of the IMC in 1952. At Willingen representatives of the ecu-

6. Stephen Neill, "How My Mind Has Changed about Mission," video recording produced by Overseas Ministries Study Center, 1984.

7. J. E. Lesslie Newbigin. *The Household of God: Lectures on the Nature of the Church* (New York: Friendship, 1954), 164–65.

8. London: International Missionary Council, 1939.

# Figure 1
## Common Conceptions of *Church* and *Mission*

| Church | Mission |
|---|---|
| • Institutionalized organization | • Individualized fellowship |
| • Based in permanent facilities | • Mobile; few permanent facilities |
| • Led by paid clergy | • Led by self-sacrificing missionaries |
| • Institution-maintaining orientation | • Entrepreneurial, risk-taking orientation |
| • A haven from the world | • Out among the world |
| • An orderly polity | • Loose, ad hoc organization |
| • Structured accountability, ownership | • Unstructured independence, volunteerism |
| • Self-serving/self-supporting | • Supported endlessly from outside |
| • Self-governing/self-propagating | • Controlled and promoted from outside |

menical missionary movement affirmed that "there is no participation in Christ without participation in His mission to the world. That by which the Church receives its existence is that by which it is also given its world mission."[9] This conviction has been echoed by many since then. For example, Thomas Torrance affirmed that "mission belongs to the nature of the Church."[10] Johannes Blauw said, "There is no other Church than the Church sent into the world, and there is no other mission than that of the Church of Christ."[11] And John R. W. Stott stated, "The Church cannot be understood rightly except in a perspective which is at once missionary and eschatological."[12]

Although we know that the two ideas are distinct, we are aware that it is impossible to understand one—or to be part of one—without being part of the other. On the one hand, mission activity is supported

9. International Missionary Council, *The Missionary Obligation of the Church* (London: Edinburgh House, 1952), 3.

10. Thomas F. Torrance, "The Mission of the Church," *Scottish Journal of Theology* 19.2 (1966): 141.

11. Johannes Blauw, *The Missionary Nature of the Church: A Survey of the Biblical Theology of Mission* (Grand Rapids: Eerdmans, 1974), 121.

12. John R. W. Stott, *One People* (Downers Grove, Ill.: Inter-Varsity, 1971), 17. See also idem, "Evangelism Through the Local Church," *World Evangelization* (March–April, 1989): 10.

by the Church, carried out by people from and in the Church, and the fruits of mission are received by the Church. On the other hand, the Church lives out its calling in the world through mission, finds its essential purpose in its participation in God's mission, and engages in a multitude of programs whose purpose is mission. The conclusion is inevitable: We cannot understand mission without viewing the nature of the Church, and we cannot understand the Church without looking at its mission. As Newbigin has said, "Just as we must insist that a Church which has ceased to be a mission has lost the essential character of a Church, so we must also say that a mission which is not at the same time truly a Church is not a true expression of the divine apostolate. An unchurchly mission is as much a monstrosity as an unmissionary church."[13]

## The Strategic Importance of the Local Congregation

During the 1960s the growing enthusiasm for the relationship of church and mission was reflected in the documents of Vatican Council II,[14] as well as in the World Council of Churches' study, *The Church for Others and the Church for the World*.[15] Unfortunately, the activism of the time ended up making church and mission nearly synonymous, defining the Church in terms of its usefulness for social change. The Church only really mattered as it contributed to radical changes in the world. The dominant phrase became, "The Church *is* mission."

But a vital component was missing, as Neill pointed out when he warned that "if everything is mission, nothing is mission."[16] Recarpeting the sanctuary, buying a new organ, calling a new pastor, or restructuring the denomination did not necessarily translate into crossing barriers from church to non-church for the communication of the gospel.

A reductionism began to occur, especially in Europe and North America. There arose a growing dissatisfaction with the institutional church, resulting in a mass exodus by the "baby boomer" generation from local congregations.[17] Although they believed themselves to be part of the Church universal, they displayed great pessimism regarding the organized churches of which they had been a part. Following J. C.

13. Newbigin, *Household*, 169.

14. Austin P. Flannery, ed., *Documents of Vatican II* (Grand Rapids: Eerdmans, 1975).

15. *The Church for Others and the Church for the World: A Quest for Structures for Missionary Congregations* (Geneva: World Council of Churches, 1968).

16. Stephen Neill, *Creative Tension* (London: Edinburgh House, 1959), 81.

17. An insightful discussion of this is given by Benton Johnson, "Is There Hope for Liberal Protestantism" in Dorothy C. Bass, Benton Johnson and Wade Clark Roof, *Mainstream Protestantism in the Twentieth Century: Its Problems and Prospects* (Louisville: Presbyterian Church USA, 1986), 13–26.

Hoekendijk's idea of *The Church Inside Out*,[18] they joined the Peace Corps, Lyndon Johnson's Great Society, and other movements aimed at transforming their world—from outside the parameters of the traditional churches. They wanted mission without church, and they would only give allegiance to the *church* insofar as it fulfilled the political and social functions they considered to be *mission*.

Eventually the results became apparent. Not only did that perspective lose touch with the larger Church; it also lost its vision for mission. By losing contact with the tangible, local, social, relational group of worshiping believers, this kind of mission became social activism but not mission. The uniqueness, qualities, and separateness of the Church's nature were swallowed up in a social activism which ultimately became purely secular. As Rodger Bassham described it, "Participation in God's mission to the world became the key to defining the function, reality, and validity of the church's existence. The understanding of church and mission underlying the phrase 'the church is mission' viewed the church as a function of the mission, not mission as a function of the church."[19]

Apparently few people were listening to David Moberg in 1962 when he insisted that, because of their essential identity, churches are agents of mission in their environment.[20] Only later would some realize the seriousness of the error of bypassing, ignoring, or forgetting the local congregation as the basic agent of the Church's mission in the world.

Toward the end of the 1970s several voices began calling for a careful reevaluation of the local congregation's role in the Church's mission in the world. When Jürgen Moltmann wrote *Hope for the Church*, he focused that hope in the local, believing community, proclaiming, "The local congregation is the future of the Church."[21] He added: "God as love . . . can only be witnessed to and experienced in a congregation small enough for members to know each other and accept each other as they

18. The E.T. of a book by Hoekendijk with that title was published in 1966 by Westminster, Philadelphia. Hoekendijk's perspective strongly influenced the World Council of Churches study, *The Church for Others and the Church for the World*, a study which sought to develop "missionary structures of the congregation." Actually, the congregations themselves were left largely untouched and uninfluenced by the study.

19. Rodger C. Bassham, "Seeking a Deeper Theological Basis for Mission," *International Review of Missions*, 67.267 (July 1978): 333.

20. Cf. David O. Moberg, *The Church as a Social Institution: The Sociology of American Religion* (Englewood Cliffs, N.J.: Prentice-Hall, 1962). Moberg makes a strong case for the "social functions of the Church," mentioning the Church's role as agent of socialization, status-giving agency, provider of social fellowship, promoter of social solidarity, function as a social stabilizer, agent of social control, agent of social reform, welfare institution, and philanthropic institution. Moberg does not mean to reduce the Church's being to its social function. Rather, he demonstrates that precisely in being the Church, God's people may have this kind of impressive social impact.

21. Nashville: Abingdon, 1979, 21.

are accepted by Christ. The gospel of Christ crucified for us puts an end to religion as power and opens up the possibility of experiencing God in the context of genuine community as the God of love."[22]

Around this same time David Wasdell,[23] Wilbert Shenk,[24] and Mady A. Thung[25] were rethinking some of the implications of the earlier missiological ecclesiology that had developed during the 1960s. Then in 1984 David A. Roozen, William McKinney, and Jackson W. Carroll, in a study of congregational presence in Hartford, Connecticut, stressed even more emphatically the vital role of the congregation in the Church's mission in the world:

> Most obvious perhaps is the role congregations play in providing sustenance for their members and participants. No other social institution has played a more important role historically in providing people with a sense of meaning for their lives and the opportunity to see their own existence in relation to a source and purpose that transcends everyday life. Through such activities as corporate worship, pastoral care, and programs of education, congregations are visibly present to their members and communities.
>
> Relatively few institutions can "mediate" effectively between society's megastructures and individuals, but congregations are clearly among them . . . We live in a time . . . in which the private-public balance has been lost and in which the church has a special bridging role to play.[26]

Interestingly, five years later Newbigin strongly supported this emphasis. After intense reflection on *The Gospel in a Pluralist Society*,[27] Newbigin found himself compelled to focus on the congregation "as hermeneutic of the gospel. . . . How is it possible that the gospel should be credible, that people should come to believe that the power which has the last word in human affairs is represented by a man hanging on a cross? I am suggesting that the only answer, the only hermeneutic of the gospel, is a congregation of men and women who believe it and live by it."[28]

22. Ibid., 42. Quoted in David A. Roozen, William McKinney and Jackson W. Carroll, eds., *Varieties of Religious Presence: Mission in Public Life* (New York: Pilgrim, 1984), 26.

23. David Wasdell, "The Evolution of Missionary Congregations," *International Review of Mission*, 66 (Oct. 1977): 366–72.

24. Wilbert Shenk, "Missionary Congregations: An Editorial Comment," *Mission Focus* (March 1978): 13–14.

25. Mady A. Thung, "An Alternative Model for a Missionary Church: An Approach to the Sociology of Organizations," *Ecumenical Review*, 30.1 (Jan. 1978): 18–31. This article should be read in conjunction with Thung's larger work, *The Precarious Organization: Sociological Explorations of the Church's Mission and Structure* (The Hague: Mouton, 1976).

26. Ibid, 26–27. Roozen, McKinney, and Carroll cite Parker J. Palmer, "Going Public," *New Congregations* (Spring 1980): 15.

27. Grand Rapids: Eerdmans, 1989.

28. Ibid., 227–32.

In other words, it is precisely because of being part of the universal Church that the local congregation is in *mission,* and as it lives out its *missionary nature* the local congregation discovers itself emerging to become the Church. We have seen the impact of theology of mission and sociology of religion on our perspective of the missionary nature of the congregation. Now we need to consider more specifically the way in which developments in modern ecclesiology have called the Church to rethink its nature, restate its relationship to the world, and reshape its participation in God's mission.

## Further Study

Barth, Karl. *Church Dogmatics,* 4.2.

Berkhof, Hendrikus. *Christian Faith: An Introduction to the Study of the Faith*, S. Woudstra, trans. Grand Rapids: Eerdmans, 1979. See 406–10.

Bright, John. *The Kingdom of God: The Biblical Concept and Its Meaning for the Church.* Nashville: Abingdon–Cokesbury, 1953. See 215–43.

Kittel, Gerhard, and Gerhard Friedrich, eds. *Theological Dictionary of the New Testament*, 10 vols., G. W. Bromiley, trans. Grand Rapids: Eerdmans, 1967, s.v., οἶκος.

Ladd, George E. *The Presence of the Future: The Eschatology of Biblical Realism.* Grand Rapids: Eerdmans, 1974. See 171–94.

Martin, Ralph P. *The Family and the Fellowship: New Testament Images of the Church*, 1st American ed. Grand Rapids: Eerdmans, 1979.

Minear, Paul S. *Images of the Church in the New Testament.* Philadelphia: Westminster, 1960.

Ridderbos, Herman N. *The Coming of the Kingdom*, H. de Jongste, trans. Philadelphia: Presbyterian and Reformed, 1962. See 334–96.

*[handwritten note:]* In order for missionaries, ch. planters and pastors to build missionary congregations, they must gain a new vision of the church in its local setting. - understand the rel. bet. ch & mission. Mission doesn't exist w/o the ch and church isn't really ch. w/o mission!

# 2

## *The Impact of Modern Ecclesiology on the Local Church*

ach person relates church and mission according to an individual perception of what the Church is. For those in the Church to see themselves as the missionary people of God they need to visualize the Christian community as simultaneously a human organization and a divinely created organism. Its mission then is both gift and task, both spiritual and social. This paradigm is a rather recent development.

Until the twentieth century the theology of the Church did not receive its share of attention. Paul S. Minear and others have pointed out that during the early centuries ecclesiology amounted to the use of various images to stimulate the Church into taking on certain characteristics. Whether the Church was viewed as body, community, servant, or bride; as vineyard, flock, household, or building—each image in its own way was meant not only to describe the Church (indicative), but within that description to represent a normative (imperative) relationship between the congregation and the Church's nature.[1] Augustine's day marks a watershed period when the Church's self-understanding moved from categories of self-examination and criticism to categories of self-congratulation and static definition, culminating in the triumphalism of the Council of Trent where there was a near-identification of the Roman Church with the Kingdom of God, and a celebration of the fact that the four attributes (one, holy, catholic, and apostolic) were to be identified within the Holy Roman See alone. During the Middle Ages Christians had set their Church on a mystical, instrumental pedestal; its mission was essentially shaped around the sacraments as a means of grace to the world.

The Protestant Reformation of the sixteenth century sought to return to a self-critical corrective with the idea of the "marks" of the Church. For example, the Belgic Confession defines the Church in article 27:

> We believe and profess one catholic or universal Church, which is a holy congregation and assembly of true Christian believers, expecting all their salvation in Jesus Christ, being washed by his blood, sanctified and sealed by the Holy Ghost.

This is followed by article 29:

> The marks by which the true Church is known are these: If the pure doctrine of the gospel is preached therein; if she maintains the pure administration of the sacraments as instituted by Christ; if church discipline is exercised in punishing of sin; in short, if all things are managed according to the pure Word of God, all things contrary thereto rejected, and Jesus Christ acknowledged as the only Head of the Church.

This view of the Church remained mostly unchallenged until Dietrich Bonhoeffer wrote *The Communion of Saints*, marking a radical change in

---

1. Minear points out that "so effective are the [images] that we hardly need to ask concerning the identity of that reality [to which they all point]. Image after image points beyond itself to a realm in which God and Jesus Christ and the Spirit are at work. It was of that work and of that realm that the New Testament writer was thinking as he spoke of Kingdom or temple or body. The study of images, therefore, reinforces the conviction that the reality of the Church is everywhere Christ." Paul S. Minear, *Images of the Church in the New Testament* (Philadelphia: Westminster, 1960), 223; see also John N. D. Kelly, *Early Christian Doctrines* (New York: Harper, 1959), 190–91; Jaroslav Pelikan, *The Christian Tradition: A History of the Development of Doctrine* (Chicago: University of Chicago Press, 1971), 1:159; G. C. Berkouwer, *The Church* (Grand Rapids: Eerdmans, 1976), 7; Hans Küng, *The Church* (New York: Seabury, 1980): 266; Avery R. Dulles, *Models of the Church: A Critical Assessment of the Church in All Its Aspects* (Garden City, N.Y.: Doubleday, 1974), 126–27; John Mackay, *A Preface to Christian Theology* (New York: Macmillan, 1943), 170, and Charles Van Engen, *The Growth of the True Church* (Amsterdam: Rodopi, 1981), 68–72, 194–202.

ecclesial perspective. Until Bonhoeffer's work, most ecclesiology involved an a priori, logical, scholastic thought process. The Church was defined and explained with such logic and reason that it had no recognizable counterpart in real-world congregations. From world-dominating churches of the Constantinian and Holy Roman Empire eras to the reforming evangelicals and Anabaptists—all had derived logical, ordered, systematic definitions for *church*, either from Scripture or from other aspects of their theology. Even reformation church leaders had no way of empirically verifying what "pure preaching of the Word," "right administration of the sacraments," or "the proper exercise of church discipline" meant in practice. Witness the divisions of early Protestantism and the use of the marks of the Church to defend one's own church as "true," and all others as something less than "true." Logical, a priori ecclesiology created a very serious chasm between the idea of what should be and the reality of what is. The result was that ecclesiology ended up having two separate natures. One nature was that of the "visible" church, which was far less than what it should be, but at least its practices were verifiable. The second nature was that of the "invisible" church, which was ideal and perfect but which could not be found in the real world.

In the early twentieth century the question of the nature and mission of the Church began to take on new urgency. Some questions came to the fore through Johannes Gustav Warneck's writings,[2] and others developed through the International Missionary Council (IMC) conference of Madras, India, in 1937.[3] What Warneck and others began questioning was the Church's relation to mission and the Church's nature in terms of its mission in the world. The questions were further refined at IMC conferences at Willingen, 1952; Evanston, 1954, and Ghana, 1957. This rethinking strived to be biblical and to take theological study seriously, but the new perspective of church and mission definitely rejected the a priori, logical assumptions. The new starting point considered the real place of the real Church in the real world.

During the nineteenth century a large share of European and North American mission sending was carried out through such specifically-focused "parachurch" missionary agencies as the China Inland Mission and the British and Foreign Bible Society. Churches were not directly involved. Warneck and others began questioning the missions' relation-

2. These include *Outline of a History of Protestant Missions from the Reformation to the Present Time: A Contribution to Modern Church History*, 7th ed., George Robson, ed. (New York: Revell, 1901), and *The Living Christ and Dying Heathenism*, 3d ed., Neil Buchanan, trans. (New York: Revell, 1909); see also W. Holsten, "Warneck, Gustav (1834–1910)" in Stephen Neill, Gerald H. Anderson, and John Goodwin, eds., *Concise Dictionary of the Christian World Mission* (Nashville: Abingdon, 1971), 643 ff.

3. For a discussion of what new ideas were at work in the IMC, see Rodger C. Bassham, *Mission Theology, 1948–1975: Years of Creative Tension—Ecumenical, Evangelical and Roman Catholic* (Pasadena, Calif.: William Carey Library, 1980), 23 ff.

ship to the churches, and the Church's mission in the world. They began to see that the Church's nature could not be defined apart from its mission, and mission could no longer be defined apart from the Church's relation in the world. The Church's nature, reason for being, and mission in the world were progressively elaborated and shaped through missionary outreach. Additional questions about the relationship of the mission churches to other religions, to developing Third World governments, to new technologies, and to Western colonial expansion called for attention. To establish self-supporting, self-governing, self-propagating churches did not seem sufficient in the light of these new questions.

## Bringing Change to Modern Ecclesiology

The forces that stimulated a new way of thinking in modern ecclesiology were varied:

1. The historic world missionary conference at Edinburgh, Scotland, in 1910, the rise of the International Missionary Council, founded at Lake Mohonk, New York, in 1921,[4] and the global Christian missionary movement all brought a missions perspective into the European and North American churches. Those involved in this new missions ideal tended to see the church as living in order to bear the fruit of mission.

2. The capitulation to the forces of evil, particularly by the European churches during the 1930s and 1940s, led to an intensely introspective period after World War II in which many theologians demanded a rethinking about the role of the national church in society.

3. As the Church developed a more mature indigenous organization and leadership in all six continents, the tremendous diversity of cultural, national, anthropological, socio-economic, and ecclesiastical forms assumed by this increasingly global Church began to impress itself on ecclesiology.[5]

4. The rise of the World Council of Churches (WCC) and various national Christian councils demanded answers to searching questions about the relation of the one Church to diverse movements seeking membership. Because they were councils of

4. The best volume to date on the history of the IMC is W. Richey Hogg, *Ecumenical Foundations: A History of the International Missionary Council and Its Nineteenth-Century Background* (New York: Harper, 1952).

5. See Steven G. Mackie, *Can Churches Be Compared?* (Geneva: World Council of Churches, 1970); and Steven Mackie, "Seven Clues for Rethinking Mission," *International Review of Mission*, 60 (1971): 324–26.

churches, it was important to know by what criteria of beliefs and organization these groups could be called churches and accepted as members. The African independent churches, the Oceania cargo cults and prophet movements, the Latin American "base ecclesial communities," socially active faith communities such as Sojourners in Washington, D.C., and the gay church all stretched known definitions of Christianity and ecclesiology. Admitting these groups to membership in a national or world council legitimized their claims as churches; but if they were churches, what is church?[6]

5. Our radically shrunken global village, the rise of the Third World nations, the increased facility in travel, and the increase in communications called for the Church to be a global Christian community, relevant to global issues to an unprecedented degree.

6. The renaissance of "faith missions" after World War II, with their "interdenominational" or "non-denominational" makeup, has forced many to ask some very searching questions about the nature of the Church. While the parachurch missions movement was vitally active from the early 1800s, since 1900 David Barrett counts "15,800 distinct and separate parachurch agencies serving the churches in their mission through manifold ministries in the 223 countries of the world, yet organizationally independent of the churches."[7] The relationship of these agencies to the Church, their own nature as Church, and the converts from these ministries who themselves became a national church has de facto redefined the nature of the Church in many countries. It was impossible to say that these parachurch agencies (or "sodalities," using Ralph Winter's term[8]) were not a part of the "one, holy, catholic, and apostolic Church"; yet the confessional and organizational makeup of their membership was very different from the traditional churches as known throughout previous church history.

7. The worldwide development of what at one time were called "younger" churches in the Third World from "mission" to "church"

6 An urgent call for new ecclesiological and missiological thinking about the church has come from a number of Roman Catholic and Protestant Latin Americans like Leonardo Boff, Juan Luis Segundo, René Padilla, and Orlando Costas.

7. David Barrett, "Five Statistical Eras of Global Mission," *Missiology*, 12.1 (Jan. 1984): 31.

8. Winter first presented the idea in "Churches Need Missions Because Modalities Need Sodalities" in *Evangelical Missions Quarterly* (Summer 1971): 193–200. He later elaborated it in "The Two Structures of God's Redemptive Mission," in *Missiology*, 2.1 (Jan. 1974): 121–39. The address was subsequently published in booklet form by William Carey Library in 1976.

has raised new issues about how to appropriately contextualize ecclesiology in the Third World, allowing relevance yet protecting biblical Christianity.[9]

8. The post-Vatican Council II ecclesiology, articulated, for example, in "Lumen Gentium" and "Ad Gentes," stressed a conception of the Church as the "People of God," and led to a broad reexamination of Roman Catholic ecclesiology.[10]

9. The rise in the United States of faith communities whose members have a high degree of personal commitment to each other, a communal style of living, a strong social activism, and creative forms of worship and common life, has demonstrated the breadth of forms and the depth of involvement possible in the Church.[11]

A new paradigm was needed to take into account these new directions. The Church's nature in confronting new realities was squarely faced by Dietrich Bonhoeffer when he considered the relation between the community of the saints (*communio sanctorum*) as a sociological entity within world society and the spiritual community (*sanctorum communio*) when viewed as the fellowship of the followers of Jesus.[12]

Though not everyone who came after Bonhoeffer followed his approach to ecclesiology, his work marks the beginning of a new viewpoint that continually wrestled with holding together *both* sides of the Church's nature—the empirical and sociological on the one hand; the a priori, biblical, and theological on the other.

## Missiological Significance of a New Paradigm

With increasing urgency pastors, missiologists, and theologians have called for redefining the Church's nature, its mission, its reason for being, its relation to the Kingdom of God, and its calling in the world. It has become increasingly difficult to separate the "visible" from the

9. See, for example, Hendrik Kraemer, *From Missionfield to Independent Church* (the Hague: Boekencentrum, 1938).

10. See, for example, Austin P. Flannery, ed., *Documents of Vatican II* (Grand Rapids: Eerdmans, 1975). The recent papal encyclical, "Redemptoris Missio" affirms this new ecclesiology. See *Origins*, 20.34 (31 Jan. 1991).

11. The Church of the Saviour in Washington, D.C.; the Boston Church of God led by Kip McKean, and the "Community of Communities," a national network of house churches representing a number of denominational backgrounds, are examples of new ways of being the church. See "Called and Committed: The Spirituality of Mission," *Today's Ministry* 2.3 (1985): 1–8.

12. See Eberhard Bethge, "Foreword," in: Dietrich Bonhoeffer, *The Communion of Saints: A Dogmatic Inquiry into the Sociology of the Church*. E.T. (New York: Harper, 1963).

"invisible," the hope from the reality. These modern Bonhoeffers have convincingly demonstrated that the Church must live out its missionary nature in the here and now.[13]

A new missiological paradigm in ecclesiology is needed so that we might see the missionary Church as an "emerging" reality which, as it is built up in the world, becomes in fact what it is in faith. By grasping and internalizing this new paradigm we will find our thinking about the Church and its mission becoming highly contextual, radically transformational, and powerfully hopeful, exercised with eternity in view. This viewpoint involves a process whereby the Church *is* and *becomes*.[14] It *is* a fully formed community, a living sacrament, and a sign before God, its members, and those outside its walls. But simultaneously it is in the process of *becoming* through carefully contextualized goal-setting, planning, and evaluation. The gap will be bridged between the Church's human, often-sinful, visible, and organizational side and its divine, holy, invisible, and organic side.

In this view the essential Church is never the same during any two days, because it is constantly becoming, developing, and "emerging." Yet in another sense the Church *is* already by nature what it is *becoming* and simply must continually change, improve, reform, and emerge. The shape this constant change develops follows well-defined and clear sociological lines, but each new form is the mysterious *creatio Dei*, directed wherever the Holy Spirit pleases to blow. We know that people join a church for social, demographic, cultural, political, and economic reasons. Yet no one joins *the Church* who is not called, elected, justified, and adopted by Jesus Christ. His Spirit mysteriously creates his Body, outside of which there is no salvation.

The Church thus emerges naturally, but with supernatural characteristics; it is a sociological entity with a spiritual nature. Churches grow because of certain internal spiritual characteristics, because members desire to grow and prioritize and strategize for such growth, and because significant social and demographic factors affect growth. This Church will continue to become what it is in the power of the Spirit, and even "the gates of Hades will not overcome it" (Matt. 16:18 NIV). This process of change reflects the desire of the Church since its inception to be in fact what it is in vision, in hope, and in potential. Paul S. Minear counts ninety-six images or word pictures used to describe the Church and notes that such images establish vision and self-concept within the body:

13. For further analysis of these paradoxical perspectives, see Charles Van Engen, *The Growth of the True Church*, "Amsterdam Studies in Theology," vol. 3 (Amsterdam: Rodopi, 1981), 47–94.

14. This issue was raised, for example, by Juan Isais in *The Other Side of the Coin*, E. P. Isais, trans. (Grand Rapids: Eerdmans, 1966).

One function of a church image is to satisfy (a need to relate dream and vision to reality). For example, we may consider the blunt, prosaic injunction: "Let the church be the church." Such a slogan implies that the church is not now fully the church. It implies that the true self-image is not at present the effectual image that it should be. But what is the church when it allows itself to become the church? Do we know? Yes. And no. We who stand within the church have allowed its true character to become obscured. Yet we know enough concerning God's design for the church to be haunted by the accusation of the church's lord: "I never knew you." So there is much about the character of the church to which the church itself is blind. . . . In every generation the use and re-use of the Biblical images has been one path by which the church has tried to learn what the church truly is, so that it could become what it is not.[15]

When Jesus left his disciples after the resurrection, his commission to them was at once a dream, an image, and a view of the "emerging" church: "You shall receive power when the Holy Spirit has come upon you; and you shall be my witnesses both in Jerusalem, and in all Judea, and Samaria, and even to the remotest part of the earth" (Acts 1:8 NASB).

Jesus' statement has been overworked in missionary theory, especially in regard to the expansion of the Church in ever-widening national, cultural, and geographic circles. But few have looked at Jesus' promise as an image of the self-understanding of the Church. Could it not be that Jesus is telling his disciples that they are a certain kind of fellowship which in its essential nature is an ever-widening, mushrooming group of missionary witnesses? It seems Jesus is telling the disciples that by the very fact of being "witnesses" they are and will be endlessly emerging into what he has made them.

W. Douglas Smith has pointed out that there is a cyclical pattern to what we are calling the emerging of the missionary Church. The cycle is one of "going, teaching, equipping, and sending."[16] In fact, the historical expansion of the Church could be described as the missionary people of God striving to emerge, not only numerically, culturally, and geographically, but also spiritually, structurally, organizationally, theologically, architecturally, musically, and economically. Clearly the human, fallen, and sinful aspect of the Church's nature has worked as a counterforce in this search for the Church's emerging to become what it is.

Hendrikus Berkhof has pointed to the emerging dynamism of the Church's nature in terms of the Church's "mediating" function:

15. Paul S. Minear, *Images of the Church in the New Testament* (Philadelphia: Westminster, 1960), 25.

16. W. Douglas Smith, *Toward Continuous Mission: Strategizing for the Evangelization of Bolivia* (Pasadena, Calif.: William Carey Library, 1978), chapter 6.

The interposition of the community between Christ and the individual gives us a clear focus on the mediating function of the church, and that is part of its twofold character. Mediation means that the church comes from somewhere and goes somewhere, in order to link the beginning and the end. She must bridge the gap between Christ and man. . . . The final goal of the church cannot possibly be the individual believer. God wants a whole humanity for himself. In the movement of the Spirit to the world, the church as the provisional terminal is at the same time a new starting-point. . . . The church thus stands between Christ and the world, being as it were equally related to both.[17]

## Seven Stages of Emerging within Missionary Congregations

This emerging characteristic of mission drives the Church toward becoming a dynamic, growing, developing reality. The same commands, experiences, images, and hope which empowered the disciples on the Day of Pentecost still goad the Church to emerge to become what Christ has been creating. Since its birth, the Church has been called to grow up to the "mature man, to the measure of the stature of the fulness of Christ" (Eph. 4:13). Since this fulness is infinite, eternal, and unchanging, the vision of the Church is never limited to seeing only what is there; it always sees what, by God's grace, could and will be there.

We can illustrate this fantastically dynamic characteristic of the Church by looking at mission history. There we see at least seven stages in the emerging of a local and national missionary church—stages that have been repeated time and again in church-planting situations. We might summarize the development of the church in a given context in this way:

1. Pioneer evangelism leads to the conversion of a number of people.
2. Initial church gatherings are led by elders and deacons, along with preachers from outside the infant body.
3. Leadership training programs choose, train, and commission indigenous pastors, supervisors and other ministry leaders.
4. Regional organizations of Christian groups develop structures, committees, youth programs, women's societies, and regional assemblies.
5. National organization, supervision of regions, and relationships with other national churches begin to form.
6. Specialized ministries grow inside and outside the church, with boards, budgets, plans, finances, buildings, and programs.

17. Hendrikus Berkhof, *Christian Faith: An Introduction to the Study of the Faith*, S. Woudstra, trans. (Grand Rapids: Eerdmans, 1979), 345–47.

7. Indigenous missionaries are sent by the daughter church for local, national, and international mission in the world, beginning the pattern all over again.[18]

The concept of emerging which lies behind those seven stages provides a clue to the interaction of missiology and ecclesiology as we apply our understanding of the dialectical tension between present reality and future hope:

The missionary Church is *becoming* what it is.

The missionary Church *is* what it is becoming.

The missionary Church cannot *become* more than what it is.

The missionary Church cannot *be* more than what it is becoming.

Thus it is important for missionaries, mission executives, pastors, and church-planters to build up the Church's missionary nature. By so doing they more completely edify the building which, though constituted by humans, is not made with human hands. This is at once the sociological theology and the theological sociology of the Church. The Church is uniquely the body of Jesus Christ who is uniquely the God-man, at once divine and human, other-worldly and this-worldly. It is not by accident but by design that the Church which is his body should be "in the world, but not of the world"; should be at once a fallen, human institution, and a perfect, divine organism. Only as we join the human and divine aspects of the Church's nature in a unified perspective can we possibly arrive at a true understanding of the Church's mission. Only as congregations intentionally live out their nature as the missionary people of God will the Church begin to emerge to become in fact what it is by faith.

---

18. The following questions may help the reader reflect on the way missionary congregations could be stimulated to emerge. At which of the stages above do you look for completion of the translation of the Bible? At which stage do you expect the new church to be self-supporting, self-governing, and self-propagating (see preface, footnote 2)? At what stage do you begin and end the infusion of outside funds and personnel? At what stage should there be a concentration on theological education? At what stage should national indigenous leaders take over the enterprises originally begun by expatriot missionaries? At what stage do you begin to build the local church as a body, with members variously gifted for ministry? What relation might exist between the stages of congregational development and the church's specialized educational, medical, or agricultural missions? What role should tribal, cultural, and national patterns of structure and organization play in the development and sequence of these stages? What role should the polity of the sending organization play in the subsequent organizational development of the new missionary congregation? What managerial principles are appropriate for missionary congregations?

## Further Study

Barth, Karl. *Church Dogmatics*, 4.2; 4.3.1; 4.3.2.

Berkhof, Hendrikus. *Christian Faith: An Introduction to the Study of the Faith*, S. Woudstra, trans. Grand Rapids: Eerdmans, 1979.

Berkouwer, G. C. *The Church*, J. Davison, trans. Grand Rapids: Eerdmans, 1976.

Bonhoeffer, Dietrich. *The Communion of Saints: A Dogmatic Inquiry into the Sociology of the Church*. E.T., New York: Harper, 1964.

Calvin, John. *Institutes of the Christian Religion*, Book 4.

Dulles, Avery R. *Models of the Church*. Garden City, N.Y.: Doubleday, 1974.

————. *A Church to Believe In: Discipleship and the Dynamics of Freedom*. New York: Crossroad, 1982.

Flannery, Austin P., ed. *Documents of Vatican II*. Grand Rapids: Eerdmans, 1975.

Hoekendijk, Johannes C. *The Church Inside Out*, I. C. Rottenberg, trans. Philadelphia: Westminster, 1966.

Küng, Hans. *The Church, Maintained in Truth*, E. Quinn, trans. New York: Seabury, 1980.

Minear, Paul S. *Images of the Church in the New Testament*. Philadelphia: Westminster, 1960.

Moltmann, Jürgen. *The Church in the Power of the Spirit*. New York: Harper, 1977.

Newbigin, J. E. Lesslie. *The Household of God: Lectures on the Nature of the Church*. New York, Friendship, 1954.

Van Engen, Charles. *The Growth of the True Church*. Amsterdam: Rodopi, 1981.

Watson, David C. K. *I Believe in the Church*, 1st American ed. Grand Rapids: Eerdmans, 1979.

Williams, Colin W. *The Church*. Philadelphia: Westminster, 1968.

*How to hold both soc & theolog sides of the church in balance*

*Dialectical tension bet. present reality and future hope - the missionary ch is becoming what it is. Impt for missionaries, mission execs, pastors & ch leaders to build up the churches missionary nature.*

**3**

# *The Essence of the Local Church in the Book of Ephesians*

A s we begin to construct a new image of the Church's missionary nature in the local congregation, we must ground it on a biblical foundation. One of the most important sources for this is Paul's letter to the Ephesians. A careful study of Ephesians offers an overview of the missionary nature of the local congregation. This discussion is not meant to be a detailed exegesis of Ephesians. Rather, we would use some principial statements found there to open a window to Paul's missionary ecclesiology. Paul saw the local church as an organism which should continually grow in the missional expression of its essential nature in the world. The words "one, holy, and catholic," as applied to the nature of the Church, can be traced back to the canons of the First Council of Constantinople in 381, and the ideas expressed go back to at least Ignatius in the early second century. Ignatius sought to apply Paul's teachings on the church, so it should not surprise us that Paul used these basic ideas in his images of the Church in Ephesians.

In dealing with the missionary ecclesiology of Ephesians we could easily become sidetracked into examining the various words which refer to the Church. Martin Luther, for example, detested the old German word *kirche* because of its institutional and hierarchical baggage. Luther preferred such words as crowd (*Haufe*), assembly or convocation (*Versammlung*), collection or set (*Sammlung*), or congregation (as a corporate community, *Gemeinde*). The actual words are not as important as is the Reformation emphasis on the nature of the Church. That emphasis is well expressed in the Apostles' Creed as "the *communion* of saints," stressing the Church as congregation, communion, fellowship, or people of God. Paul's definition of the Church drew this same focus from the Old Testament's view of the people of God.[1] The New Testament uses the word *ekklēsia* at least seventy-three times, and invariably the meaning involves the idea of an assembly—either the gathering or the individuals gathered.[2]

But a semantic study does little to enrich our understanding of the nature of the Church. Linguistic anthropologists have suggested that, in order to understand a given concept in its cultural milieu, it is helpful to search for dynamic equivalents of thought, image, and feeling. One aspect of this method involves word pictures which graphically convey certain meanings. Paul S. Minear found ninety-six different word images representing the Church in the New Testament.[3] A careful analysis of the images of the Church in Ephesians can be particularly helpful for understanding Paul's view of the Church's mission.

In Ephesians the word *ekklēsia* appears only nine times. This is surprising when we consider that Ephesians is usually regarded as expressing the height of Paul's view of the Church. The absence of the word *ekklēsia*, then, should make us aware that Paul is here developing his thought with Hebrew-style pictorial representation or images, rather than with Greek logical propositions. A closer look reveals that at least fifteen different word pictures are employed. The most important of these are *saints* (used nine times), *body* (used eight times), *soldier with armor* (used eight times), and *wife* (used seven times). A series of lesser images embellish the major conceptions: *chosen people of God* (used four times), *sons* or *family* (used four times), *workmanship, building,* or

---

1. For a discussion of Paul's use of the Old Testament view of the Church, see Paul D. Hanson, *The People Called: The Growth of Community in the Bible* (New York: Harper and Row, 1986).

2. See, for example, Gerhard Kittel and Gerhard Friedrich, eds., *Theological Dictionary of the New Testament*, G. W. Bromiley, trans., 10 vols. (Grand Rapids: Eerdmans, 1965), s.v., "ἐκκλησία" (espec. 3.501–13); Walter Bauer, *A Greek-English Lexicon of the New Testament and Other Early Christian Literature*, W. F. Arndt and F. W. Gingrich, and F. W. Danker, trans. and rev. (Chicago: University of Chicago Press, 1979), s.v., "ἐκκλησία."

3. Paul S. Minear, *The Images of the Church in the New Testament* (Philadelphia: Westminster, 1960).

*temple* (used three times), a *song of praise* or *offering* (used two times), a *new man*, or *new self* (used two times). Finally a whole range of images flash once: *the breadth, length, height and depth of love, imitators of God, kingdom of Christ, children of light, wise men,* and *ambassadors.*

These lucid verbal photographs help us understand the nature of the Church and illuminate a background scene around the ancient confessional words, "one, holy, and catholic." We must begin at the very heart of the epistle, where the creed also begins—with the concept of the unity of the body of Christ.

## The Church's Mission in Unity (Eph. 4:1–16)

The apostle Paul states categorically, "There is one body and one Spirit, as there is also one hope held out in God's call to you; one Lord, one faith, one baptism; one God and Father of all, who is over all and through all and in all" (Eph. 4:4–6). We do not confess "holy catholic church*es*" or "famil*ies* of God" or "people*s* of God" or "bod*ies* of Christ" or "New Israel*s*." In the biblical view of the church the plural only refers to geographical location of churches, not existential being of the Church. In its essence there is only one Church. In Ephesians *ekklēsia* appears only in the singular.

We receive by faith the *oneness* of the Church. This oneness is something given by God, not fabricated by humans. It is a oneness bonded by the Spirit of God who gathers the Church. The Church remains the mysterious *creatio Dei* of elected, justified sinners. Paul speaks of the fact that the Church comes into being just as a building is put together—and God through Son and Holy Spirit is the divine builder (Eph. 2:10, 21–22). The means of God's building activity is mission, and the fruit of God's building activity is the unity of the body of Christ. As Karl Barth has put it, we cannot justify, spiritually or biblically, "the existence of a plurality of churches genuinely separated . . . and mutually excluding one another internally and therefore externally. A plurality of churches in this sense means a plurality of lords, a plurality of spirits, a plurality of gods."[4]

The Church's oneness is a faith affirmation, because in the midst of our brokenness and dividedness the Church's oneness is not an obvious fact to be observed. We are all "Gentiles," "strangers," and "aliens," held apart by the "dividing wall" (Eph. 2:11–14). Yet we accept by faith the fact of one body because we believe in one God, in one Jesus Christ, and in one Holy Spirit.

This confession has practical significance. Because we receive by faith the oneness of the Church, we therefore strive to achieve that oneness (Eph. 4:1–3). Paul exhorts us that we walk "worthy of our calling" in

---

4. Karl Barth, *Church Dogmatics*, 4.1. Barth goes to great lengths to affirm the work of Christ and the Holy Spirit in creating the Church as his body.

that we be "humble, gentle, patient, and forbearing." Another translation puts it that we are to "spare no effort to make fast with bonds of peace the unity which the Spirit gives" (Eph. 4:3). This oneness of the body is more profoundly an internal unanimity than an external, institutional, organizational unity. Paul speaks of this unified spirit in Philippians 2:1–11 and 1 Corinthians 1:12–13. This is a matter of being members one of another as in 1 Corinthians 12, whereby the joys and the honors, the griefs and the pains of each member have repercussions among all members, for all are *one* body. In Ephesians Paul does not speak of denomination or council or association. Paul speaks of body. He wants us to see that we receive by faith the oneness of a universal Church and strive to achieve it *in the exercise of our gifts in service to the world.*[5] What it means to be one, as expressed by Paul in Ephesians 4:1–6, is explained more fully in 4:7–16 in the idea of a body with members who exercise their gifts as part of that body. Each member has been given a gift (4:7). The Giver is the Christ who has "filled the universe" (4:8–10). The gifts themselves involve apostles, prophets, evangelists, pastors, and teachers (4:11–12). The purpose of the gifts is to equip the saints for diaconal service, for the building up of the body of Christ (4:12).

So the idea of *oneness* does not involve putting individuals or denominations together like pieces of a puzzle to get a larger whole. Paul's concept is that the whole defines the identity of the parts and is more than the sum of the parts. In this respect the Church is like a clan or tribe. Individuals have significance in themselves, but as they relate to the body of Christ they derive their ultimate meaning from their place in the whole. As Paul expressed it in 1 Corinthians 12:14–27, a dismembered hand or a disjointed ear or eye have no significance, no task, and no identity in themselves. They take on importance by the fact that God has made them a functional part of the whole body.

This concept of the body equally denigrates Western individualism and Marxist conformism. Individuals are extremely important and unique as God's creatures, but their value within the Church is in and through their special participation in the whole, through the exercise of their own gifts, according to the grace given to them. This is the correct sense in which we may understand Cyprian's dictum, *"extra ecclesiam nulla salus"* ("outside the church there is no salvation"). Apart from the body no members can maintain their walk with God, their identity, or their purpose.

The oneness of the Church is at once introverted and extroverted. The gifts are given by the Holy Spirit "to equip the saints" so they may carry out the Spirit's outward purpose, *"ergon diakonias"* ("the work of service," 4:12). Verse 4:12 goes on to say that in this effort all the saints

---

5. See Barth, *Church Dogmatics*, 4.2. Barth uses the phrase "being for the world."

together work "eis oikodomen tou somatos tou Xristou" ("toward the upbuilding of the body of Christ"). This is the oneness of "the church inside out."[6] Here the members exercise their various gifts to prepare each other for mission and ministry in the world. This oneness is not an introverted club of like-minded enthusiasts. Here is a body of apostles, prophets, evangelists, pastors, and teachers who assist and enable each other in the proclamation of the gospel in the world around them. It is the body which exploded into action in those early years, going to all the nations making disciples, preaching, teaching, and baptizing (Matt. 28:19–20). This body was known to hold "all things in common" (Acts 4:32); to be concerned about the sick and to look after the widows, the orphans, and the poor. This is an externalized oneness which searches the highways and byways of the world with an invitation to the great feast (Matt. 22:9–10).

Jesus emphasized this externalized perspective of oneness in his high priestly prayer. "And the glory which Thou hast given Me I have given to them; that they may be one, just as We are one; I in them, and Thou in Me, that the *world* may know that Thou didst send Me and didst love them even as Thou didst love Me" (John 17:22–23 NASB, emphasis added).

The overriding purpose of it all is that the Church may grow to be one in "the unity inherent in our faith and our knowledge of the Son of God—to mature manhood, measured by nothing less than the full stature of Christ. . . . Let us speak the truth in love; so shall we fully grow up into Christ. He is the head, and on him the whole body depends. Bonded and knit together by every constituent joint, the whole frame grows through the due activity of each part, and builds itself up in love" (Eph. 4:13, 15–16 NEB).

This is growth in greater oneness[7] through the incorporation of members into the body (numerical growth); growth through the spiritual development of the members of the body as they exercise their gifts for the sake of the world (organic and spiritual growth); growth through the increased impact of the body of Christ in the world to which it has been sent (growth in *diakonia*); and growth through an enhanced understanding of the lordship of Christ in the Church, preventing us from being "tossed by the waves and whirled about by every fresh gust of teaching" (theological growth, Eph. 4:14).

Mission and unity are wedded in Paul's view of the Church. One day we will have grown to such an extent that Christ will "present the church to himself all glorious, with no stain or wrinkle or anything of the

---

6. Johannes C. Hoekendijk strongly defends this view in *The Church Inside Out*, I. C. Rottenberg, trans. (Philadelphia: Westminster, 1966).

7. Barth, *Church Dogmatics*, 4.2; pages 641–60 deal with the "upbuilding" of the communion.

sort, but holy and without blemish" (Eph. 5:27 NEB; cf. Rev. 21:9–10, 25–26).

## The Church's Mission Is Mission in Holiness
## (Eph. 1:1–14; 4:17–5:5; 5:6–6:20; 3:14–21)

To speak of the holiness of the Church is deeply disturbing. In ecclesiology we have had to create some careful distinctions—such as visible vs. invisible; form vs. essence; ideal vs. real; institution vs. community, and imperfect vs. perfect—to make sense out of the pain we feel concerning the lack of holiness of the Church. In Ephesians the water of holiness flows deep and strong. As we have seen, "saints" is a very dominant image in Ephesians. Further, Paul's call to holy living (5:1–21), the call to being light in darkness (5:8–14), the exhortation to battle evil and the powers of the air as a soldier outfitted for war (6:10–18)—all these reinforce the Constantinopolitan confession concerning the holiness of the Church.

We receive by faith the *holiness* of the Church (Eph. 1:1–14). It is a gift of God, affirmed by God as his purpose for us. Paul opens his epistle with what might be described as an ancient hymn extolling ten individual blessings which have implications for the Kingdom as a whole. The thoughts may be arranged as a litany of praise to the work of the three Persons of the Trinity. What has God done for us? We are:

> By the Father: (1) chosen, (2) to be made holy, (3) predestined, (4) adopted . . .
>
> **to the praise of his glory**
>
> By the Son: (5) redeemed, (6) pardoned, (7) made to know the mystery, (8) united in Christ, (9) heirs with him . . .
>
> **to the praise of his glory**
>
> By the Spirit: (10) sealed . . .
>
> **to the praise of his glory**

In the language of poetry and song this is who we are as a holy people of God. We receive this affirmation by faith, for we cannot see it. When we look into our individual lives, we do not see much holiness. With the mouth we confess that we are saints (as in Eph. 1:1)—with the heart we feel that we are sinners ("futile in our thinking," as in Eph. 4:17).

Thus we strive individually and corporately to achieve the holiness which expresses the body of Christ (Eph. 4:17–5:14). Paul, the apostle to the Gentiles, calls into condemnation a whole series of practices done by the Gentiles. He shines the searchlight of the Word upon the cultural makeup of his followers and points out the human practices which must be modified precisely because now there is a "new self" (4:24). Corporately the collection of transformed individuals creates a transformed culture. Paul deals with some very personal things here: sensuality, lust, and immorality (4:19, 22; 5:3); greed (4:19, 28; 5:3); stealing (4:28); diligence in work (4:28); foul language (4:29; 5:4); bitterness and anger (4:26–27, 31); lying (4:25), and coveting (5:5). Paul calls members of the congregation to be "children of light," each one shining forth the "fruits of goodness, righteousness, and truth," so that their light might expose the darkness in the lives of others and call them to "wake up" and "rise from the dead" so that "Christ will shine" on them (Eph. 5:8–14).

From the context of this section it seems obvious that Paul is speaking about more than individual behavior. He wants us to know that the church as congregation is directly affected by how we speak, how we work at our jobs, how we use or abuse our bodies, how we think and evaluate, how we relate to those in need. By implication even the holiness of the essential Church is directly related to the life of each "new self" of its body in the world. How we pay our income tax, how we manage our family and business finances, how we vote politically, and what we say in public and private all have a bearing on the holiness of the Church. By the fact that we are members of the body, when we confess belief in the holiness of the Church, we confess a commitment to our own holiness. This involves righteous conduct which calls for the transformation of our culture, our economics, our politics, our education, and even our lifestyles.[8] Paul wants us to recognize that we exercise our holiness within our individual life situations as an expression of the holiness of the Church (Eph. 5:6–6:20). The Church as a community of "children of light" (5:8) illumines the farthest reaches of the darkness of the world through the holiness of its members, both individually and corporately (Matt. 5:14). Further, the holiness of the Church has to do with holiness in worship (Eph. 5:19–20), holiness in local church organization and submission[9] (5:21), holiness in marital relationships (5:22–33), holiness in parenting (6:1–4), and holiness at work (6:5–9).

The Church's holiness in society is our point of battle, "not against human foes, but against cosmic powers, against the authorities and potentates of this dark world, against the superhuman forces of evil in the heavens" (6:12 NEB). In the midst of great individual and corporate

---

8. See, for example, Ronald J. Sider, *Rich Christians in an Age of Hunger* (Downers Grove, Ill.: Inter–Varsity, 1977); idem, ed., *Cry Justice! The Bible on Hunger and Poverty* (New York: Paulist, 1980).

9. *A Greek-English Lexicon of the New Testament* translates *hypotassomenoi* here as "voluntary yielding in love."

evil, the Church must never think that political and economic strength may replace the strength of holiness in the Lord. The Church—as well as those comprising it—must hold the truth, encompassing it like a belt, set righteousness at the heart of all its relationships, put on the gospel as its running shoes and faith as a defense against oppression and pessimism. It must proclaim salvation as something certain, the Word of God as the offensive stroke against evil, and prayer as the watchword which presents to God the needs of the world (Eph. 6:10–20). Once the Church is clothed in the armor Paul describes, it is ready to begin changing the world through the exercise of true missionary holiness.

True holiness is growth in love (Eph. 3:17b–19). In Ephesians 3:14–21 Paul pictures holiness as "power through his Spirit in the inner person" (3:16), as "Christ dwelling in your hearts through faith" (3:17), and as being "filled up to all the fulness of God" (3:19). What is at the very center of that holy presence of God in the Church? Love! "By this will all know that you are my disciples," Jesus had said (John 13:35; see John 15:10–12). There is no other activity which so completely identifies the Christian and the Church with its Lord than love. What is the sum of all the law and the prophets? *Love* of God and *love* of neighbor. And the church in Ephesus also is called to holiness by being "rooted and grounded in *love*," in order that they might "comprehend with all saints what is the breadth and length and height and depth of the *love* of Christ" (3:17–19). Love is the Church's power in the world. As church historian Kenneth Scott Latourette has shown, love was the Church's radically transforming power which unleashed such tremendous energy in the disciples of Jesus that they eventually conquered the Roman Empire.[10] "Greater love has no one than this, that one lay down one's life for one's friends" (John 15:13). And herein lies the *holiness* of the Church. "This I command you," Jesus said, "that you *love* one another" (John 15:17). It is a sobering thought to say with the creed, "*I believe the holy catholic Church, the communion of saints.*"

## The Church's Mission Is Mission to All
## (Eph. 1:15–23; 2:1–22; 3:1–13)

Ephesians follows its song of redemption with one of the most cosmic Christologies (apart from Colossians 1 which parallels it) to be found in the New Testament. Paul wants us to know about the Church by knowing about the Head of the Church. For the Church derives life, nature, and mission from the Person of Jesus Christ. As Barth has put it,

10. See Kenneth S. Latourette, *A History of the Expansion of Christianity*, 7 vols., vol. 1, *The First Five Centuries* (New York: Harper, 1937–45; repr. ed., Grand Rapids: Zondervan, 1970), 163–69; idem, *A History of Christianity* (New York: Harper and Row, 1953), 105–8.

> In the first instance it is not the community which is called a body, or compared to it, but Christ Himself. He is a body. By nature He is not simply one (for a body is the unity of many members), but one in many. It is not that σωμα is a good image for the community as such, but that Jesus Christ is by nature σωμα. . . . The community is not σωμα because it is a social grouping which as such has something of the nature of an organism, which reminds us of an organism. . . . It is σωμα because it actually derives from Jesus Christ, because of Him it exists as His body. The relationship to Him, or rather from Him, is everywhere evident: "ηοι πολλοι εν σωμα εσμεν εν χριστωι" (Rom. 12:5). He is the "Head" of this body, the centre which constitutes its unity, organises its plurality, and guarantees both (Col. 1:18, Eph. 5:23). . . . Apart from Jesus Christ there is no other principle or τελος to constitute and organise and guarantee this body.[11]

So when we read the full-blown Christology of Ephesians 1, we should have the "eyes of our heart enlightened" (1:18), and recognize that we are being told something about the body which is the Church. What we are told is fantastic! What was done in Christ is precisely the "surpassing greatness of His power toward us who believe" (1:19 NASB). Christ has been raised from the dead, seated at God the Father's right hand in heavenly places, placed far above all rule and authority, power and dominion, and given the rule over every name that is named in every age. All things have been placed in subjection under his feet; he is given to the Church as Ruler over all things, and he is the Head of the body, the Church. In him all fulness is manifested. He fills *all in all* (1:20–24).

Now if this cosmic Christology is applied to the Body of which Christ is the Head, we are faced with a far-reaching universality. We receive by faith the universality of the Church because we recognize it as an expression of the universal intention of God in Jesus Christ.[12] In choosing a people, God intended to reach out to the whole world. As Johannes Verkuyl has reminded us concerning Israel, "In choosing Israel as segment of all humanity, God never took his eye off the other nations; Israel was the *pars pro toto*, a minority called to serve the majority. God's election of Abraham and Israel concerns the whole world."[13]

We receive the Church's catholicity by faith because we do not yet see it. True, there are more than a billion people around the world who may be counted within the Christian Church in one way or another. And yet there are more than three billion others who are outside the

---

11. Barth, *Church Dogmatics*, 4.1.

12. Cf. Herman N. Ridderbos, *Paul: An Outline of His Theology*, J. R. de Witt, trans. (Grand Rapids: Eerdmans, 1975), 387–92.

13. Johannes Verkuyl, *Contemporary Missiology: An Introduction*, D. Cooper, trans. (Grand Rapids: Eerdmans, 1978), 91–92.

Shepherd's fold. If the *Church* is for everyone, why is not *everyone* in the Church?

We confess the Church's universality in Jesus Christ, so we strive to achieve it in the world (Eph. 2:1–13). In Ephesians 2 Paul says that all of us who were far from God, "dead in our transgressions," have been raised up with Him—in order that "He might show the surpassing riches of His grace in kindness toward us" who have been brought nigh (2:5–7 NASB). "Remember," Paul says, "that you were at that time (when we were Gentiles according to faith) separate from Christ, excluded . . . strangers . . . having no hope . . . without God in the world. But now in Christ Jesus you who formerly were far off have been brought near by the blood of Christ" (2:11–13 NASB).

Because it is for all people, the Church may never cease to call, to invite, to draw everyone to him. The Church catholic rightly belongs in the highways and byways as the messenger carrying a special invitation. The Church catholic is a completely open fellowship, with its doors always spread wide, open to all. The Church catholic cannot diminish its universality by exclusivism, be it social, economic, racial, sexual, cultural, or national. The Church catholic is by its very nature missionary, sent to all people precisely because the Head of the Church "fills all in all."

Since we receive the Church's universality by faith and strive to achieve it in the world, we understand that our Christian lives are an expression of the catholicity of the Church (Eph. 2:13–22). We begin to see ourselves as world Christians when we see the dividing wall demolished in his flesh (2:13–15). Now all ethnic and social distinctions have been abolished in the fulness of one body, reconciled through the death and resurrection of Jesus, through participation in the death and resurrection of the believer in Christ (2:16–18). We "are no longer strangers and aliens, but . . . fellow-citizens with the saints, and are of God's household" (2:19 NASB) within the structure of the building God is constructing (2:20–22). Christians have sometimes interpreted this to mean they should homogenize away ethnic and cultural diversity. But this unity is so much more penetrating. Under its ideal members may joyfully express differences in background as gifts from God, confident enough in their acceptance in Christ to let others do the same.

All of us have been drawn into the Church catholic so that the Church may become increasingly universal. Then we are sent out to make disciples of others. The Church is not an exclusive club of privilege, neither is it a place to rest from our labors. We have been brought in so that we may gather others into this Kingdom of grace. We have been drawn "in order that in the ages to come He might show [to everyone else] the surpassing riches of His grace in kindness toward us in Christ Jesus" (2:7 NASB).

As the Church becomes more universal, its body grows as the Church catholic (Eph. 3:1–13). Paul's exposition of the missionary nature of the Church in Ephesians is at once profound and simple. Recognized by faith, universality becomes something toward which the people strive. The natural consequence is growth. As "God's household," a "holy temple" (2:19, 21), the Church continues to grow geographically, culturally, numerically, ethnically, and socially. Here lies the "mystery" of God's purpose for all peoples, revealed to Paul, of which he is "a servant" (3:2–12).

Taken prisoner by the universal intention of Christ Jesus, Paul is sent out "for the sake of the Gentiles" (3:1). Paul is made the steward of the mystery: "that the Gentiles are fellow-heirs and fellow-members of the Body" (3:6). The mystery revealed to Paul is that God's will establishes the *catholicity* of the Church. He is to preach to the Gentiles the unfathomable riches of the cosmic lordship of Christ (3:8), "in order that the manifold wisdom of God might now be made known *through the Church*." Paul says that God's wisdom is being shown in the catholic Church, even to the spiritual forces of heaven, in accordance with his eternal, universal purpose (3:10–11). Living at the crossroads of Asia Minor, in a cosmopolitan city filled with people of many races, colors, and languages, the Ephesian Christians, though formerly strangers, are now part of that great throng "from whom every family in heaven and on earth derives its name" (3:15 NASB; cf. Phil. 2:9–10).

We have studied the missionary nature of the Church through the images afforded us by Paul in Ephesians, and have allowed those images to become a confession of God's glorious purpose. By so doing we have been confronted with a powerful vision of the local congregation in mission. By the very act of confessing our faith in "one holy catholic Church, the communion of saints," we intentionally and unavoidably commit ourselves to participate in God's mission in the world.

## Further Study

Allen, Roland. *The Spontaneous Expansion of the Church*. Grand Rapids: Eerdmans, 1962.

Banks, Robert. *Paul's Idea of Community: The Early House Churches in Their Historical Setting*. Grand Rapids: Eerdmans, 1980.

Barth, Karl. *Church Dogmatics*, 4.1.

Berkhof, Hendrikus, and Philip Potter. *Key Words of the Gospel*. London: SCM, 1964.

Blauw, Johannes. *The Missionary Nature of the Church*. New York: McGraw-Hill, 1962.

Boer, Harry. *Pentecost and Missions*. Grand Rapids: Eerdmans, 1961.

Gilliland, Dean. *Pauline Theology and Mission Practice*. Grand Rapids: Baker, 1983.

Minear, Paul S. *Images of the Church*. Philadelphia: Westminster, 1960.

Neill, Stephen. *Fulfill Thy Ministry*. New York: Harper, 1952.

Newbigin, J. E. Lesslie. *The Household of God*. New York: Friendship, 1954.

_____. *The Open Secret*. Grand Rapids: Eerdmans, 1978.

Piet, John. *The Road Ahead: A Theology for the Church in Mission*. Grand Rapids: Eerdmans, 1970.

Ridderbos, Herman N. *The Coming of the Kingdom*. Philadelphia: Presbyterian and Reformed, 1962.

_____. *Paul: An Outline of His Theology*. Grand Rapids: Eerdmans, 1975.

This chapter is adapted from the author's article in *Reformed Review* 37.3 (Spring 1984): 187–201; used by permission.

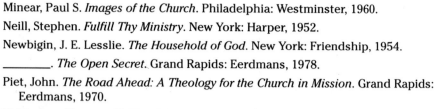

# 4

# The Essence
# of the Local Church
# in Historical Perspective

**P**aul's energizing vision of a missionary church as one, holy, and catholic underwent significant modification during the ensuing centuries. Although the three concepts were affirmed and a fourth—"apostolic"—was added at the First Council of Constantinople in 381, the Church struggled, rather unsuccessfully, during the next millennium to maintain an organic, outward-directed missional view.

Paul had demonstrated that in its openness to God, humanity, and the future, the Church stands in a tension between what it is and what it should be. But this tension itself can be the driving force to move the Church to become what it is, to "emerge" from seed to full-grown tree. As Christians who reflect on the nature and mission of the Church, we are inquiring about the essential nature of the Church. This would seem an easy matter; at least Martin Luther apparently thought so when he wrote in the Smalcald Articles in 1537:

> Thank God a seven-year-old child knows what the church is, namely holy believers and sheep who hear the voice of their shepherd

59

(John 10:3). So children pray, "I believe the one holy Christian Church." Its holiness does not consist of surplices, tonsures, albs, or other ceremonies of theirs (the papists) which they have invented over and above the Holy Scriptures, but it consists of the Word of God and true faith.[1]

More recently, Hendrik Kraemer came close to Luther's simplicity of definition when he said, "Where there is a group of baptized Christians, there is the Church."[2]

Yet the matter is not that simple. Even Luther was compelled to include the ancient confessional phrase, "*I believe* the Church." The element of belief tells us there is more to the Church than can be seen, more than exists at this moment, more than our feeble faith can encompass, and more than the attributes describe about the Church.[3] G. C. Berkouwer pointed out:

> Whoever feels urged to reflect on the Church, on her reality for faith (*credo ecclesiam*), finds himself face to face with a long series of varied questions, all closely linked to the fact that there are so many churches as well as so many differing views of the essence of the Church. In our day, especially, still another question looms behind these questions: in view of the Church's place in the world today, is such reflection really relevant? The more the Church claims to be, the more the question arises as to how obvious the statements made about the Church really are. Are such statements really credible?
>
> Even though one emphasizes that the Church may never be explained from her historical, psychological, and social components, one may still not deny that the intention of the credo ecclesiam is to point to nothing other than what is customarily called the "empirical" Church.[4]

## Invisible Ideal and Visible Reality

The Church has understood that when the words *one*, *holy*, *catholic*, and *apostolic* refer to the nature of the Church, "they have to be visible qualities of the Church as it actually exists."[5] We cannot build abstract ideas from the attributes of the Church's essence without losing touch

---

1. Lehmann, Helmut T., gen. ed., *Luther's Works*, 53 vols. (Philadelphia: Fortress, 1955), Introduction to vol. 39.

2. Quoted in International Missionary Council, *The Missionary Obligation of the Church* (London: Edinburgh, 1952).

3. Charles Van Engen, *The Growth of the True Church* (Amsterdam: Rodopi, 1981), 48–94.

4. G. C. Berkouwer, *The Church*, J. E. Davison, trans. (Grand Rapids: Eerdmans, 1976), 7.

5. Avery R. Dulles, *Models of the Church: A Critical Assessment of the Church in All Its Aspects* (New York: Doubleday, 1974), 126.

with its life on this earth. And yet neither will we seek to describe the institution purely as it is. Rather we must search for the marks of the true community in its nature as fellowship, institutionally organized. The only way we can measure a church is by what we can see.[6] Paradoxically, we also know that the Church is not what we see; she is holy but sinful, one but divided, universal but particular, apostolic but steeped in the thought structures of her own time.

The Church has seldom differentiated between the logical meaning of the formula and the visible reality. J. N. D. Kelly remarks that *holy* "expresses the conviction that [the Church] is God's chosen people and is indwelt by His Spirit. As regards 'Catholic,' its original meaning was 'universal' or 'general' and in this sense Justin can speak of 'the catholic resurrection.' As applied to the Church, its primary significance was to underline its universality as opposed to the local character of the individual congregations."[7]

Early theologians did not distinguish the visible from the invisible Church. This universal fellowship or communion was almost always conceived of as an empirical, visible society. This was the real, existing fellowship of Christ, called by the Spirit, open to all people in all the world.[8] In the early Church's self-perception unity, holiness, catholicity, and apostolicity were assumed criteria by which to measure various errors as they appeared. Later confessions fixed them as points of reference by which to measure truth.

With time, however, credal signs began to be considered properties (*proprietas*), then criteria, and finally the marks of the church (*notae ecclesiae*)—the recognizable elements of the Roman Church which constituted the basis for defending the status quo. They were misused to declare that only the Roman See was holy, perfect, complete, and God-given. They formed the rationale for defending the Roman institution called "church" from the Eastern communion, the Waldensians, or any other "churches."

By the reign of Pope Gregory IX in the 1200s the Roman Church believed God's gifts were its exclusive property. Ultimately the ideas of unity, holiness, catholicity, and apostolicity became self-justification rather than self-examination, support for the authenticity of the Roman Church. Eventually Vatican Council I (1869–1870) could state that the Church is in itself "a great and lasting motive for its credibility and divine mission."[9]

6. Gene A. Getz, *The Measure of a Church* (Glendale, Calif.: Regal, 1975), 16.

7. J. N. D. Kelly, *Early Christian Doctrines* (New York: Harper and Row, 1978), 190.

8. Ibid., 190–91. Kelly cites Clement of Rome, Justin, Ignatius, 2 Clement, and Hermas in this regard.

9. Hans Küng, *The Church: Maintained in Truth*, E. Quinn, trans. (New York: Seabury, 1980), 266.

Because of the static, self-justifying appropriation of the four attributes by the Roman Church, the Reformers felt that it was important to draw a sharp distinction between attributes and marks or *notae*. As Berkouwer explains, surveying church history . . .

> we meet with a striking distinction . . . between the attributes and marks of the Church. At first sight, the distinction is quite unclear, since one might expect that the Church can be known and precisely demarcated by means of her "attributes." However, closer inspection shows that there is an explicit motive underlying this distinction, which played a far reaching role in the controversy between Rome and the Reformation and was related to the question of how one ought to view the Church's attributes. . . .[10] In speaking of the marks of the Church, the *notae ecclesiae*, the Reformation introduced a criterion by which the Church could be, and had to be, *tested* as to whether she was truly the Church. This motif of testing in ecclesiology adds an entirely new and important perspective to the doctrine of the Church's attributes, and it is of decisive significance for the nature of the Church and her attributes.[11]

The issue at stake in this very important distinction is the function of these "attributes" of the church. *One, holy, catholic,* and *apostolic* reflected an ecclesiology in which everything was decided simply on the basis that a local church existed and by virtue of that existence possessed a number of unassailable "attributes." There was no thought as to whether these attributes actually functioned in the life of the church. The Reformers found this use of the words totally unacceptable. They felt the need to suggest something more profound, a test which would demonstrate the proximity or distance of a local church from its Center in Jesus Christ.[12] This pushed the Reformers to search for a new paradigm which would help them verify the presence or absence in fact and in reality of the Church's essence. As Berkouwer explains it,

> it is striking in this connection that the four words themselves were never disputed, since the Reformers did not opt for other "attributes." There is a common attachment everywhere to the description of the Church in the Nicene Creed: one, holy, catholic, and apostolic. . . . Whether the Church is truly one and catholic, apostolic and holy, is not asked; rather, a number of marks are mentioned, viz. the pure preaching of the gospel, the pure administration of the sacraments, and the exercise of church discipline. . . . The decisive

10. Berkouwer cites Herman Bavinck, *Gereformeerde Dogmatiek*, 4 vols. (Kampen, the Netherlands: Kok, 1895–1901), 4.304.

11. Berkouwer, *The Church*, 13; emphasis author's.

12. Hendrikus Berkhof, *Christian Faith: An Introduction to the Study of the Faith* (Grand Rapids: Eerdmans, 1979), 409.

point is this: the Church is and must remain subject to the authority of Christ, to the voice of her Lord. And in this subjection she is tested by Him. That is the common Reformation motive underlying the *notae*.[13]

Thus for the Reformers the three marks of the Church were ways by which members of a local body could ascertain their proximity to Jesus Christ, the one and only true Center of the Church's deep essence. Pure preaching of the Word, right administration of the sacraments, and proper exercise of discipline were tests by which the entire Church could be measured as to its faithfulness to its Lord. The presence of the Lord of the Church in its midst would test all the Church's activities, dogmas, and postures of discipline. The Reformers wanted to point to something behind and beyond the four attributes to the Center, to Jesus Christ, to whom the Church owed its life and nature. Since the four "attributes" had lost their testing function, Word and sacrament were needed to bring back a reference to the one Ground of the Church's being and truth. Jesus Christ would be known as the gospel was proclaimed in word and deed in the life and worship of the Church. This would redirect the Church to a dynamic view of the four attributes as well. Avery Dulles notes, "The gospel, to be sure, is one and holy. Being directed to all men, it is catholic. Since it can never be changed into a 'different gospel' (cf. Gal. 1:6), it remains 'apostolic.' The Church, insofar as it lives out the gospel, would share these attributes. The Church, however, does not proclaim itself. . . . The Church is considered to stand under the gospel and be judged by it."[14]

The Reformers felt that it did no good if the Church claimed to be one, holy, catholic, and apostolic—and yet was not directed to the one Head of the body, Jesus Christ, as the Ground and Goal of the four ancient words.[15]

Unfortunately, soon after the Reformers, the Reformation "marks" themselves became means for destroying unity, true holiness, and catholicity. Luther and John Calvin originally intended these marks to be dynamic, inclusive means by which greater unity, holiness, and catholicity might be achieved. Sadly, the children of the Reformation stressed the other, darker side of these marks—their introverted, exclusivistic tendency. As Richard de Ridder (following John Piet) has shown, the later Reformed churches used the marks to signify the *place* where certain things were done, rather than the *tasks* to be carried out in the

13. Ibid., 14–15.
14. Dulles, *Models*, 126–27; see also Küng, *The Church*, 268.
15. Cf. Van Engen, *Growth of the True Church*, 237–39.

world.[16] Thus, they too became dogmatic, polemical tools for differentiating one church as "true" and another as "false." Increasingly in post-Reformation Protestantism they also lost their self-examining, dynamic function. So the problem of defining a living and dynamic ecclesiology was not solved. John Piet well describes the flaw inherent in these marks:

> First, it is clear that all definitions of the church written during the sixteenth century were influenced by social and religious factors prevalent at that time. . . . Secondly, the marks of the church carry one only so far, since their interpretation can vary considerably. Lutherans differ from Calvinists, some Lutherans from other Lutherans, and some Calvinists from other Calvinists, precisely because each group places its own connotation upon such words as "rightly" and "purely."
>
> Thirdly, although all reformational definitions have their point of departure in Scripture, they are not necessarily "scriptural," because scriptural descriptions of the Church arise from the context of mission, whereas Reformational definitions arise from a given situation in society. . . . Lastly, the effect of reformational thinking upon the present must be seen for what it is, and recognized wherever it appears. One effect is that anyone who adheres rigidly to Reformation concepts of the church stands in danger of having a stationary or static view of the Church. . . . The Church must look to God and to the world and find its reason for being as God's people in God's world.[17]

This development in ecclesiology contributed to the twentieth-century tendency for neither Roman Catholics nor Protestants to be sure of where they stand in proximity to the dynamic, living essence of the Church. The Church lost the objectivity to maintain a constantly-reforming ecclesiology. Christians had no bases on which to evaluate oneness, holiness, catholicity, and apostolicity in actual experience; there was a growing suspicion that a one-nature perspective was not adequate. Could the Church truly be viewed as having only one nature, either divine or human?[18] Ecclesiologists began to seek a way to view the local church as *both*

16. See Richard de Ridder, *Discipling the Nations* (Grand Rapids: Baker, 1971), 212–14; Van Engen, *Growth of the True Church*, 243–48; John Piet, *The Road Ahead: A Theology for the Church in Mission* (Grand Rapids: Eerdmans, 1970), 24; Colin Williams, *Where in the World?: Changing Forms in the Church's Witness* (New York: National Council of Churches, 1963), 52, and idem, *What in the World?* (New York: National Council of Churches, 1964), 44.

17. Piet, *The Road Ahead*, 28–29.

18. For example, the Third World Conference on Faith and Order (1952) stated, "We are agreed that there are not two churches, one visible and the other invisible, but *one Church which must find visible expression on earth*" (Lukas Vischer, *A Documentary History of the Faith and Order Movement* [St. Louis: Bethany, 1963], 103). Abraham Kuyper wrote a major paragraph defending a similar perspective in *Tractaat van de Reformatie der Kerken*, entitled, "*Waarom de eene zelfde kerk op aarde tegelijk onzichtbaar en zichtbaar zij.*"

human and divine, organism and organization, fellowship and institution. This, in turn, demanded that they return to the Nicene attributes and the Protestant marks, perceiving them as both gifts and tasks.

## A New Look at the Four Distinctives

Such diverse theologians as Hans Küng, Berkouwer, Dulles, Hendrikus Berkhof, and Karl Barth all called for a reexamination, a way of measuring reality by the ideal of the four concepts. The words expressed both gifts and tasks and so might define the idea of the Church as emerging toward the full manifestation of its true nature. Thus the *gift* that the Church's nature is *one* embodies the *task* to strive toward unity, to live as one, to unite itself around its Lord. The *gift* that the Church's nature is *holy* accompanies the *task* to strive toward holiness in its members, in its organizations, in its life in the world, in its reception and expression of the Word of God. The *gift* that the Church is *catholic* means that the Church's *task* is to grow in its geographical, cultural, racial, spiritual, numerical, and temporal universality around the Lord of lords who speaks his Word to all creatures. The *gift* that the Church is *apostolic* would itself be a *task* for applying the apostolic gospel, living in the apostolic way, and being sent as apostles to the world.

This perspective begins to find a way in which the Church which we confess by faith becomes somewhat recognizable in its actual life in the world. This view offers exciting new possibilities for the Church in mission. Beyond that, David Watson writes, "the old order of the established and organized church, relying on its structures and traditions instead of the renewing of the Spirit of God, will not do. The formularies and creeds of the church, devoid of spiritual life, will never satisfy those who in their own different ways are searching for the living God." Watson continues that if the Church can rediscover its God-given identity, and become alive in spirituality, the most exhilarating part of its history may lie ahead. "Everything depends on our ability to catch a new vision of the church as it ought to be, on our willingness to change where necessary, and above all on our determination to keep our lives continually open to spiritual renewal."[19] There must be movement and development from our conception of what the Church is toward our commitment to what the Church must become.[20]

If the four words are understood as both gifts and tasks, we are no longer restricted within the confines of an institution which may or may not reflect the Nicene and Reformation qualities. Our concept of *Church*

19. David Watson, *I Believe in the Church* (1st American ed., Grand Rapids: Eerdmans, 1979), 37–38.

20. See Jürgen Moltmann, *The Church in the Power of the Spirit* (New York: Harper and Row, 1977), 2.

## Figure 2
### A Dynamic View of the Four Attributes

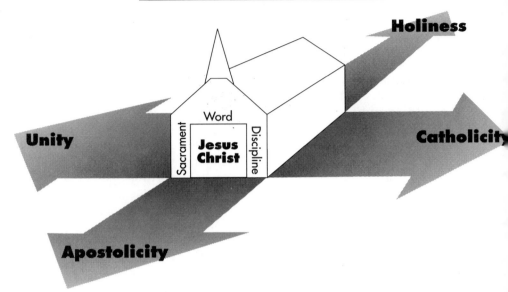

reaches beyond what *is* to what *could be* as we maintain more intimate contact with the essence of the Church's nature. In its essence, the Church begins to reach out beyond itself. The Church truly begins to be turned "inside out," as Johannes C. Hoekendijk has advocated. This kind of dynamic movement outward from the attributes of the Church might be illustrated by the diagram which follows (see figure 2).

In figure 2 Jesus Christ can be seen to be the very Center of the definition of the Church, recognized in the Reformation "marks," and expressed in the Church's nature through four planes which represent the four attributes of the Church. However, those attributes themselves cannot express the reality of the presence of Christ in the Church unless they also are given an expanding direction as both gifts and tasks of the Church's life. When this happens, the four attributes can be seen to expand outward, into the world.[21]

### The Four Attributes in Action

Missiologically we cannot stop there. We must look for another way of maintaining a dynamic, missional understanding of the four words. The Küng-Berkouwer perspective of "gift and task" was deficient in this

21. J. E. Lesslie Newbigin emphasizes this in *The Household of God: Lectures on the Nature of the Church* (New York: Friendship, 1954), 47–60.

regard because it tended to look mostly inward at the Church and ignored the world in which the Church lives, for which the Church exists, and to which the Church is sent. Jürgen Moltmann was one of the first of a number of more recent ecclesiologists to call for a look outward to the world in which the Church is to be the Church. That world, says Moltmann, is divided, embattled, unjust, and inhumane. "We cannot therefore merely give the marks of the church bearings that tend in an inward direction, understanding them in the light of word and sacrament; we must to the same degree give them outward direction and see them in reference to the world. They are not merely important for the internal activities of the church; they are even more important for the witness of the church's form in the world."[22]

For Moltmann, of course, the close identification between Jesus and the oppressed calls for a radical missional response to the four distinctives: "The church's unity is its unity in freedom. The church's holiness is its holiness in poverty. The church's apostolicity bears the sign of the cross and its catholicity is linked with its partisan support for the oppressed."[23]

Jon Sobrino followed Moltmann's thinking in *The True Church and the Poor*,[24] developing his more strongly missiological view along the ideas of "the unity of the church of the poor, the holiness of the church of the poor, the catholicity of the church of the poor, and the apostolicity of the church of the poor. . . . I believe," says Sobrino, "that the church of the poor is an authentically missionary church dedicated to evangelization. Mission is much more important than in the past; it has changed the very being of the Church."[25]

Such thinking has had great impact on Latin American Roman Catholics, but similar ideas have been echoed by Protestants as well. Across a wide spectrum of theological and social thought there is a growing sense that we must infuse the ancient four words with a new missiological emphasis. For example, Howard Snyder, in speaking about the unity of the Church, suggests a four-step movement in the Church's missional expression: "(1) The primary purpose of the unity of the Church is that God may be glorified. (2) The secondary purpose of the

22. Moltmann, *Church in the Power*, 341–42.
23. Ibid., 341.
24. M. J. O'Connell , trans. (Maryknoll, N.Y.: Orbis, 1984).
25. Ibid., 117–18. See also Leonardo Boff. *Ecclesiogenesis: The Base Communities Reinvent the Church*, R. Barr, trans. (Maryknoll, N.Y.: Orbis, 1986); idem, *Church, Charism, and Power: Liberation Theology and the Institutional Church*, J. Dierksmeyer, trans. (New York: Crossroad, 1986); Juan Luis Segundo, *Theology and the Church: A Response to Cardinal Ratzinger* (London: Winston-Seabury, 1985); Sergio Torres and John Eagleson, eds., *The Challenge of Basic Christian Communities*, J. Drury, trans. (Maryknoll, N.Y.: Orbis, 1981), and Gustavo Gutiérrez, *A Theology of Liberation* (Maryknoll, N.Y.: Orbis, 1973), 255–85.

unity of the Church is the authentic communication of the Good News.
(3) Unity in truth is unity with Christ and thus with the Trinity. (4) This
unity in truth means both unity of belief and unity of life, both orthodoxy and orthopraxis."[26]

Maybe it is time we begin to see the four words of Nicea not as adjec-
tives which modify a thing we know as the Church, but as adverbs
which describe the missionary action of the Church's essential life in
the world. This would make the four be more than static "attributes,"
more than testing "marks," and even more than dynamic "gifts and
tasks." It would see the four as planetary orbits of the Church's missionary life in the world.

As can be seen in figure 3, this perspective would provide us with a
radically new way of affirming the congregation's missionary nature—
and would give us very concrete ways of understanding the Church as an
event or movement of missional significance.

First, *the one Church of Jesus Christ would be seen as a unifying force.*
Its life would be occupied with gathering, inviting, and incorporating. The
biblical images of organic cohesion, body life, and wedding feast would
be translated into missionary action which would seek to "preserve the
unity of the Spirit in the bond of peace" (Eph. 4:3). Second, *the holy
Church of Jesus Christ would be seen as a sanctifying force.* The Church
lives so that people can be forgiven and healed and the presence of the
holy can be experienced. Israel's Tabernacle in the wilderness is a dominant image, given fullest expression in Jesus Christ . . . Emanuel . . . God
with us. Third, *the catholic Church of Jesus Christ would be seen as a reconciling force.* This is the bridge-building movement which shows the
way to renewal and fellowship with God for fractured, alienated humanity. Here is the Church as ambassador, calling the world to be reconciled
to God (2 Cor. 5). Fourth, *the apostolic Church of Jesus Christ would be
seen as a proclaiming force.* Only in the Church is truth and certainty
available and the offer of structure and stability finally practical. The
Church is the fellowship of disciples who know, love, and serve each

26. Howard A. Snyder, "Co-operation in Evangelism," in: C. René Padilla, ed., *The New
Face of Evangelicalism: An International Symposium on the Lausanne Covenant* (Downers
Grove, Ill.: Inter-Varsity, 1976): 113–34. See also José Miguez Bonino, "Fundamental
Questions in Ecclesiology," in Sergio Torres and John Eagleson, eds., *The Challenge of
Basic Christian Communities: Papers from the International Ecumenical Congress of
Theology, February 20–March 2, 1980, São Paulo, Brazil,* J. Drury, trans. (Maryknoll, N.Y.:
Orbis, 1981): 145–59; C. René Padilla, "A New Ecclesiology in Latin America,"
*International Bulletin of Missionary Research,* 11.4 (Oct. 1987), 156–64; Guillermo Cook,
"Grassroots Churches and Reformation in Central America," in *Latin American Pastoral
Issues,* 14.1 (June 1987), 5–23; Orlando Costas, *Christ Outside the Gate* (Maryknoll, N.Y.:
Orbis, 1978); Robert L. Wilson, "How the Church Takes Shape," in *Global Church Growth,*
20.6 (Nov.–Dec. 1983), 325–27, and John R. Welsh, "Comunidades Eclesiais de Base: A
New Way to Be Church," *America,* 154.5 (8 Feb. 1986), 85–88.

# Figure 3
## The Four Attributes in Missional Perspective

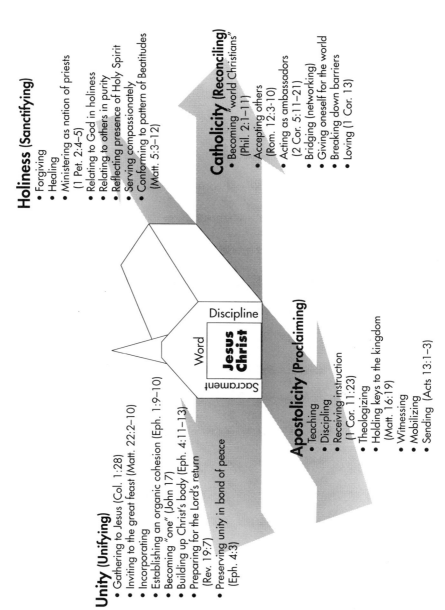

**Holiness (Sanctifying)**
- Forgiving
- Healing
- Ministering as nation of priests (1 Pet. 2:4–5)
- Relating to God in holiness
- Relating to others in purity
- Reflecting presence of Holy Spirit
- Serving compassionately
- Conforming to pattern of Beatitudes (Matt. 5:3–12)

**Catholicity (Reconciling)**
- Becoming "world Christians" (Phil. 2:1–11)
- Accepting others (Rom. 12:3–10)
- Acting as ambassadors (2 Cor. 5:11–21)
- Bridging (networking)
- Giving oneself for the world
- Breaking down barriers
- Loving (1 Cor. 13)

**Apostolicity (Proclaiming)**
- Teaching
- Discipling
- Receiving instruction (1 Cor. 11:23)
- Theologizing
- Holding keys to the kingdom (Matt. 16:19)
- Witnessing
- Mobilizing
- Sending (Acts 13:1–3)

**Unity (Unifying)**
- Gathering to Jesus (Col. 1:28)
- Inviting to the great feast (Matt. 22:2–10)
- Incorporating
- Establishing an organic cohesion (Eph. 1:9–10)
- Becoming "one" (John 17)
- Building up Christ's body (Eph. 4:11–13)
- Preparing for the Lord's return (Rev. 19:7)
- Preserving unity in bond of peace (Eph. 4:3)

Jesus Christ

Word
Sacrament
Discipline

other because they know, love, and serve their Master. This is the witnessing, mobilizing, and teaching fellowship which, based on the teaching of the apostles and prophets, proclaims God's Word in the world.

Viewed this way the four ancient concepts are not only activities the Church does, but the totality of existence. Therefore, they should be the concerns that set the agenda in the local congregation. What is the Church? It is the unifying, sanctifying, reconciling, and proclaiming activity of Jesus Christ in the world. Mission cannot be something separate from or added to the essence of the Church. The essential nature of the local congregation is, in and of itself, mission, or else the congregation is not really the Church.

Notice that this description is a far cry from saying that "everything the church does is mission." What the church does internally with no intention of impacting the world outside itself is not mission. But when a local congregation understands that it is, by its nature, a constellation of mission activities, and it intentionally lives its life as a missionary body, then it begins to emerge toward becoming the authentic Church of Jesus Christ. This leads us to the next chapter, where we will explore the concept of "missional intention," and examine some new words which may serve us as concrete expressions of the local congregation's missional existence in the world.

## Further Study

Barth, Karl. *The Church and the Churches*. Grand Rapids: Eerdmans, 1936. See 27–28.

Berkouwer, G. C. *The Second Vatican Council and the New Catholicism*, L. B. Smedes, trans. Grand Rapids: Eerdmans, 1965. See chapter 3.

Congar, Georges Yves. *The Mystery of the Church*, A. V. Littledale, trans. Baltimore: Helicon, 1960. See chapter 2.

Cook, Guillermo. "Grassroots Churches and Reformation in Central America," *Latin American Pastoral Issues*, 14.1 (June 1987), 5–23.

_____. *The Expectation of the Poor: Latin American Base Ecclesial Communities in Protestant Perspective*. Maryknoll, N.Y.: Orbis, 1985. See 95–104.

_____. "The Protestant Predicament: From Base Ecclesial Community to Established Church—A Brazilian Case Study," *International Bulletin of Missionary Research*, 8.3 (July 1984), 98–102.

Dulles, Avery R. *A Church to Believe In: Discipleship and the Dynamics of Freedom*. New York: Crossroad, 1982. See chapter 2.

_____. *Models of the Church*. Garden City, N.Y.: Doubleday, 1974. See chapter 2.

Grabowski, Stanislaus J. *The Church: An Introduction to the Theology of St. Augustine*. St. Louis: Herder, 1957. See chapter 3.

Hoekendijk, Johannes C. "The Church in Missionary Thinking." *International Review of Missions* (July 1952): 324–37.

_____. *The Church Inside Out*, I. C. Rottenberg, trans. Philadelphia: Westminster, 1966.

Johnson, Douglas W. *Managing Change in the Church*. New York: Friendship, 1974.

Kelley, Arleon L. *Your Church: A Dynamic Community*. Philadelphia: Westminster, 1982.

Kelley, Dean M. *Why Conservative Churches Are Growing: A Study in the Sociology of Religion,* rev. ed. New York: Harper and Row, 1977. See chapter 5.

Mayers, Marvin K. *Christianity Confronts Culture: A Strategy for Cross-Cultural Evangelism*. Grand Rapids: Zondervan, 1974. See chapter 1.

Schlink, Edmund. *The Coming Christ and the Coming Church*. Philadelphia: Fortress, 1968. See part 2.

Schmemann, Alexander. *Church, World, Mission: Reflections on Orthodox in the West*. Crestwood, N.Y.: St. Vladimir's Seminary Press, 1979. See chapter 8.

Sexton, Virgil. *Listening to the Church: A Realistic Profile of Grass Roots Opinion*. Nashville: Abingdon, 1971.

Visser 'T Hooft, W. A. *The Pressure of Our Common Calling*. New York: Doubleday, 1959.

Watson, David. *I Believe in the Church*. Grand Rapids: Eerdmans, 1979. See 331–68.

Williams, Colin W. *Where in the World?: Changing Forms of the Church's Witness*. New York: National Council of Churches of Christ in the U.S.A., 1963. See 21–71.

*Church's agenda should be to utilize the great task aspects of 4 concepts (one holy Catholic apostolic)*

# 5

# *Restating the Missionary Intention of the Local Church*

hen Dietrich Bonhoeffer wrote *Communio Sanctorum*[1] he introduced other ideas—new, concrete, recognizable distinctives—that might direct the local church toward its life and mission in the world. Bonhoeffer essentially pointed back to the four ancient concepts we studied in chapter 4. But these four credal attributes, tested by the three Reformation marks, have never constituted an exhaustive list of pointers to the Church's ultimate nature and reality, according to G. C. Berkouwer.

Yet Berkouwer wonders if the new indicators being suggested are not simply stating the implications of the Nicean attributes: "Here we cannot help thinking of the many images and characterizations of the Church in the Scriptures, especially in the New Testament. . . . This multiplicity itself can guard us from onesidedness. It is good to remember this when we reflect on the attributes of the Church, since the whole life of the

---

1. E.T., Dietrich Bonhoeffer, *The Communion of Saints: A Dogmatic Inquiry into the Sociology of the Church*, trans. from 3d German ed. (New York: Harper, 1964).

Church is at stake in the pure understanding of the *credo ecclesiam*, the one reality of the Church."[2]

We must hold two very different but complementary truths in dialectical tension: First, we must be open to new ways of perceiving the Church's nature within a specific time and historical context. Second, given the Church's continuity of message and purpose through history, we must assert that there is only one reality, and the same Lord of the Church yesterday, today, and forever (Heb. 13:8). Thus every new description needs to be seen in relation to the four attributes, tested by Scripture and recognized in the Reformation marks of the Church. Each new suggestion must be a concrete, testable, and visible means of recognizing the presence of the one, holy, catholic, and apostolic community of Jesus Christ today.

Between Pentecost and Parousia the Church is a movement which is becoming . . . an emerging reality. Its actions within a historical situation (what some theologians prefer to call *praxis*), as well as its ever-changing place and nature in the world, dictate that we constantly look for new ways to express the concept of *Church*. Reflecting on what this means for the modern era, Jürgen Moltmann says, "we find that Christianity's new answer to the altered situation in the world was: (i) a missionary church; (ii) the will to ecumenical fellowship between the divided churches; (iii) the discovery of the universality of the Kingdom of God; and (iv) the lay apostleship."[3]

In its sameness, then, the Church must continually change its mode of expression, for it is historically oriented to an constantly-changing world. The new ideas should enhance and strengthen the missiological dimensions of the Church's nature as those are given concrete expression in today's world. The new concepts we will now look at are *being for the world, identification with the oppressed, mission, proclamation witness,* and *yearning for numerical growth.*

## Being for the World

In his *Letters and Papers from Prison*, Dietrich Bonhoeffer said, "The Church is the Church only when it exists for others."[4] The Church exists for humanity in that it is the spiritual body of Christ, and—like Jesus—it is sent to be a servant. As the Father sent Jesus, so Jesus sends his disciples into the world for the sake of the world. The disciples who would

---

2. G. C. Berkouwer, *The Church*, J. Davison, trans. (Grand Rapids: Eerdmans, 1976), 24. See also Hans Küng, The Church: *Maintained in Truth*, E. Quinn, trans. (New York: Seabury, 1980), 359; Jürgen Moltmann, *The Church in the Power of the Holy Spirit* (New York: Harper and Row, 1977), 340, and Hendrikus Berkhof, *Christian Faith: An Introduction to the Study of the Faith*, S. Woudstra, trans. (Grand Rapids: Eerdmans, 1979), 409–10.

3. Moltmann, *Church in the Power*, 9.

4. Dietrich Bonhoeffer, *Letters and Papers from Prison* (New York: Macmillan, 1953), 203.

save their lives will lose them, but those who would spend their lives in the world for the sake of the gospel of reconciliation shall find them (cf. John 15:13; 20:21; Matt. 10:39). Moltmann developed his view of the Church along similar lines in his introduction to *The Church in the Power of the Spirit*. Observing that a variety of changes and conflicts were breeding insecurity in society, he noted:

> When its traditions are imperilled by insecurity, the church is thrown back to its roots. It will take its bearings even more emphatically than before from Jesus, his history, his presence and his future. As "the church of Jesus Christ" it is fundamentally dependent on him, and on him alone. . . . I do not believe that there is any other way in which the church can proclaim the gospel responsibly, theologically speaking, or can celebrate the Lord's supper, baptize with the sign of the new beginning, and live in the friendship of Jesus [than by pointing to the people's own communal church among the people]. Missionary churches, confessing churches and "churches under the cross" are fellowship churches, or inescapably become so. They do not stray into social isolation but become a living hope in the midst of the people.[5]

We can find a similar emphasis on the Church's existence for the world in a number of late-twentieth-century missiologists and theologians. We could mention Helmut Thielicke,[6] John Piet,[7] Hans Küng,[8] Albert Theodore Eastman,[9] the World Council of Churches,[10] and the Roman Catholic documents *Lumen Gentium* (1964) and *Ad Gentes Divinitus* (1965).[11] More recently a similar view was elaborated in the Papal Encyclical, *Evangelii Nuntiandi* (1975) and *Redemptoris Missio* (1991).[12] The amazing agreement concerning the Church's "being for the

5. Moltmann, *Church in the Power,* xiii–xvi.

6. *The Evangelical Faith,* vol. 1, G. W. Bromiley, trans. and ed. (Grand Rapids: Eerdmans, 1974), 345, 362.

7. *The Road Ahead: A Theology for the Church in Mission* (Grand Rapids: Eerdmans, 1970), 101.

8. *The Church,* 485–86.

9. *Chosen and Sent: Calling the Church to Mission* (Grand Rapids: Eerdmans, 1971), 129, 132–33.

10. *The Church for Others and The Church for the World: A Quest for Structures for Missionary Congregations* (Geneva: World Council of Churches, 1968).

11. These are two of several very important documents which came out of Vatican Council II. See Austin P. Flannery, ed. *Documents of Vatican II* (Grand Rapids: Eerdmans, 1975).

12. "*Evangelii Nuntiandi*" was a result of the fourth synod of bishops, which gathered in Rome in September 1974. Pope Paul VI issued this major encyclical in December 1975. See *The Pope Speaks* 21 (Spring 1976): 4–51, and Michael Walsh and Brian Davies, eds., *Proclaiming Justice and Peace: Documents from John XXIII–John Paul II* (Mystic, Conn.: Twenty-Third, 1984), 204–42. This encyclical compares favorably in its missional approach with the most recent, "*Redemptoris Missio,*" issued by John Paul II in Jan. 1991. See also "Origins," *CNS Documentary Service* 20.34 (31 Jan. 1991), 541–68.

world," in spite of the diversity represented by these writers, ought to make us give the matter some serious consideration. They have emphasized that the Church's characteristic of existing for the world is not optional; it is part of the Church's being.

This "new word" is related to two of the traditional attributes of the Church, apostolicity and catholicity. First, being for the world is an expression of the Church's "sentness," which in turn is related to the Church's apostolicity. Just as Jesus gathered his disciples around him, so also he sent them. Particularly in Matthew 10:5–42, in the various Gospel forms of the great commission (Matt. 28:19–20; Mark 16:16; Luke 24:49; John 20:21), and in Acts 13:2–4 this "sentness" is emphasized. Discipleship must always be discipleship-in-movement-to-the-world. The disciple who will not lay down life for the world and for the gospel of reconciliation is not worthy of being a follower of Jesus Christ.

Second, the Church's being for the world is related to the Church's universality. If the scope of the kingdom is as broad as we believe it is, and if the extent of Christ's Lordship encompasses "all power and authority" (Matt. 28:18, Eph. 1:19–23, and Col. 1:15–20), then we must understand the Church's existence also within that universal scope. The Church as the body of Christ can be nothing else than for the world, for the Church's being for the world is itself an incomplete expression of the breadth of the Lordship of Christ, its Head.

The twentieth-century theologian who most fully developed the theme of the Church's being for the world was Karl Barth. In *Church Dogmatics*[13] Barth devoted an entire section to the issue of "The Community for the World." Barth's thesis was this:

> The community of Jesus Christ is itself creature and therefore world. Hence, as it exists for men and the world, it also exists for itself. . . . Even within the world to which it belongs, it does not exist ecstatically or eccentrically with reference to itself, but wholly with reference to them, to the world around. It saves and maintains its own life as it interposes and gives itself for all other human creatures.[14]

## Identification with the Oppressed

Moltmann makes a case for another characteristic of the church which may serve as a window through which we may see the missionary essence of the Church:

13. Edinburgh: T and T Clark, 1958, 762–63.
14. Ibid., 4.3.2, para. 72.

> Where is the true Church? In the fellowship manifest in word and
> sacrament, or in the latent brotherhood of the Judge hidden in the
> poor? Can the two coincide? If we take the promises of Christ's pres-
> ence seriously, we must talk about the brotherhood of believers and
> a brotherhood of the least of his brethren with Christ. "He who
> hears you hears me"—"He who visits them, visits me.". . . If the
> Church appeals to the crucified and risen Christ, must it not repre-
> sent this double brotherhood of Christ in itself and be present with
> work and Spirit, sacrament, fellowship and all creative powers
> among the poor, the hungry and the captives? . . . Then the Church
> with its mission would be present where Christ awaits it, amid the
> downtrodden, the sick and the captives. The apostolate says what
> the Church is. The least of Christ's brethren say where the Church
> belongs.[15]

A strong echo of these words could be heard at the Uppsala
(Switzerland) Assembly of the World Council of Churches (July 1968).
There many voices joined in a choral emphasis upon "humanization,"
"the new humanity," "new mankind," "true humanity," "mature manhood," and "renewed mankind." It is not our aim to argue whether political and social action are appropriate aims for the mission of the
Church. What is of interest is the close intertwining at Uppsala of ecclesiology and mission, a specific perception of the nature of the Church as
being for the world.

A radically-horizontal view of mission was espoused at Uppsala, yet
one need not follow such a theology to realize that the Church has as
much of a debt to the poor and oppressed, and as much responsibility
for the state of the world, as in any previous age. In Acts 6 the widows
were neglected by the church, and the church did something about it.
James 1:27 called for visiting orphans and widows as a demonstration of
true religion. The emphasis on mercy and compassion for the poor in
the New Testament is built on solid Old Testament exhortations found,
for example, in Malachi and Isaiah. God was displeased with pre-exilic
Israelite life when the many temple sacrifices were used to avoid helping
the poor, the oppressed, and the needy.

David Barrett highlights this in a fascinating article concerning the
financial state of the Christian Church today, entitled, "Silver and Gold
Have I None: Church of the Poor or Church of the Rich?"[16] Barrett
reported that at the time he wrote the global Christian Church had an
income of about $5.9 trillion (U.S.) a year. Of this only 3 percent was
given in donations for both Christian and nonChristian causes. The
global world mission enterprise is funded by 5 percent of that tiny 3 percent of all global giving. Barrett's conclusion? "To a large extent the

15. Moltmann, *Church in the Power*, 128–29.
16. *International Bulletin of Missionary Research*, 7.4 (Oct. 1983): 146–51.

global sharing by Christians of money, wealth, property, and goods could solve most of (the world's) problems, including those of famine, poverty, disease, unemployment, dangerous water supply, and so on. Because this is so, there is a sense in which Christians are to blame for the persistence of the present disastrous state of affairs."[17]

Is identification with the oppressed optional for the Church today? Or is it an essential part of its nature as the body of Christ in the world? For those who take the latter view, the true Church would not be found so much inside the Church walls where the Word is purely preached, the sacraments rightly administered, and church discipline exercised—but would be found where Christians are struggling on the side of the oppressed for economic, political, social, and human liberation. Is liberation theology a way of pointing to the essence of the Church? It is important that we at least struggle more deeply to define biblically and theologically how *identification with the oppressed* is related to the Church's essential nature.

## Mission

We have already mentioned the relationship between the Church's sentness and apostolicity. *Mission* seeks to strengthen the implications of that apostolicity. As the apostles are sent by Jesus, the Church is sent by her Lord. And it is in the going, in the sentness itself, that the Church emerges toward the world and toward the continuing office of the apostolate. Arnold A. Van Ruler and Johannes C. Hoekendijk, among others, reminded us of the Church's apostolate—not as an optional matter, but as an essential element of the Church's being.

The biblical theology of the Word-made-flesh, Jesus Christ, contains the concept of "sentness." The incarnation was a sending forth. John 1 teaches us that Jesus Christ as the Word was sent into the world as light in darkness. Though the darkness did not understand nor accept the light, yet that does not invalidate the sending forth and the diffusion of the light. The Word-made-flesh created, through the operation of the Holy Spirit, an apostolic band of 12, then 3000, then 5000, then 8000—a community of faith to whom Jesus says, "You are the light of the world" (Matt. 5:14). The Church becomes *mission* in following the Lord as an apostolic community that is in constant, dynamic movement, proclaiming the gospel of the kingdom of light in the midst of the kingdom of darkness.

Vatican Council II in *Ad Gentes Divinitus* stressed this essence of "mission" when it said that the nature of the Church is missionary, "since, according to the plan of the Father, it has its origin in the mission of the

17. Ibid., 151.

Son and the Holy Spirit. This plan flows from 'fountain-like love,' the love of God the Father." Therefore, missionary activity flows from the very nature of the Church; "the theology of mission is to become so much a part of theology . . . that the missionary nature of the Church will be clearly understood."[18]

The twentieth-century author who has probably stressed this view of the Church more than anyone else is Johannes Blauw in *The Missionary Nature of the Church*.[19] "There is no other Church," Blauw wrote, "than the Church sent into the world, and there is no other mission than that of the Church of Christ." He refocuses attention on mission to the world:

> If one wants to maintain a specific theological meaning of the term mission as "foreign mission," its significance is, in my opinion, that it keeps calling the Church to think over its essential nature as a community *sent* forth into the world. Seen in that light missionary work is not just one of its activities, but *the criterion for all its activities*. . . . It is exactly by going outside itself that the Church *is* itself and comes to itself.[20]

So we are justified in asking whether *mission* is not one of the new conceptions by which we may perceive the essence of the Church. It is, of course, legitimate and necessary to relate this term as we redefine it to the attribute of the apostolicity of the Church, as well as to see this mark as a natural consequence of the proclamation of the Word which is sent into the world.

Missionaries and pastors have not given enough weight to this "new word." Far too often mission is relegated to one of those "wishful-thinking" categories that we hope to get to some day in our ministry. The newer third-world churches are supposedly not ready to engage in mission on their own until they reach a certain level of maturity—that

18. Flannery, ed., *Documents of Vatican II*, 814, 820, 857. See also, *Vatican II*, "*Ad Gentes Divinitus*," 2, 5; and Paul VI, "*Ecclesiae Sanctae III*" (6 Aug. 1966). It is fascinating to see the large number of missiologists and theologians today who would echo agreement with the sentiment expressed at Vatican II. Johannes Verkuyl, for instance, mentions Karl Barth's thesis that "if the Church fails her missionary obligations, she is no longer Church" (*Contemporary Missiology: An Introduction*, D. Cooper, trans. [Grand Rapids: Eerdmans, 1978], 61, citing idem, *Church Dogmatics*, 4.2, 3); see also idem, *Credo: A Presentation of the Chief Problems of Dogmatics with Reference to the Apostles' Creed*, J. S. McNab, trans. (New York: Scribners, 1936), 145. Similar ideas have been presented by J. H. Bavinck, Hendrik Kraemer, Arnold A. van Ruler, and in Colin W. Williams, *New Directions in Theology Today: The Church* (vol. 4 of William Hordern, ed., *New Directions in Theology Today*, 6 vols. [Philadelphia: Westminster, 1968], 80).

19. *The Missionary Nature of the Church: A Survey of the Biblical Theology of Missions* (New York: McGraw-Hill, 1962).

20. Ibid., 121–22 (author's emphasis). See also idem, "The Mission of the People of God," in Charles C. West and David M. Paton, eds., *The Missionary Church in East and West* (London: SCM, 1959).

maturity often judged by Westerners, based on Western standards. Meanwhile the North American and European congregations often relegate "mission" to the leftover category, with the internal necessities of congregation and membership receiving higher priority. Mission calls us to radical reexamination. If mission is part of the essence of the Church's nature as the body of Christ and the people of God, then it ought to be at the top of the list.

## Proclamation Witness

A number of years ago Blauw called Barth "the first, and up to now the only, systematic theologian who sees the existence and task of the Christian to lie in witness."[21] Blauw was pointing to Barth's strong emphasis on the Word of God, relating revelation to the mission of the Church.[22] Barth said it this way:

> The community is the human fellowship which in a particular way provisionally forms the natural and historical environment of the man Jesus Christ. Its particularity consists in the fact that by its existence it has a witness to Him in face of the whole world, to summon the whole world to faith in Him. Its provisional character consists in the fact that in virtue of this office and commission it points beyond itself to the fellowship of all men in face of which it is a witness and herald.[23]

In this day when there is so much confusion concerning the Church's reason for being and relation to the world, we must understand proclamation as something which is done not only inside the Church but also outside the confines of the Church to those for whom Christ died. This is stressed by Lesslie Newbigin, who related the converting work of the Spirit to the being of the Church by saying that "it is the Spirit who converts, not the Church." Then he asks, "Where, then, does the Church come into the picture?" His answer is that "the Church comes into the picture at the point where it is on trial for its faith, at the point where it confesses the sole lordship of Jesus in the face of the overwhelming power of that which denies it, at the point—therefore—where it bears the marks of the Cross, at the point of marturia."[24]

*Proclamation witness* as a mark of the Church attempts to restore the outward and upward direction of the Church. Proclamation witness takes place, most profoundly, in the world, where the Church is a wit-

21. Blauw, *Missionary Nature*, 169.
22. Blauw was referring primarily to *Church Dogmatics*, 4.2.
23. *Church Dogmatics*, 2.2.
24. J. E. Lesslie Newbigin, "Context and Conversion," *International Review of Mission*, 68.271 (July 1979): 307.

ness of Jesus Christ. This serves as a corrective to the Reformation's highly internalized use of preaching, sacrament, and discipline as something done within the midst of the Church, where the presence of Christ is manifested through the "marks" understood introvertedly. Whereas the Reformation perspective on the marks was essentially inward-looking, proclamation witness directs the marks outward. Thus proclamation witness turns the Church inside out, externalizing its life so that its essence becomes the bridge between God and humanity. In this view the Church would be compared with the slaves in the parable of the marriage feast (Matt. 22:1–14). The Church is being obedient when it can be found out in the main thoroughfares and streets inviting everyone to the eschatological wedding feast of the Lamb. Here can be found the Church of Jesus Christ known and tested by her proclamation witness.

## Yearning for Numerical Growth

As we have seen, in the twentieth century Protestants and Catholics alike felt the need to redefine, reformulate, rethink, and reshape their ecclesiology. As a result, some found that the credal "four" could be infused with new and dynamic meaning to again test the life of the Church—as they were originally intended. Others realized, however, that there was a need to rethink the situation of the Church in the world. These new ideas are actually reflections or restatements of the four attributes and the three Reformation marks. But, more significantly, they are ways in which the Church can be pointed back to its Center and critiqued according to its distance from that Center.

In this evaluating process we should add one more concept to the list. In *The Growth of the True Church*[25] it was demonstrated that *yearning for numerical growth* is an essential mark of the presence of the true Church. Yearning for numerical growth originates in a number of important motifs found in Scripture, all of which point to the same essential reality. The *universal intention* of God in the Old Testament, the *gathering* in the New Testament, the *finding* of the lost sheep, the *building* toward fulness, and the picture of *growth* all point to something in the Church's nature which makes it yearn to incorporate more and more people within itself. There are likewise many biblical images of the Church which suggest this earnest desire. Whether the Church is viewed as the people of God, the new Israel, the sheepfold, the planting, the building, or the body, there is always a driving energy within it. This is the growth principle by which the Church has always expressed her nature in "yearning" to incorporate more and more men and women within the bounds of God's grace. It is a movement, a spirit, a presence

25. Charles Van Engen, *The Growth of the True Church* (Amsterdam: Rodopi, 1981), 142.

which has pushed the Church from Pentecost to the present in an ever-widening, ever-outward, ever-enlarging sphere of life and influence in the world. This "yearning" element is found in Isaiah 55:11–13; 56:8 (NEB). The word of YHWH, it promises,

> shall not return to me fruitless without accomplishing my purpose or succeeding in the task I gave it. You shall indeed go out with joy and be led forth in peace. Before you mountains and hills shall break into cries of joy, and all the trees of the wild shall clap their hands, pine-trees shall shoot up in place of camel-thorn, myrtles instead of briars; all this shall win the Lord a great name, imperishable, a sign for all time. . . . This is the very word of the Lord God, who brings home the outcasts of Israel; I will yet bring home all that remain to be brought in.

Yearning by Christians for numerical growth involves an attitude about the Church, its place in the mission of God, and its role in the world. It is the attitude portrayed by Paul when he said, "For I could even pray to be outcast from Christ myself for the sake of my brothers, my natural kinsfolk" (Rom. 9:3 NEB). Newbigin said, "Anyone who knows Jesus Christ as his Lord and Saviour must *desire ardently* that others should share that knowledge and must rejoice when the number of those who do is multiplied. Where this desire and this rejoicing are absent, we must ask whether something is not wrong at the very center of the church's life."[26]

In a sense this last "new concept" is the concrete manifestation of all four credal attributes. *The one Church yearns* to incorporate more and more men and women and unite everything and everyone at the feet of Jesus Christ (Col. 1). *The holy Church yearns* to bring the holiness of God to bear in the lives of all sinful humanity. *The catholic Church yearns* to spread her universal fellowship of loving believers to include all those who will believe on the Lord Jesus Christ. *The apostolic Church yearns* to go and make disciples of all peoples, because there, among all the nations, Christ has promised to be present. This yearning Church knows that it has been assembled to serve, and it assembles others to serve together with it, in the world. These disciples come hoping, praying, desiring, yearning that those who are "not-my-people" will come to experience the joy of becoming the people of God (1 Pet. 2:9–10). This yearning is the basic characteristic of the Church which gives rise to its apostolate.

We summarize this chapter in figure 4. The reader will remember that in previous chapters we examined the four credal attributes surrounding the three Reformation marks, and understood them as both gifts and

---

26. James E. Lesslie Newbigin, *The Open Secret: Sketches for a Missionary Theology* (Grand Rapids: Eerdmans, 1978), 142.

# Figure 4
## New Words of Church-in-Mission

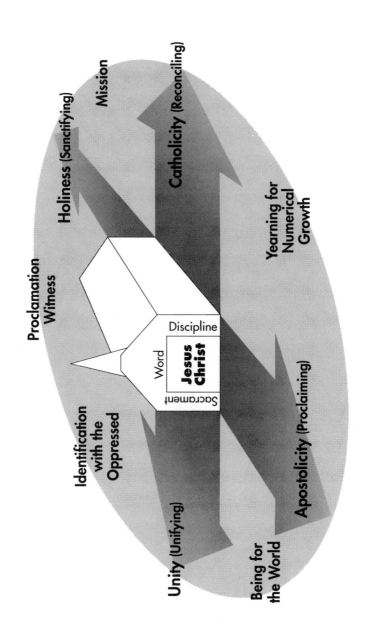

Proclamation
Witness

Holiness (Sanctifying)

Mission

Catholicity (Reconciling)

Yearning for
Numerical
Growth

Discipline

Word

**Jesus
Christ**

Sacrament

Apostolicity (Proclaiming)

Identification
with the
Oppressed

Unity (Unifying)

Being for
the World

tasks, as movements outward from the center to the edge of the Church's missionary being in the world. As soon as we began to be involved in this movement, we were faced with other perspectives which brought us into that emerging, changing, growing, dynamic area where the Church meets the world. In this new arena of the Church's nature we found that some "new words" better expressed what the Church is because they demonstrate what the Church is becoming in its missional calling to the world. Thus the Church emerges from its Center, Jesus Christ, moves toward the world, and there finds dynamically described its marching orders for a missionary presence in the world.

## Further Study

### *Identification with the Oppressed*

Arias, Mortimer. *Salvación es Liberación*. Buenos Aires: Aurora, 1973.

Arias, Esther and Mortimer. *The Cry of My People*. New York: Friendship, 1980.

Gutiérrez, Gustavo. *We Drink from Our Own Wells: The Spiritual Journey of a People*, M. J. O'Connell, trans. Maryknoll, N.Y.: Orbis, 1984.

Padilla, C. René. *Mission Between the Times: The Essays of C. René Padilla*. Grand Rapids: Eerdmans, 1985, 170–85.

Segundo, Juan Luis. *The Community Called Church*, J. Drury, trans. Maryknoll, N.Y.: Orbis, 1973.

Verkuyl, Johannes. *Break Down the Walls: A Christian Cry for Racial Justice*. Grand Rapids: Eerdmans, 1973.

### *Mission*

Bosch, David. "Mission in Jesus' Way: a Perspective from Luke's Gospel." *Missionalia* 17.1 (April 1989), 3–21.

Avis, Paul D. L. *The Church in the Theology of the Reformers*, P. Toon and R. Martin, eds. Atlanta: John Knox, 1981.

Hall, Francis J. *The Church and the Sacramental System*. New York: Longmans, Green, 1920. See chapters 3, 5, and 6.

Miller, Donald G. *The Nature and Mission of the Church*. Atlanta: John Knox, 1957.

Peters, George. *A Biblical Theology of Missions*. Chicago: Moody, 1972. See chapter 6.

Scott, Waldron. *Karl Barth's Theology of Mission*. Downers Grove, Ill.: Inter-Varsity, 1978. See 31ff.

Van den Heuvel, Albert H. *The Humiliation of the Church*. Philadelphia: Westminster, 1966. See chapter 3.

Wilson, Frederick. *The San Antonio Report: Your Will Be Done. Mission in Christ's Way*. Geneva: World Council of Churches, 1990.

*[handwritten note: Essence of ch - Mission, proclamation witness, yearn for numerical growth]*

PART **2**

# Local Churches

## *A New Vision of God's Missionary People*

# 6

# *The Purpose of the Local Church*

As we expand the horizons of the Church's missionary nature we are directed outward from Jesus Christ, the Head of the Church, through the three Reformation marks, through the four credal attributes of the Church, to new attributes which today may show us where the Church is truly God's missionary people in the world. And once out in that land of intercession and intermediacy we are faced with one of the more difficult questions about the Church: Why does it exist in the world?

The answer cannot revolve around what we *want* the Church's purpose to be, or *what we think the world desires or needs* the Church's purpose to be. Rather, the Church's purpose can be derived authentically only from the will of Jesus Christ, its Head; from the Spirit who gives it life; from the Father who has adopted it, and from the trinitarian mission of God.[1]

---

1. James E. Lesslie Newbigin demonstrates this relationship between the church's purpose and the Trinity in *The Open Secret: Sketches for a Missionary Theology* (Grand Rapids: Eerdmans, 1978).

87

The question of the Church's purpose is extremely important. Whether at the level of the local congregation, or at the regional, national, or international and cross-cultural levels, the same question faces all of the Church's life and activity. How we answer determines how we set goals, define objectives, and lay out strategies. Edward Dayton and Theodore Engstrom have spoken of "the awesome power of goals."[2] Alvin Lindgren has emphasized that "contemporary pressures require the Church to define its nature":

> Defining the nature and purpose of the Church is an intensely personal matter for the minister, since the concept of ministry emerges directly from the concept of the Church. . . . We are saying that the very content of the gospel predetermines the vehicles which are suitable for carrying it. . . . Achievement of God's purpose, not activism, is the sole concern of church administration. . . . Let it be clear that our concern is with a definition of *what the church ought to be*, its essential nature and purpose, rather than a description of what it now is, or for that matter what the church has been, either in church history or even in the New Testament. . . . The Church ought to be whatever God intended it to be, and we search the Scriptures to discover God's intention for the Church.[3]

Karl Barth observed that the Church's essential nature is not only perceived, but in fact comes to be, when the Church fulfils the purpose for which it exists. Barth spoke of the Church's purpose in relation to "the doctrine of reconciliation" as this leads toward "the being of the community" of reconciled persons.[4]

The Church is there because Jesus Christ lives in the midst of the members of the community. As John MacKay has said, "We share the view that the Christian Church is basically a Fellowship, that it is the community of those for whom Jesus Christ is Lord. We believe that the essential reality of the Church is community and that community is more basic to the Church's reality than organization or structure, both of which are secondary."[5]

---

2. Edward R. Dayton and Theodore W. Engstrom, *Strategy for Leadership* (Old Tappan, N.J.: Revel, 1979), 51.

3. Alvin J. Lindgren, *Foundations for Purposeful Church Administration* (Nashville: Abingdon, 1980), 281–33. Emphasis author's.

4. Karl Barth, *Church Dogmatics* (Edinburgh: T and T Clark, 1958), 4.1.650–51.

5. John MacKay, "The Witness of the Reformed Church in the World Today," *Theology Today*, 11 (Oct. 1954): 375. See also Charles Van Engen, *The Growth of the True Church* (Amsterdam: Rodopi, 1981), 166; Ralph P. Martin, *The Family and the Fellowship: New Testament Images of the Church* (Grand Rapids: Eerdmans, 1979); Paul D. Hanson, *The People Called: The Growth of Community in the Bible* (San Francisco: Harper and Row, 1986).

This community perspective of the Church as the people of God was a dramatic new development in Roman Catholic thought at Vatican Council II. Gregory Baum pointed this out in his introduction to *The Teachings of the Second Vatican Council*[6] and in his commentary on *De Ecclesia*.[7] He stated that the constitution on the Church from Vatican II represents a radical shift from an institutional view of the Church to a perspective on the Church as a community, fellowship, and people of God. When we read the documents we begin to discover the tremendous doctrinal riches contained in this major achievement.[8]

So it is important for us to examine the purpose of the Church's life in the world, as that is derived from the Church's nature as a fellowship of the redeemed. At this point we are reminded of some well-known scriptural words which reflect a many-sided description of the Church's reason for being. Four of these may be easily recognized by the reader: *koinonia*, *kerygma*, *diakonia*, and *martyria*. The thesis of this chapter is that the missionary Church emerges when its members increasingly participate in the Church's being-in-the-world through *koinonia*, *kerygma*, *diakonia*, and *martyria*. We need to take a closer look, therefore, at these words, viewing them from a biblical perspective. Coupled with each word is a biblical statement which might summarize that particular aspect of the Church's reason-for-being in the world.

κοινωνία:   "Love one another" (John 13:34–35; Rom. 13:8; 1 Pet. 1:22).

κήρυγμα:   "Jesus is Lord" (Rom. 10:9; 1 Cor. 12:3).

διακονία:   "The least of these my brethren" (Matt. 25:30, 45).

μαρτυρία:   "You shall be my witnesses; be reconciled to God" (Isa. 43:10, 12; 44:8; Acts 1:8; 2 Cor. 5:20).

As we approach the New Testament Church we must remember that we are studying self-images of a fellowship which was gathered around Jesus Christ. The New Testament Church considered the presence of

---

6. Gregory Baum, "Introduction" in *The Teachings of the Second Vatican Council: Complete Texts of the Constitutions, Decrees, and Declarations* (Westminster, Md.: Newman, 1966), vii–xi.

7. Idem, "Commentary," in Edward H. Peters, ed., *De Ecclesia, The Constitution on the Church of Vatican Council II Proclaimed by Pope Paul VI on November 21, 1964* (Glen Rock, N.J.: Paulist, 1965), 18.

8. Some of Baum's subsequent works draw out the implications of this new ecclesiology, e.g., *The Credibility of the Church Today: A Reply to Charles Davis* (New York: Herder and Herder, 1968), chapter 1, and *Man Becoming: God in Secular Language* (New York: Herder and Herder, 1970), chapter 3. Baum should be read in context with Karl Rahner, Hans Küng, and other Vatican II theologians who have drawn similar implications from the Council's shift in ecclesiology.

Christ the supreme authenticating sign of its own existence. Besides being a promise, the words "I am with you always" (Matt. 28:20) also described the nature of the community of those who had walked personally with Jesus of Nazareth.

### Koinonia: "Love One Another"

One of the simplest but most complex words describing the Church is the command of Jesus: *love*. Not only did the disciples of Jesus understand *agape* love to be the way of life expected of the people of God; it had been the church's duty from ancient times. Love of neighbor can be found early in the Old Testament (Lev. 19:18; Prov. 20:22; 24:29). In fact, love of God and neighbor is the summary of Torah (Mark 12:29–31).

But Jesus brought an astounding new dimension to this Old Testament truth. "I give you a *new* commandment: Love one another; as I have loved you, so you are to love one another" (John 13:34 NEB). So what was really "new" about this commandment? Charles K. Barrett tells us that the commandment is new in that "it corresponds to the command that regulates the relation between Jesus and the Father [John 10:18, 12:49–50, 15:10]; the love of the disciples for one another is not merely edifying, it reveals the Father and the Son."[9]

Here is the revolutionary factor injected by Jesus: This type of love was new in kind, though it had a continuity from the Old Testament. It now meant a transformed kind of life, qualitatively new in its outward, sacrificial, self-giving sense.[10] "His followers are to reproduce," said Charles H. Dodd, "in their mutual love, the love which the Father showed in sending the Son, the love which the Son showed in laying down his life."[11] This love is not a sentiment spoken from emotion alone, but rather *a certain type of action* which Father and Son have taken upon themselves for the sake of the world. This self-denying response is commanded of the disciples.

The *new* commandment is incarnational. "Anyone who loves me will heed what I say [in the new commandment to love]; then my Father will love him, and *we will come to him*, and make our dwelling with him" (John 14:23 NEB). Barrett comments that this promises an indwelling by both Father and Son, "the parousia upon which John's interest is concentrated, and it is the interval, unforeseen by apocalyptic Christianity, between the resurrection and the consummation that he proposes to explain."[12]

9. Charles K. Barrett, *The Gospel According to Saint John: An Introduction with Commentary and Notes on the Greek Text* (Philadelphia: Westminster, 1978), 451.

10. Charles Van Engen, *Growth of the True Church* (Amsterdam: Rodopi, 1981), 167.

11. Charles H. Dodd, *The Interpretation of the Fourth Gospel* (Cambridge: Cambridge University Press, 1953), 405.

12. Barrett, *Gospel According to Saint John*, 466.

This is how the promise "I will be with you always" is fulfilled, and the sense in which the Church in the time-between-the-times becomes profoundly the body of Christ. That continuing presence bridges between the "already" and the "not yet" of the kingdom. It is in the mutual love of the disciples that there is parousia, the Lord's coming—after Jesus' first coming, and before his second. And it is in this new presence of Jesus that the disciples and all those who follow after them can discover the presence of Jesus, though they do not see him; for where they are gathered in loving *koinonia*, he will be there. And where the Head of the Church is present in the midst of his disciples, there the Church exists.

Jesus Christ's new presence in the loving fellowship (*koinonia*) of the disciples constitutes the Church. Without this presence of Christ, there is no Church. How do we so easily forget that it is only in the context of the love of disciple for Lord and disciple for disciple that the Church has life at all? What Paul said in 1 Corinthians 13 applies: If the Church is one, holy, universally catholic, and apostolic but has no love, it is nothing. Undergirding all else lies the supreme mark of the people of God—love. Unless the Church is first of all the community of love, Word and sacrament are an empty mockery. In this "time between the times" the Church must hear again the voice of its Lord:

> I give you a new commandment: love one another; as I have loved you, so you are to love one another. If there is this love among you, then all will know that you are my disciples [John 13:34–35 NEB].

Likewise, being for the world, identification with the oppressed, mission, proclamation witness, and yearning for numerical growth are meaningless outside the light of this supreme mark of the Church. The Church's *koinonia* as a fellowship of love is also the foundation for *diakonia*, *kerygma*, and *martyria*. But the absence of *diakonia*, *kerygma*, or *martyria* may mean that the Church has turned inward upon itself to such an extent that there is no longer the kind of *koinonia* of which Jesus spoke. We cannot forget that *all people* will know if the disciples love each other within the Church, because this love is to be *externalized*. Otherwise, we would fall into the unhealthy situation C. Peter Wagner calls "koinonitis":

> Fellowship, by definition, involves interpersonal relationships. It happens when Christian believers get to know one another, to enjoy one another, and to care for one another. But as the disease develops, and koinonia becomes koinonitis, these interpersonal relationships become so deep and so mutually absorbing, they can provide the focal point for almost all church activity and involvement.

Church activities and relationships become centripetal [introverted].[13]

*Koinonia becomes koinonitis when the purpose for which the fellowship exists is lost.* The church loses sight of why there is a Sunday school class, a prayer group, or neighborhood calling. Introversion occurs unless love is lived out in fellowship, service, and self-sacrifice. Churches who lose *koinonia* lose fellowship with the Christ who linked the promise "I am with you always" with the command to "go and make disciples."

### Kerygma: "Jesus Is Lord"

At Pentecost we see an explosion of the disciples who upon receiving the Holy Spirit, immediately move outward to the streets to proclaim the truth which has changed their lives. The koinonia fellowship itself embodies a proclamation of the lordship of Jesus of Nazareth.

The confession that Jesus is Lord was probably one of the earliest rallying points of the New Testament Church. We know that it reflects the very ancient Old Testament understanding of the people of God as the people of YHWH, translated in the Septuagint as *kyrios*, and associated with the divine name in the minds of the disciples of Jesus. Oscar Cullmann asserts that the New Testament Church adopted "Jesus is Lord" as the central element of its faith and identity.[14] The earliest Christian creed took the form, "Jesus is Lord."

The lordship of Christ drives the Church outward in its proclamation of the gospel to the world. The confession has some amazingly broad ramifications and sharp implications. Harry Boer, for example, makes a case for linking the New Testament's teaching of the lordship of Christ with God's universal intent. He cites such texts as Romans 11:25, 26; 16:25; Ephesians 1:9-10, 3:3-11, 5:32; Colossians 1:26-27, and 1 Timothy 3:16 to show that the lordship of Christ is not simply lordship in the Church and over individual believers, but rather *lordship with cosmic and universal proportions*[15] (Acts 4:25-30). The apostle Paul, writing to the Christians in Colossae, brought together the fullest implications of the confession, "Jesus is Lord," in the high christology of Colossians 1.

The Gospels begin with a major emphasis on the *kerygma*. John the Baptist comes proclaiming, "The kingdom of heaven is near" (Matt. 3:2). Jesus declares that the reason he has been sent is to "preach the good

---

13. C. Peter Wagner, *Your Church Can Be Healthy* (Nashville: Abingdon, 1979), 78.
14. Oscar Cullmann, *The Earliest Christian Confessions* (London: SCM, 1949). See also Harry R. Boer, *Pentecost and Missions* (Grand Rapids: Eerdmans, 1961), 144.
15. Boer, *Pentecost and Mission*, 153–55.

news of the kingdom of God" (Luke 4:43). No sooner does the Holy Spirit come at Pentecost, than the disciples take to the streets and Peter proclaims, "God has made this Jesus, whom you crucified, both Lord and Christ" (Acts 2:37). Paul's first sermon emphatically repeats the point: "I want you to know that through Jesus the forgiveness of sins is proclaimed to you. Through him everyone who believes is justified from everything you could not be justified from by the law of Moses. . . . For this is what the Lord has commanded us, 'I have made you a light for the Gentiles'" (Acts 13:38-39, 47; cf. Luke 2:32, Isa. 49:6). Years later, under house arrest in Rome, Paul continued to proclaim the same message. "Boldly and without hindrance he preached the kingdom of God and taught about the Lord Jesus Christ" (Acts 28:31).

The Church's purposive existence in this world as the kerygmatic fellowship of the disciples who confess that Jesus is Lord was described by Rudolf Schnackenburg as a necessary mission, "willed by Christ to bring the world of men and with this the whole creation under his rule." He explained that the "cosmic ecclesiology" of the Pauline Epistles "throws light on the special attitude that was seen by and imposed itself on the early Church as soon as it grasped the notion of Christ's position as Lord, his heavenly exaltation and establishment in sovereign power and reflected upon all its consequences. Christ's rule here and now over Church and world is the manner in which the kingship of God is realized in the present era of salvation between fulfillment and completion."[16]

The kerygmatic confession "Jesus is Lord" necessarily involves movement outward toward the world as the arena and recipient of the Church's kerygmatic proclamation. The Church recognized that the reconciling, redeeming, and renewing kingdom of this Lord is a universal kingdom which includes all nations. "Jesus is Lord" means "Jesus is Lord of the world." The Church cannot escape the fact that to confess Jesus as Lord moves it profoundly toward its own universality—a movement outward to the nations. This is climactically presented to us in the Great Commission of Matthew 28:19–20: "Full authority in heaven and on earth has been committed to me. Go forth therefore and make all nations my disciples."

The Church of Jesus Christ exists when people confess with their mouth and believe in their heart that Jesus is Lord—Lord of the Church, of all people, and of all creation (cf. Col. 1:15–20). Through this confession the Church emerges to become what it is, the missionary fellowship of disciples of the Lord Jesus Christ.

16. Rudolf Schnackenburg, *God's Rule and Kingdom*, J. Murray, trans. (New York: Herder and Herder, 1963), 316–17. See also Geerhardus Vos, *The Teaching of Jesus Concerning the Kingdom of God and the Church* (Grand Rapids: Eerdmans, 1958); George Ladd, *The Gospel of the Kingdom* (Grand Rapids: Eerdmans, 1959), and Herman N. Ridderbos, *The Coming of the Kingdom*, H. de Jongste, trans. (Philadelphia: Presbyterian and Reformed, 1962).

Thus the mission of Jesus becomes inescapable and utterly binding for all of his disciples. They cannot confess Jesus is Lord without at the same time proclaiming his lordship over all people. The implication of this intimate, inseparable connection between confession and commission is that the fulfilling of the commission to the world over which Christ is Lord *is itself a mark of the missionary Church* (see Phil. 2:9–11).

Here is where worship and liturgy need to fit into the perception and program of missionary congregations. Even the Eucharist is for Paul a matter of proclaiming Christ's death until he comes again (1 Cor. 11:26). The verbal proclamation of the gospel in the *kerygma* and the visual proclamation of the gospel in the sacraments empower the Church's confession that Jesus is Lord. What we too often forget, however, is that it makes no sense for evangelistic proclamation to be made by Christ's disciples only to Christ's disciples within the confines of the local church. The proclamation is only kerygmatic when it is intentionally addressed to those who have not accepted Jesus as Lord.[17]

So Jesus Christ, the Lord of all people, all creation, and Lord of the Church, sends his people to a radical encounter with the world. This creates a necessity and an energy which impels the Church forward in its emerging out of love, through confession, to action—that is, to *diakonia*.

### Diakonia: "The Least of These My Brethren"

As the loving fellowship of the disciples of Jesus Christ, the Church is the fellowship of the crucified, as Donald A. McGavran has pointed out.[18] "The slave (*doulos*) is no greater than his lord (*kuriou autou*)" (Matt. 10:24; John 13:16, 15:20). Therefore the disciple who confesses that Jesus is Lord can expect to live a certain lifestyle and go through certain experiences as the servant of the master. Matthew 10:18 connects discipleship with being brought before governors and kings for Christ's sake as a witness to them and to the Gentiles (*eis martyrion autois kai tois ethnesin*; compare this with the call of Saul of Tarsus in Acts 9:15–16). John 13:16 adds that no servant is greater than his or her master as he washes the disciples' feet—the lowest task of the lowliest servant. Such an attitude of humble service is thus also required of his disciples. Then in John 15:20 the relation of slave to master is associated with Christ's choosing of his disciples, their oneness with him as his friends (*philoi*), and the persecution which results from being

17. Harvie Conn, *Evangelism: Doing Justice and Preaching Grace* (Grand Rapids: Zondervan, 1982), and John R. W. Stott, *Christian Mission in the Modern World* (Downers Grove, Ill.: Inter-Varsity, 1975), 48–51.

18. Donald A. McGavran and Winfield C. Arn, *Back to Basics in Church Growth* (Wheaton: Tyndale, 1981), chapter 5.

friends with Jesus the crucified Messiah among those for whom Jesus died.

Here three different aspects of discipleship fill the idea of being a servant: witness; personal service to each other, and suffering for Christ's sake (compare the beatitudes in Matt. 5:1–16 with Luke 6:17–26 regarding this discipleship).

*The Theological Dictionary of the New Testament* tells us that there are several words which we might find in the New Testament dealing with the concept of *service*:

| | |
|---|---|
| δουλεύω | Service as a slave. |
| θεραπεύω | Willingness for service. |
| λατρεύω | Service for wages (in the New Testament primarily religious duties). |
| ὑπηρετέω | Service to the master. |
| διακονέω | Very personal service to another.[19] |

Behind such terms lies the self-portrait by which the early followers of Jesus understood their discipleship. Matthew follows a certain progression of thought: Chapters 24–25 unite both didactic material and parables to focus on the vision Jesus shares for discipleship in the here-and-now. Interestingly, the last major portion of this teaching deals with *diakonia* (Matt. 25:31–36).

The image is one of stewards reporting to their master. In their role as servants, Jesus does not speak of disciples being judged on the basis of good conduct, sacrifices, religious life, liturgy, theology, or racial makeup. *As servants they are judged by what they did or did not do for those in their world who were obviously in need.* They are judged on the basis of their *diakonia* as servants of the Master who gave his life a ransom for many. This gives us the concrete meaning of the new commandment to "love one another"—the supreme test of discipleship. No wonder the concept of *diakonia* received such strong emphasis in the life of the early Church. Immediately after Pentecost the disciples begin working miracles, healing the sick, and caring for the needy. When the disciples could not attend to diaconal work efficiently, a new model for ministry developed—the deacon.[20] This aspect of discipleship quickly spread; Luke tells of Dorcas, whose *diakonia* service was so valued by those at Joppa that Peter had to be summoned from Lydda to bring her back to life (Acts 9:36–42). The poor could not do without the clothing

19. Gerhard Kittel and Gerhard Friedrich, eds., *Theological Dictionary of the New Testament*, G. W. Bromiley, trans., 10 vols. (Grand Rapids: Eerdmans, 1964–76): s.v., "διακονέω, διακονία, διάκονος."

20. See Ralph P. Martin, *Family and the Fellowship*, 62.

she provided for them. Paul presents *diakonia* as a full-fledged, multi-faceted ministry, writing to the Corinthians, for example, that the Holy Spirit dispenses to Christians a variety of *diakonias*—ministries of discipleship (1 Cor. 12:5). The deacon became a Church official,[21] and diaconal work an accepted ministry of worship by which the Church expressed discipleship in following the Crucified One. The Church's ministry of *diakonia* still witnesses to the Church's authenticity and contributes to the emergence of the missionary Church, the loving diaconal fellowship of those who confess allegiance to Christ.

Paul further emphasizes diaconal ministry in his second letter to the Corinthians, when he attempts to inspire them to give liberally toward the needs of the people suffering in Jerusalem. In that case Paul calls it "*tēn charin kai tēn koinōnian tēs diakonias tēs eis tous hagious*"—"the grace of sharing (or participation) in the service to the saints" (8:4). And Paul clearly associates the diaconate with discipleship in a life of dependence on God's loving provision (9:10–15). Paul couples the nature of the Church as a loving fellowship to its exercise of ministry, the act of providing for the physical needs of those who are suffering by sharing the gifts of the collection about which Paul writes.

James restores to Christian importance a very old part of the Judaic faith when he states, "The kind of religion which is without stain or fault in the sight of God our Father is this: to go to the help of orphans and widows in their distress, and keep oneself untarnished by the world" (1:27; compare this, for example, with Deut. 14:29; Job 31:16, 17, 21; Ps. 146:9; Isa. 1:17, 23). One hears echoes of the Old Testament Year of Jubilee (see Lev. 25:8–55) which Jesus spread as a backdrop for his messianic mission when he stood to read Isaiah 61:1–2 in the synagogue in Nazareth (Luke 4:18–19, 21).

All of this should be well-established in our theology of ministry, but we often fail to understand that *diaconal ministry is an inevitable and necessary expression of the Church's essential nature as the fellowship of the disciples of Jesus*. To confess Jesus is Lord is inescapably joined to the diaconal call of Jesus Christ to look after "the least of these my brethren," for in them we see the face of our Savior. Only within this context may we meaningfully discuss the Church's role in establishing justice, righteousness, and *shalom*. The New Testament teaching assumes that the diaconal ministry extends beyond addressing the needs of the believing community. *Diakonia* also calls the Church to demonstrate and contribute to the creation of a new world order where peace, justice, and mercy reign under the lordship of Jesus. *Diakonia* is not simply an extra good thing to do, or even simply a necessary outreach to the world we live in; it is the essential nature of the Christian

---

21. Kittel and Friedrich, *Theological Dictionary*, 2:89–93.

Church to minister to anyone and everyone in need. When God's missionary Church ceases to be involved in diaconal ministry, something about her missionary nature ceases to emerge.[22]

## Martyria: "You Shall Be My Witnesses"

Just before his ascension, Jesus told his disciples in Acts 1:8, "You shall be my witnesses" (*kai esesthe mou martyres*), beginning in Jerusalem and spreading outward geographically and culturally to the ends of the earth (*eōs eschatou tēs gēs*). Much has been made of this commission in terms of the geographic and cultural expansion of the Church. But maybe we have missed the full weight of Christ's words: "You shall be my *witnesses*." The Church's existence shall be one of witness in all those places and cultures.

Acts provides a detailed description of the earliest days of the Church. It is made clear that loving *koinonia* fellowship, a communal life, a kerygmatic proclamation that Jesus is Lord, a sharing with those in need through a loving diaconal ministry all brought about *marturia*—a powerful witness to the Church's missionary nature.[23] J. Herbert Kane has stated that the Church's nature in the world involves declaring and demonstrating—truth and power—as components of the Church's existence and mission in the world.[24] *Martys* has several uses in Scripture:

1. witness to facts in a legal sense
2. witness to facts in a confession of faith
3. declaration of fact as an eyewitness to an event
4. the evangelistic witness to Christ's nature and significance
5. martyrdom[25]

Within the scope of these meanings the purpose of the body of Christ is to make the fact that Jesus Christ is present in the world tangible, real, visible, and effective. The people who do not know Jesus are to come to know him in the presence, the proclamation, and the persuading acts and words of the Church. God's missionary Church witnesses to the fact that Jesus is alive and that he is the Head of the body, the Church, through loving *koinonia* fellowship, through confession that Jesus is Lord, and through actions of diaconal service. God's missionary

22. David B. Barrett discusses this relationship in "Silver and Gold Have I None: Church of the Poor or Church of the Rich?" in *International Bulletin for Missionary Research* 7.4 (Oct. 1983): 146–51.

23. Van Engen, *Growth of the True Church*, 178–90.

24. J. Herbert Kane, *The Christian World Mission* (London: Lutterworth, 1963), chapter 4.

25. Kittel and Friedrich, *Theological Dictionary*: s.v., "μάρτυς . . . ."

# Figure 5
## Purposes for an Emerging Church

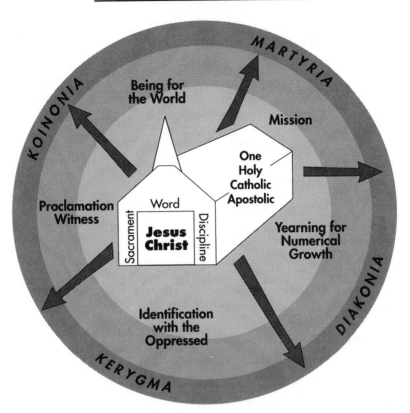

people are to be a reconciled community who witness to the possibility of reconciliation in an alienated world. So in 2 Corinthians 5:18–21 Paul asserts that members of the Church are ambassadors through the diaconal ministry of reconciliation (*tēn diakonian tās katallagēs*).

The missionary Church itself becomes the "righteousness of God" in Christ in exercising the ministry of reconciliation. The work of bringing God's reconciliation to the world is the heart and soul of the Church's witness. Through its loving *koinonia*, which expresses its faith in *kerygma* and *diakonia* the Church witnesses by saying to the world: "Be reconciled to God."[26]

26. It is interesting to note that *presbyteros* derives from the verb "to ambassador" (*presbeuō*). Paul uses it in 2 Cor. 5:20 to describe the reconciliation that is to be carried out in the world. . . not in the church. What does this say about our concept of ministry? What is this passage is the purpose of having elders? See W. A. Visser T'Hooft, *The Pressure of Our Common Calling* (New York: Doubleday, 1959), 39.

Now we begin to see the full breadth of the Church's nature. At the level of the local congregation the missionary Church discovers its reason for being in the world as it becomes the loving koinonia fellowship of disciples of the crucified Jesus, confessing in word and deed that Jesus is Lord, and witnessing to the greatest event of all time—God with us. Is this the reason for which your congregation, mission church, or denomination exists in the world today?

*[handwritten: Summarize 4 greek words that define the four reasons for the Church's being in the world]*

## Further Study

### Koinonia

Many have written on this subject, but from the congregational view helpful resource readings include:

Arn, Winfield C., and Charles Arn. *Who Cares About Love?* Pasadena, Calif.: Church Growth, 1986.

Barth, Karl. *Church Dogmatics*, 4.2.68.

Berkouwer, G. C. *The Church*, J. Davison, trans. Grand Rapids: Eerdmans, 1976. See 45–46.

Getz, Gene A. *The Measure of a Church*. Glendale, Calif.: Regal, 1975. See 22–67.

Kittel, Gerhard, and Gerhard Friedrich, eds. *Theological Dictionary of the New Testament*, G. W. Bromiley, trans., 10 vols. Grand Rapids: Eerdmans, 1964–76. s.v., "καινος . . . "; s.v., "κοινωνος . . . ."

"*Lumen Gentium*," in Austin P. Flannery. *Documents of Vatican II*. Grand Rapids: Eerdmans, 1975.

Martin, Ralph P. *The Family and The Fellowship: New Testament Images of the Church*. Grand Rapids: Eerdmans, 1979. See chapter 3.

Schaeffer, Francis. *The Mark of the Christian*. Downers Grove, Ill.: Inter-Varsity, 1969.

Snyder, Howard A. *The Community of the King*. Downers Grove, Ill.: Inter-Varsity, 1977. See 45–95.

Tillapaugh, Frank. *The Church Unleashed: Getting God's People Out Where the Needs Are*. Ventura, Calif.: Regal, 1982.

Watson, David. *I Believe in the Church*, 1st American ed. Grand Rapids: Eerdmans, 1979. See chapter 19.

### Kerygma

Green, E. Michael B. *Evangelism in the Early Church*. Grand Rapids: Eerdmans, 1970. See 49ff.

Hoekendijk, Johannes C. "The Call to Evangelism" in *International Review of Missions*, 39 (April 1950): 162–75.

Kittel and Friedrich, eds. *Theological Dictionary of the New Testament*. s.v., "κήρυγμα": 3.714–18.

Kraemer, Hendrik. *The Communication of the Christian Faith*. Philadelphia: Westminster, 1956.

McGavran, Donald A., and Winfield C. Arn. *Ten Steps for Church Growth*. San Francisco: Harper and Row, 1977. See chapters 5, 6.

Schlink, Edmund. *The Coming Christ and the Coming Church*. Philadelphia: Fortress, 1968.

### Diakonia

Bosch, David. "The Scope of Mission," *International Review of Mission*, 73.289 (Jan. 1984): 17–32.

Kraybill, Donald B. *The Upside-Down Kingdom*. Scottdale, Pa.: Herald, 1978.

McKee, Elsie Anne. *Diakonia in the Classical Reformed Tradition and Today*. Grand Rapids: Eerdmans, 1989.

Sine, Tom. *The Mustard Seed Conspiracy: You Can Make a Difference in Tomorrow's Troubled World*. Waco, Tex.: Word, 1981.

Van Klinken, Jaap. *Diakonia: Mutual Helping with Justice and Compassion*. Grand Rapids: Eerdmans, 1989.

Wallis, Jim. *Agenda for Biblical People*. New York: Harper and Row, 1976.

Yoder, John. "The Experiential Etiology of Evangelical Dualism" in *Missiology*, 11.4 (Oct. 1983): 449–59.

_____. *The Politics of Jesus: vicit Agnus noster*. Grand Rapids: Eerdmans, 1972. See 115–92.

*Your Kingdom Come: Mission Perspectives; Report on the World Conference on Mission and Evangelism, Melbourne, Australia, 12–25 May, 1980*. Geneva: World Council of Churches, 1980.

See also Ronald Sider's works.

### Martyria

Kraemer. *Communication of the Christian Faith*. See 116ff.

Kittel and Friedrich, eds. *Theological Dictionary of the New Testament*, s.v., "ἀλλάσσω"; s.v., "πρέσβυς . . . ."

MacNair, Donald J. *The Growing Local Church*. Grand Rapids: Baker, 1975. See chapters 1, 10, 11.

Metz, Donald. *New Congregations: Security and Mission in Conflict*. Philadelphia: Westminster, 1967. See chapter 3.

Schillebeeckx, Edward C. "The Church and Mankind," in Edward J. Dirkswager, Jr., comp. *Readings in the Theology of the Church*. Englewood Cliffs, N.J.: Prentice-Hall, 1970.

Schlink, Edmund. *The Coming Christ and the Coming Church*. Philadelphia: Fortress, 1968. See 102ff.

# 7

## *The Local Church and the Kingdom of God*

od's grace drops us into the pond of the world to create ever-widening ripples. Our vision of mission begins at the center, Jesus Christ, and is bound to the Word of God, proclaimed verbally and represented sacramentally. Like small waves, the faith of the one, holy, catholic, and apostolic community of believers spreads inevitably outward toward the world. This missionary faith is defined through some "new words" that give form to the way we expand further outward: *koinonia, kerygma, diakonia,* and *martyria.*

We have not yet reached the point of missionary encounter between Church and world, however, for we must also consider the relation of the covenant community to the kingdom of God in the life of the local congregation. *Koinonia, kerygma, diakonia,* and *martyria* derive from a larger perspective of the kingdom of God in a world that is created, sustained, governed, and redeemed by Jesus Christ, the King. We cannot fully understand the breadth or depth of the congregation's mission unless we see it in relation to the kingdom of God in the world (see figure 6). As the missionary people of God, local congregations are branch offices of the kingdom, the principal instrument, anticipatory sign, and primary locus of the coming of the kingdom.

101

## Figure 6
### The Covenant Community of the King

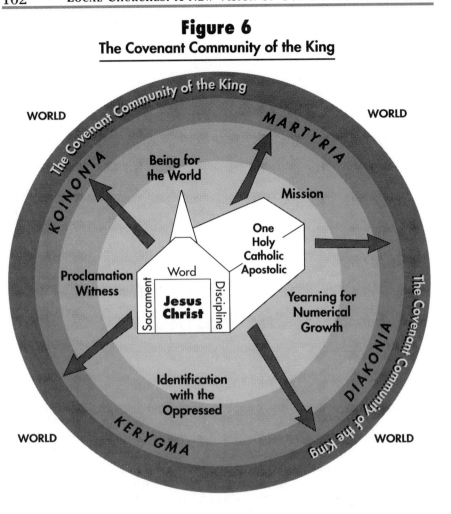

## The Covenant Community in Scripture

Missionary congregations are local manifestations of the covenant community of the King. The people of God have been seen as the covenant community since the Abrahamic covenant (Gen. 15) and the beginning of Israel's self-consciousness as a unique people, described, for example, in Deuteronomy 10:15. We can see in the Old Testament a very strong realization on the part of the Israelites that they were a special people because of the direct acts of the God-over-all. Theirs was a realization that this God-Creator-of-all elected them to be a special people with a unique heritage, mission, and hope.

Israel increasingly understood its reason-for-being within the framework of a covenantal relationship with YHWH. This relationship involved both blessing and cursing, two sides of the same covenant which spelled out Israel's nature as the special people of YHWH. The people accepted the negative with the positive, convinced by historical experiences that God held Israel in particular esteem as his special people. At the same time Israel became increasingly conscious of the fact that God was not to be owned or controlled. He was Lord of all and within the covenant had given to Israel a special purpose in relation to other nations. To be bound in covenant to YHWH meant, therefore, to be a participant in YHWH's universal purpose for the whole world. Israel could not remain forever exclusive because YHWH's desire was to bless all peoples. To be the people of YHWH meant a commitment to be an instrument on behalf of all the nations within the universal scope of YHWH's lordship over all the world.[1] Daniel T. Niles summed up this world relationship with four principles:

1. God's concern for the salvation of the nations underlies his call of Abraham.
2. Israel is formed out of the nations and so is not a nation like any other. Israel is a nation within and out of the nations and addressed to them.
3. The God who chose Israel out of the nations remained always the God of all the nations.
4. Because of this threefold emphasis, Israel's life and mission affect not only its national history but also the history of the world.[2]

"Such a conception of Israel's life and mission," Niles said, "demanded on the one hand that it guard its identity in the world, and on the other hand that it serve the world towards which its mission was set."[3]

Throughout its history Israel continually struggled to balance the particular and the universal aspects of its nature. Israel was a special people, yet its mission was to represent before God all the peoples of the earth. As one of the nations, chosen from out of the nations and standing alongside them, Israel had no special merit and significance. Its uniqueness did not stem from its ancestry, nor its history, race, culture,

1. On this lordship see, for example, Johannes Blauw, *The Missionary Nature of the Church: A Survey of the Biblical Theology of Mission* (Grand Rapids: Eerdmans, 1974); Richard R. De Ridder, *Discipling the Nations: The Biblical Basis for Missions* (Grand Rapids: Baker, 1975); Suzanne De Dietrich, *The Witnessing Community: The Biblical Record of God's Purpose* (Philadelphia: Westminster, 1968).

2. Daniel T. Niles, *Upon the Earth: The Mission of God and the Missionary Enterprise of the Churches* (New York: McGraw-Hill, 1962), 250.

3. Ibid., 251.

or language. It stemmed from YHWH's unique call. Yet precisely because of YHWH's unique purpose, Israel considered itself different, having a special destiny, a unique mission which set it apart from all other races, cultures, tribes, families, and nations.[4]

Jesus adapted this concept in his call to the disciples. He told them that they were in the world but not of the world because their allegiance, values, goals, and hope were not of the world. They were sent to be a part of the world, but they were sent as sheep among wolves, to be hated and persecuted just as he was (Matt. 10:16–25). They represented the world and were sent to the world, and yet they were uniquely separated from the world by God's call to discipleship.

Paul picked up this theme during his first missionary journey when he preached his first sermon in Pisidian Antioch (Acts 13:16–41). Paul saw his mission as an apostolate, derived from Jesus' messianic mission (Luke 4:17–27), now transferred to the disciples: to be a "light to the Gentiles" (Acts 13:47). Peter reminded his readers that they were "a chosen people, a royal priesthood, a holy nation, a people belonging to God, that you may declare the praises of him who called you out of darkness into his wonderful light" (1 Pet. 2:9). The result of the Church's chosenness would be that the "pagans" would "see your good deeds and glorify God on the day he visits us" (1 Pet. 2:12). Light for the Gentiles . . . priests for the nations—here is the special calling and identity of missionary congregations. They are the missionary people of God whose uniqueness derives directly from God's instrumental purposes for them. They are God's special people who, because of God's call, emerge in human history as the covenant community of the King, a branch chapter of the kingdom of God. Anyone who downplays the importance of the local congregation in relation to mission must carefully consider its unique identity and purpose in the world as a *covenant community of the King*.

## The Covenant Community in Church History

Such a perspective of the local church was practically lost during the medieval period, as ecclesiology became imprisoned in the institutional church, due in part to Constantine's wedding of church, society, and state. By the Late Middle Ages, the *ecclesia docens* (teaching church) was considered to be far superior to the *ecclesia audiens* (listening church). Only the missionary orders stood with even a qualified challenge to the assertion that the essence of the gospel of the kingdom was found in the ecclesiastical hierarchy.

4. See, for example, Paul D. Hanson, *The People Called: The Growth of Community in the Bible* (New York: Harper and Row, 1986), and Blauw, *Missionary Nature*.

The Orthodox churches were not so bound as the West to hierarchy, but in the East the concept of the people of God was lost under heavy sacramental baggage. Sacrament and ritualistic worship defined the Church with little reference to people or to world.

The people-of-God concept was rediscovered by the Protestant Reformation and given strong impetus by the Radical Reformation of the Anabaptists. The essence of the Church was again understood not as hierarchy and institution, but as people in community, through the perspective Martin Luther brought to ecclesiology.[5] For Luther's day this was revolutionary. With the exception of the Eastern Church, whose relation to Rome was understood differently, Luther saw only one Church. That Church was the "ark" wherein salvation was to be found—and he had little tolerance for those who would reject it. But that church was bankrupt, spiritually and morally.[6] Luther found himself in a terrible dilemma when he was compelled to break with what he had always believed was the one and only true Church. He first wrestled with the question that Protestants have been asked ever since: "Where was your Church before Luther?"[7]

In general his answer was that the evangelicals are the "old" Church, the continuing people of God. This people, like a sun that had been hiding behind the clouds, was again bursting forth. This true Church was a spiritual communion called by God through the gospel, and gathered in a crowd (*Hauffe*), a convocation (Versammlung), an assembly (*Sammlung*), or a congregation (*Gemeinde*). The communion of saints gathered around the Word was the true Church.[8] We have one baptism, one gospel, and one faith—and we are all Christians alike, for baptism, gospel, and faith alone make a spiritual and Christian people.[9] Therefore the Church must be understood as consisting primarily of people—it is not so much Church in the sense of *Kirche*. The people comprise the "holy believers and the lambs who hear their shepherd's voice."[10] This emphasis on the Church as the people of God was at times misused, but it was always there. Nearly every Protestant group of the sixteenth and

5. Hendrik Kraemer emphasized again for our time the importance of this aspect of Reformation ecclesiology in *A Theology of the Laity* (Philadelphia: Westminster, 1958).

6. See, for example, Luther's description in the "Ninety-Five Theses" (1517); "Appeal to the German Nobility" (1520); and "On the Councils and the Church" (1539).

7. Karl Barth made a point of this in a lecture in 1928 before an assembly of Protestants and Roman Catholics. See Barth's *Theology and Church* (New York: Harper and Row, 1962), 312.

8. See Martin Luther, *Luther's Works* (Philadelphia: Fortress, 1955): 41.179, and 39:65–69, 71.

9. See "Appeal to the German Nobility" in Henry Bettenson, ed., *Documents of the Christian Church* (London: Oxford, 1963), 193.

10. "Smalcald Articles" (1537) in *Luther's Works*, 39:xi.

seventeenth centuries agreed that the Church is the communion of saints, the people of God.

In reaction, the Counter-Reformation of the Roman Church disavowed this view. The Council of Trent (1545–63) and Vatican Council I (1870) strongly equated the institution and hierarchy of the Roman Church with the true Church. The view of the Church as the community of the faithful was finally given its due in Roman Catholic circles at Vatican Council II (1965). Gregory Baum, a major Roman Catholic ecclesiologist, called this astounding revolution the "principal achievement" of Vatican II: "This self-reflection of the Church on her own nature is the basis for the reform and renewal of Catholic life, which is the purpose of the entire Council. By remembering in faith who we, the Church, are . . . we come to realize anew what is God's will for his people. . . . The Constitution on the Church is the basic charter for the reform of the Church in our century."[11]

At about the same time this revolution in thinking was sweeping the Roman Catholic church, Protestants were finding that they needed to reaffirm the same concept. Churches associated with the World Council of Churches began emphasizing the "structures of missionary congregations" and rediscovered the fact that these structures could not take shape except through the membership—the people of God. The conservative evangelicals began to move strongly in the direction of parachurch agencies involved in mission—and found that this type of mission is primarily an expression of the life of members of the congregations.

These Protestant streams simply reaffirmed what many had been saying all along. The Radical Reformation emphasized this ecclesiology, as did the German pietists, the Awakenings of the eighteenth and nineteenth centuries, the Pentecostals at the beginning of the twentieth century, and the charismatics after 1960. All these groups developed around a view of the Church which strongly emphasized the role of the people of God as God's agents of mission in the world. During the 1960s as this new interest in the church as the people of God arose, a parallel emphasis began to be articulated. Theologians came to a remarkable consensus that the kingdom of God existed in both "already" and "not-yet" dimensions.

At Vatican II the Roman Catholic Church ceased to define the kingdom of God as identical with the Church.[12] Protestant thinkers were

11. Gregory Baum, "Introduction," in Austin P. Flannery, *Documents of Vatican II* (Grand Rapids: Eerdmans, 1975), 15, 25–26. See also Avery R. Dulles, *Models of the Church: A Critical Assessment of the Church in All Its Aspects* (Garden City, N.Y.: Doubleday, 1974), and Hans Küng, *The Church*, R. Ockenden, trans. (New York: Sheed and Ward, 1967).

12. Hans Küng gives a helpful historical survey of the association of kingdom and Church in *Church*, 90–92. Leonardo Boff drew out the implications of Vatican II's ecclesiology at this point in *Ecclesiogenesis: The Base Communities Reinvent the Church*, J. Dierksmeyer, trans. (Maryknoll, N.Y.: Orbis, 1986); and idem, *Church, Charism and Power: Liberation Theology and the Institutional Church*, J. Dierksmeyer, trans. (New York: Crossroad, 1985).

increasingly coming to see that the eschatological questions regarding the kingdom affected their view of the relationship between the kingdom and the Church. The kingdom of God could no longer be seen as identical with the Church. As Philip Schaff noted already in 1950, "in many passages [of Scripture] we could not possibly substitute the one [the church] for the other [the kingdom of God] without manifest impropriety."[13] In scope, time, and state the kingdom was seen to be deeper, more extensive, and purer than the Church. Yet the "already-not-yet" aspect of the kingdom was also true of the Church. As Herman N. Ridderbos, George Eldon Ladd, Oscar Cullmann, John Bright, and others demonstrated, the kingdom, the rule of Jesus Christ, is already present, but not yet complete; it has come but is coming. So also with the Church.[14] Ridderbos said it this way:

> The basileia [kingdom of God] is the great divine work of salvation in its fulfillment and consummation in Christ; the ekklesia [Church] is the people elected and called by God and sharing in the bliss of the basileia. The former, therefore, has a much more comprehensive content. It represents the all-embracing perspective, it denotes the consummation of all history, brings both grace and judgment, has cosmic dimensions, fills time and eternity. The ekklesia in all this is the people who in this great drama have been placed on the side of God in Christ by virtue of the divine election and covenant. . . . Insofar as the basileia is already a present reality, the ekklesia is also the place where the gifts and powers of the basileia are granted and received. It is, further, the gathering of those who, as the instruments of the basileia, are called upon to make profession of Jesus as the Christ, to obey his commandments, to perform the missionary task of the preaching of the gospel throughout the world. In every respect the church is surrounded and impelled by the revelation, the progress, the future of the kingdom of God without, however, itself being the basileia, and without ever being identified with it.[15]

13. Philip Schaff, *History of the Christian Church*, vol. 1 (Grand Rapids: Eerdmans, 1950), 509. Schaff mentions as examples Matt. 6:9; Mark 10:14; Luke 17:21; 1 Cor. 6:10, and Rom. 15:17, where the substitution of the word *church* for *kingdom* does not make sense. That *church* and *kingdom* do not coincide is agreed upon by many theologians. See, for example, Herman N. Ridderbos, *The Coming of the Kingdom*, H. de Jongste, trans. (Philadelphia: Presbyterian and Reformed, 1962), 347; David J. Bosch, *Witness to the World: The Christian Mission in Theological Perspective* (Atlanta: John Knox, 1980), 219; Johannes Blauw, *The Missionary Nature of the Church: A Survey of the Biblical Theology of Mission* (New York: McGraw-Hill, 1962), 79, and Küng, *Church*, 94.

14. See, for example, Ridderbos, *Coming of the Kingdom*, 342–45; George Eldon Ladd, *The Presence of the Future* (Grand Rapids: Eerdmans, 1974), and Jürgen Moltmann, *The Church in the Power of the Spirit* (New York: Harper and Row, 1977), 98–196.

15. Ridderbos, *Coming of the Kingdom*, 354–56. See also Ladd, *Presence of the Future*, 193–94.

These twin strands of a renewed conception of the Church as the people of God, together with a new view of the relationship of Church and kingdom, came together in the missiology of the 1960s and 1970s. Protestant missiologists began to see the concept of the *missio dei* as "the work of God through which everything that He has in mind for [humanity's] salvation—the complete fulness of his Kingdom of redemption—is offered through those whom He has sent."[16] Johannes Verkuyl went so far as to affirm that "missiology is more and more coming to see the kingdom of God as the hub around which all mission work revolves."[17]

The kingdom of God and the Church are interrelated precisely in the person of Jesus Christ, who is at once King of the kingdom and Head of the Church. The believer in Jesus is brought into God's *kingdom* in space and time through redemption in Jesus Christ, the "head of the body, the *church*." This transfer is made by the Father who dwells in Christ in his "complete being" (Col. 1:13–19). Thus Church, mission, and the kingdom of God are to build one another. They are not identical, yet intimately intertwine in God's mission through God's people in God's world. The Church, therefore, must be understood to be the missionary community of the disciples of the King.[18]

These developments have far-reaching consequences for the way we view missionary congregations. Missionary congregations need constant reminders that their identity and calling do not derive from denominational affiliation, nor from institutional structures. They exist because they are the covenant community of the King, called to be God's instruments for blessing the nations.

## Defining the Church in Terms of the Kingdom of God

The tendency for Christian thinkers to view Church and kingdom as neither identical, nor completely dissociated has led to what Ridderbos calls a "new consensus" regarding the nature of the kingdom.[19] The consensus defines the kingdom as both present, inaugurated, and begun, and at the same time eschatological and coming. This kingdom is not

---

16. George Vicedom, *The Mission of God* (St. Louis: Concordia, 1965), 45; quoted also by Eugene Rugingh, *Sons of Tiv* (Grand Rapids: Baker, 1969), 23.

17. Johannes Verkuyl, *Contemporary Missiology: An Introduction*, D. Cooper, trans. (Grand Rapids: Eerdmans 1978), 203; reprinted in *International Review of Missions*, 68.270 (Apr. 1979): 168–76.

18. This has been a consistent theme of Arthur M. Glasser's writing, especially evident in his articles and book chapters emanating from his participation at conferences and symposia. It is especially clear in an unpublished syllabus which has influenced the thinking of hundreds of his students at Fuller Theological Seminary, Pasadena, Calif.: "Kingdom and Mission: A Biblical Study of the Kingdom of God and the World Mission of His People."

19. Ridderbos. *Coming of the Kingdom*, 342.

viewed spatially nor institutionally, but rather as the dynamic, active rule of God through Jesus Christ and the Holy Spirit. The gospel is thus the good news of the kingdom which has come. God is with humanity (Immanuel), and God reigns over humanity. The signs of the kingdom's coming were summarized by Jesus when he explained his Messianic credentials to the disciples of John the Baptist (compare Matt. 11:4–6 with Isa. 61:1–3 and Luke 4:18–19).

Thus the kingdom has already drawn near but is not yet fully come. Although the Church is not what it ought to be, it is nevertheless the primary locus of the kingdom between the ascension and the parousia. The kingdom is coming and local churches are signs that point the world to the coming King.

## The Church Is the Community Ruled by the King

In all cultural settings missionary congregations need to see themselves as a unique community of those who acknowledge the authority of Jesus as the Christ and their King. These men and women are different from all other men and women who might be within the larger realm of the reign of Christ. *They stand apart because they are in-the-know.* They consciously, freely, and willingly commit themselves and their lives to the fact that Jesus is Lord.[20]

## The Church Is the Central Locus of the Rule of the King

Cullmann has spoken of two concentric circles of the rule of Christ, with Christ at the center. The first and smaller circle might be called $R^1$, for it encompasses the rule of Christ in the *Church*. The second, larger circle, $R^2$, constitutes the rule of Christ over *all things* as seen in Ephesians 1 and Colossians 1. A third circle, $R^3$, might be added to Cullmann's example to represent the rule of Christ over all unseen spiritual forces, the "principalities and powers" that are beyond the pale of that which is seen. Following Cullmann's point that $R^1+R^2=$**Total Reign** (of Christ), we would affirm that $R^1+R^2+R^3=$**Total Reign**. The "circles" here are all "**R**" because each represents the dynamic, active rule of the King. But each represents a slightly different way in which Christ rules. We might even say that essentially the kingdom is best described as a realm or reign.[21] As Rudolf Schnackenburg has pointed out, the fulness of God that dwells bodily in Christ (Col. 1:9) "passes through Christ also into Christians, but at the same time Christ, ruling the cosmos, also

---

20. Charles Van Engen, *The Growth of the True Church* (Amsterdam: Rodopi, 1981), 282–83.

21. George Eldon Ladd expands on this imagery in *The Presence of the Future: The Eschatology of Biblical Realism* (Grand Rapids: Eerdmans, 1974), 122ff.

chooses the Church as his direct sphere of operation, into which his divine blessings stream. We must, therefore, conclude that Christ's reign over the world is realized in a special manner in the Church and becomes there a concrete reality of grace."[22]

Whatever else they are, missionary congregations are central to the rule of the King because uniquely in them Christ rules as Head of the body, the Church. He rules nowhere else in that fashion; only the Church can be the body of Christ.[23] As each missionary church emerges, therefore, the boundary line of $R^1$ enlarges into $R^2$. Through the proclamation of the Gospel and resulting conversion of people, those who have previously been in $R^2$ are translated into $R^1$ (Rom. 6:15–22; Col. 1:9–14). This conversion or translation of people from being unwilling subjects to willing subjects of the King happens uniquely in missionary congregations. This conversion is at the heart of the local congregation's identity as the covenant community of the King.

Furthermore, whenever the Church arrives at new places, new cultures, and new spheres in the midst of humanity, the Church will find that the $R^2$ authority of the King is already long established. As the Church proclaims the gospel of the kingdom, the churches emerge to become what they are—the body of Christ the Lord. Thus $R^1$ is constantly growing into $R^2$, and even "the gates of hell shall not prevail against it [will not be able to withstand its advance]" (Matt. 16:13–20; 28:16–20). The integral growth of congregations is therefore a sign of the coming of the kingdom.

### The Church Is the Anticipatory Sign of the Rule of the King

Because missionary congregations are communities of those who live out the reign of God in their lives and in society, they are uniquely suited to be the anticipatory "first-fruits" of the kingdom in the world.[24] The Church is not the kingdom in its fulness, but as anticipatory sign Christians live in anxious waiting and suspenseful hope. Missionary congregations *know* that "the sufferings we now endure bear no comparison with the splendor as yet unrevealed, which is in store for us. For the created universe waits with eager expectation for God's Son to be revealed" (Rom. 8:18–19). Hans Küng has said it so eloquently:

> The Church on its pilgrimage is not deserted or forgotten by God; it is not wandering totally in the dark. Even though it is not the kingdom of God which is to come, it is already under the reign of God

22. Rudolf Schnackenburg, *God's Rule and Kingdom*, J. Murray, trans. (New York: Herder and Herder, 1963), 313.

23. See Karl Barth, *Credo: A Presentation of the Chief Problems of Dogmatics with Reference to the Apostles' Creed*, J. S. McNab, trans. (New York: Scribners, 1936), 140–41.

24. Cf. Karl Barth, *Church Dogmatics*, 4.3.2.

which has begun; though looking forward to the final victory of the reign of God, it can look back to the decisive victory in Jesus Christ; while still wandering in the shadow of death, it has the resurrection not only ahead of it, but in its decisive form behind it in Jesus the risen Kyrios. . . . Thus the Church may be termed the fellowship of aspirants to the Kingdom of God. . . .

[The Church] is not the bringer or the bearer of the reign of God which is to come and is at the same time already present, but its voice, its announcer, its herald. God alone can bring his reign; the Church is devoted entirely to its service.[25]

Missionary congregations emerge as they increasingly practice, announce, herald, and illustrate the coming of a kingdom which is already present. As eschatological heralds of that which is coming, local congregations experience the rule of the King. The *already* gradually moves toward the anticipated not-yet as the Church heralds its coming.

### The Church's Mission Is to Spread the Knowledge of the Rule of the King

In Mexico City in 1963 the Commission on World Mission and Evangelism of the World Council of Churches expressed the conviction "that the God whose world this is has revealed Himself in Jesus Christ; that all men have a right to know this and those who do know it are committed to making it known."[26]

As the anticipatory focal point of Christ's reign, missionary congregations are called to spread throughout the world the knowledge of the rule of the King. This means local churches cannot be ends in themselves, for the Church is not the final goal of mission. Local churches are, rather, the instruments of something much greater than themselves: They are tools of the kingdom of God. Ladd says that "if the Kingdom of God is primarily God's kingly rule, and secondarily the spiritual sphere of his rule, there can be no objection to the recognition that the church is the organ of the Kingdom as it works in the world."[27]

The Church cannot create, bring in, or build the kingdom, but it can and does witness to it. Clearly this witness happens in word and deed,[28] in miracles, in signs and wonders, in the transformation of the lives of people, in the presence of the Holy Spirit, in the radical recreation of

25. Hans Küng, *The Church, Maintained in Truth*, E. Quinn, trans. (New York: Seabury, 1980), 95–96.

26. Quoted in Charles W. Ranson, "Mexico City, 1963," *International Review of Missions*, 53 (1964): 140.

27. Ladd, *Presence of the Future*, 269. (For further documentation on this point, see Van Engen, *Growth*, 287ff.)

28. See Harvie Conn, *Evangelism: Doing Justice and Preaching Grace* (Grand Rapids: Zondervan, 1982).

humanity. A local congregation's witness to the rule of the King is itself a part of the content of the reign of Christ which is proclaimed. The kingdom comes as Jesus Christ is made known. So local churches build the Church toward the coming kingdom as they preach, proclaim, and live out their allegiance and obedience to the King. Local congregations participate in the coming of the kingdom as they live out their lives as covenant communities of disciples of the King, as branch offices of the kingdom. As the number increases of those who know and acknowledge the rule of the King, the Church becomes the anticipatory instrument of the already-but-not-yet kingdom of God.

The Church cannot bring in the kingdom—only the King can do that. What the Church can do is proclaim, gather, and grow in expectation of that day when all people will bow the knee and confess with the lips that Jesus is Lord (Phil. 2:10). The New Testament imagery of this truth may be found in the kingdom parables of growth, in the parable of the talents, the parable of the ten maidens and the oil lamps, the wedding feast, and in the teaching of Jesus concerning the judgment day in Matthew 24 and 25.

The total development of the missionary Church then aims at realizing the kingdom by pushing outward the primary sphere of Christ's rule—local missionary churches incarnated in a particular time, place, and culture. The Church, not the kingdom, is the Bride of Christ (Eph. 5:25–27). The Church, not the kingdom, is the New Jerusalem (Revelation 21). The Church, not the kingdom, is composed of those who have washed their robes in the blood of the Lamb (Rev. 7:14), whom Christ will present without spot or wrinkle (Eph. 5:27; Jude 24). So in this "time between the times" we focus on the Church because we understand that when we build missionary congregations we are already participating in our final goal, the coming of the kingdom (cf. Col. 1:13–20 ).

## Defining the Kingdom in Terms of the Church

On the other side of the coin, if we restrict our perspective of the kingdom only to what we see in the Church we do injustice to the total realm and reign of the King. As Herman Bavinck points out, the kingdom cannot be defined only as the gathering of the subjects of the King; it is rather a whole composite of spiritual goods and blessings.[29]

No one sign or witness unveils the entire scope of the kingdom. No message encompasses Christ's total reign over all things. The Church never achieves within itself the totality of the kingdom. No "signs of the times" can box-in the coming of the kingdom. No "new words" suffi-

---

29. Herman Bavinck, *Our Reasonable Faith: A Survey of Christian Doctrine*, H. Zylstra, trans. (Grand Rapids: Baker, 1986), 527.

ciently describe the kingdom. The Church ever anticipates something more, because the kingdom is so much more than has been experienced. Individual spiritual life, salvation, struggles against oppression, the alleviation of economic poverty, the building up of the Church qualitatively and quantitatively, warfare against spiritual powers—each of these separately and all of them together are incomplete manifestations of the working of the kingdom in the world. When the kingdom comes in fact and reality all must change—creation, humankind, the social order, heaven, and earth.

The missionary Church grows, not toward some human utopia, nor toward individual salvation, perfect fellowship, or spiritual identification with the values of justice, truth, joy, and love. The Church points to something far more magnificent—the rule and reign of the King over the cosmos. The Church points simultaneously to the beginning ("In the beginning was the Word," John 1:1) and to the end ("I saw no temple in the city, for its temple was the sovereign Lord God and the Lamb," Rev. 21:22). Thus as the Church emerges it moves toward Christ as *Alpha and Omega*" (Rev. 1:8), the One who is both King of all and Head of the Church.

There is a sense, therefore, in which all we have written thus far to describe the Church does not point to a reality in the Church as such, but rather to the kingdom of God. The Church stands for something more fundamental, more perfect, and more pervasive than itself. In describing the Church's attributes, "new words," and purpose in the world we only discover what criteria to use in determining how close the Church as a provisional sign comes to the real kingdom it signifies. These criteria are also commands, calling missionary congregations to grow towards the kingdom of God. Because the kingdom is more inclusive, more extensive, more perfect, and more comprehensive than the Church, the Church must be understood as the servant of the kingdom. Precisely in this service the Church becomes uniquely meaningful.[30] As servants, missionary congregations are communities of mediation which bridge the chasm from the kingdom to the world. Missionary churches have a special function as those who point the world to "the absolute claims of the kingdom to the total obedience, total priority, total self-abnegation of [humanity]."[31] The community of the King, then, is to model before the world all for which the kingdom of God stands. Although envisioning the kingdom in its fulness might tend to make us underemphasize the Church, we must remember that the kingdom has come but is not yet here. In the mystery of this time between the times, *the Church is uniquely the instrument of the kingdom in the world.*

30. Cf. Avery R. Dulles, *Models of the Church: A Critical Assessment of the Church in All Its Aspects* (New York: Doubleday, 1974), 128.
31. De Ridder, *Discipling*, 139.

## The Relation of Church, Kingdom, and World

As missionary congregations seek to manifest the kingdom of God they are continually faced with the world, especially since the kingdom is larger than the Church in spatial, temporal, spiritual, and influential terms. As the Church is caught up in that movement outward generated by its missionary nature, it finds that it is being sent into the world of people. In the mid-1960s J. C. Hoekendijk and the World Council of Churches[32] stressed that in any discussion about God, Church, and kingdom the world must be at the forefront of our conversation. "The world must set the agenda," it was said. However, the extreme pessimism regarding the Church which Hoekendijk and others demonstrated meant the nearly total eclipse of the Church and the kingdom. Replacing the biblical order of God's mission (God-Church-world) with a new order (God-world-Church) worked out in the end to rob the Church of its own involvement in mission. What God was supposedly doing in the *world* was what mattered. Thus many of us in the "baby-boomer" generation opted for Lyndon Johnson's "Great Society" programs of social reform, for the Peace Corps, and for political activism. However, years later we discovered that in turning our backs on the Church, on spirituality, on fellowship, and on discipleship in the midst of the people of God, we ended up with empty activism that had little purpose and minimal impact. In opting only for the world and ignoring the Church, we lost our true involvement in the kingdom of God. Only as we understand the relationship of the *Church* to the *kingdom* can we begin to understand the missional relationship of the Church to the world—understood within the scope and time of the kingdom of God.

The basic lines of the relationship between Church, kingdom, and world were drawn out by Ridderbos in a paper read at the Second International Conference of Institutions for Christian Higher Education in Grand Rapids, Michigan.[33] In his presentation, Ridderbos called for new ways of openness in the relation of Church to world. First, the Church is called to Christian liberty—to be open to the right position of each individual in society as the "cradle of human liberties and political rights." Second, the whole of the Church's life of service to the kingdom means service to the world. Thus Paul begins the ethical section of the Epistle to the Romans (chapters 12–16) with the concept of "spiritual service," an act of worship that presents our bodies for missional action through the exercise of our gifts as the Church in ministry in the world (12:1). The

32. Hoekendijk's perspective was especially influential in the results of the studies of missionary structures of the congregation, published in *The Church for Others and the Church for the World: A Quest for the Missionary Structures of Congregations* (Geneva: World Council of Churches, 1968).

33. This was published in booklet form by the Instituut vir die Befordering van Calvinisme, Potchefstroom, South Africa, Sept. 1979.

uniqueness of the local congregation does not separate it from the world, but rather gives it liberty to be the King's servant in the world.

In practice this means that missionary congregations live out their spiritual life not only as the Church, but also as God's people in the world, as a force to transform society to more closely resemble the kingdom of God. Local churches have a certain institutional responsibility for their context. To transform the institutional church into a cultural or political movement would wipe out the boundaries between Church and world. The Church is definitely called, however, to preach the whole gospel of the kingdom, a gospel which has social and political justice implications for the greater society. These implications cannot be restricted either to individualistic spiritual categories or to strictly socio-economic liberation categories. The gospel of the kingdom deals with all of life as a whole and transforms all of life under the lordship of Jesus Christ.

World-transforming objectives also must be understood as provisional. As Ridderbos says, "there is a powerful presence of Christ and his Kingdom also in the present world; but it is the power and the presence of the Spirit, which counts now. It is not yet the Kingdom in its heavenly glory. . . . For the Spirit itself has yet to wait and pray with the Church: 'Come, Lord Jesus.'"[34]

The provisionality of the presence of the kingdom in this world should impel local churches to continual evaluation as they reject both the present status quo and any suggested this-worldly utopia. They recognize that they are in the world because they have been sent into the world by the Lord and King of both the world and the Church. Although the presence of Christ in the world through missionary congregations is only a provisional presence, it still commands power as a compelling, transforming presence. To be free for service to the kingdom in the world is a task of the individual believer, the congregation as community, and the Church as a body. Any talk of Church and kingdom drives us into the world. This has far-reaching implications for missionary congregations.

In the first place the interrelation of Church-kingdom-world serves to show us the very limited view of the Venn-Anderson "three-self formula."[35] Henry Venn and Rufus Anderson may not have intended their

34. Ibid., 15.
35. The "three-self formula" advocated by Henry Venn and Rufus Anderson toward the end of the nineteenth century stated that mission agencies should strive to develop the young national churches in the two-thirds world until they would become self-supporting, self-propagating, and self-governing. At that time the work of the mission agency would be finished. Ironically, this formula was never applied to the mother churches or their denominational structures in England and North America. Sadly, the formula has predominantly created a self-centeredness and introversion in the younger churches of Africa, Asia, and Latin America—characteristics they are just now beginning to leave behind.

concept to become an all-encompassing theology of the Church, but efforts in cross-cultural mission, Third-World churches, and North American church planting have followed the formula as a goal in establishing local churches. The three-self formula has become the ideal. But alongside the Church-kingdom-world model its failings are apparent. The three-self view is narrow, shallow, and self-centered. As covenant communities of the King and provisional representations of the kingdom, local congregations are so much more than money, administration, and converts. As a provisional sign of the kingdom they are so much more than cultural contextualization, or indigenization of the gospel. Though these issues are important, they are only a part of a much larger whole which involves the rule of the King in the world and uniquely in the Church through its local missionary communities of the King.

Second, as we will see in chapter 12, the Church-kingdom-world relationship helps us discover new, missional administrative structures. Especially in a systems approach (see chapter 9) we will see that our church administration cannot follow an introverted, self-serving, encapsulated agenda if we wish to create missionary churches that properly reflect the kingdom of God. Missionary congregations must have an administrative system which explodes outward into the world on the way to the coming kingdom of God.

Third, in *Christianity in Culture*, Charles Kraft has reminded us again of the relationship of the Church to its surrounding culture:

> It is crucial that new generations and cultures experience the process of producing in their own cultural forms an appropriate church vehicle for the transmission of God's meanings. A contemporary church, like a contemporary translation, should impress the uniniti-ated observer as an original production in the contemporary culture, not as a badly fitted import from somewhere else. . . . The priority must be for conveying in the receptor culture a content that is equivalent to that conveyed in the original culture. . . . As with the translation, so with the transculturation of the church.[36]

This kind of approach, apart from the excellent, important, and appropriate anthropology it represents, is a practical application of the perspective which sees a dynamic relationship between Church, kingdom, and world. The meanings themselves are derived from the individual methods through which the Church becomes a sign of the kingdom in the midst of a given culture. Accepting the fact that the world is fallen and that no culture is wholly worth preserving, we must also emphasize the other side of the coin, "for God so loved the world, that He gave His

36. Charles H. Kraft, Christianity in Culture: A Study in Dynamic Biblical Theologizing in Cross-Cultural Perspective (Maryknoll, NY: Orbis, 1979), 318–26.

only son (John 3:16)." It was not the Church for which Christ gave His life, but the *world*. It was not the kingdom to which Christ was sent as a living sacrificial Lamb, but the *world*. In the future reality of a world Church surrounding the globe and encompassing thousands of different cultures, it will be necessary for all of us to find new ways to contextualize local congregations wherever we find them, calling them to become more fully who they are, covenant communities of the King.

## Further Study

Anderson, Gerald H., ed. *Witnessing to the Kingdom—Melbourne and Beyond.* New York: Orbis, 1982.

Arias, Mortimer. *Announcing the Reign of God: Evangelization and the Subversive Memory of Jesus.* Philadelphia: Fortress, 1984. See chapter 7.

Cullmann, Oscar. *Christ and Time: The Primitive Christian Conception of Time and History*, F. V. Filson, trans. Philadelphia: Westminster, 1964.

Freytag, Walter. "The Meaning and Purpose of the Christian Mission," in *International Review of Missions*, 39 (April 1950): 153–61.

Gibbs, Eddie. *I Believe in Church Growth.* Grand Rapids, Eerdmans, 1982. See chapter 2.

Hoge, Dean R., and David A. Roozen, eds. *Understanding Church Growth and Decline, 1950–78.* New York: Pilgrim, 1979.

Kelley, Dean M. *Why Conservative Churches are Growing: A Study in the Sociology of Religion*, rev. ed. New York: Harper and Row, 1977.

Klemme, Huber F. *Your Church and Your Community.* Philadelphia: Christian Education, 1957.

Kraft, Charles H. *Christianity in Culture: A Study in Dynamic Biblical Theologizing in Cross-Cultural Perspective.* Maryknoll, N.Y.: Orbis, 1979. See chapter 16.

Ladd, George Eldon. *The Presence of the Future: The Eschatology of Biblical Realism.* Grand Rapids: Eerdmans, 1974.

Latourette, Kenneth S., et al. *Church and Community.* Chicago: Willett, Clark, 1938. See 3ff.

Luzbetak, Louis J. *The Church and Cultures: New Perspectives in Missiological Anthropology.* Maryknoll, N.Y.: Orbis, 1989. See chapter 1.

McBrien, Richard P. *The Church in the Thought of Bishop John Robinson.* Philadelphia: Westminster, 1966. See chapters 2–6.

McGavran, Donald A., and Winfield C. Arn. *How to Grow a Church.* Glendale, Calif.: Regal, 1973. See chapter 3.

Newbigin, J. E. Lesslie. *Sign of the Kingdom.* Grand Rapids: Eerdmans, 1981. See 42ff.

_____. *The Open Secret: Sketches for a Missionary Theology.* Grand Rapids: Eerdmans, 1978. See chapters 4, 8, 9.

Nicholls, Bruce J., and Kenneth Kantzer. *In Word and Deed: Evangelism and*

*Social Responsibility*. Grand Rapids: Eerdmans, 1986.

Pannenberg, Wolfhart; Avery Dulles, and Carl E. Braaten. *Spirit, Faith, and Church*. Philadelphia: Westminster, 1970. See chapter 6.

Price, Peter. *The Church as the Kingdom: A New Way of Being the Church*. London: Marshal, Morgan, and Scott, 1987.

Ridderbos, Herman N. *The Coming of the Kingdom*, H. de Jongste, trans. Philadelphia: Presbyterian and Reformed, 1962.

Snyder, Howard A. *The Community of the King*. Downers Grove, Ill.: Inter-Varsity, 1977.

Taylor, John V. "The Church Witnesses to the Kingdom," in *Your Kingdom Come: Mission Perspectives; Report on the World Conference on Mission and Evangelism, Melbourne, Australia, 12–25 May, 1980*. Geneva: World Council of Churches, 1980.

Vos, Geerhardus. *The Teaching of Jesus Concerning the Kingdom of God and the Church*. New York: American Tract Society, 1903.

Wagner, C. Peter. *Church Growth and the Whole Gospel: A Biblical Mandate*. San Francisco: Harper and Row, 1981. See chapter 1.

*[handwritten margin note: and gets its purpose and is ruled by]*

*[handwritten note: Church is covenant community that claims Jesus is king]*

# 8

## The Role of the Local Church in the World

**W**hen missionary congregations begin to see themselves as branch offices of the kingdom of God, they are often led to examine more closely their role and function in the world and to study the passages which show Jesus' mission, work of revelation, reconciliation, and lordship. All of these are normally associated with Christ's offices as Prophet, Priest, and King. The role of the local church in the world involves the Church in an apostolate received from, guided by, and patterned after the mission of Jesus.

### The Transferred Apostolate

One of the most significant passages describing Jesus' mission is Luke 4:14–21. According to Luke 4, Jesus spelled out his role in the world at the beginning of his ministry by using the familiar words of Isaiah 61:1–3. Luke places these words in a particular context, showing how Jesus chose to announce his messianic mission in his own country where a prophet has no honor (Luke 4:24), a choice of platform Luke seems to have considered important.

119

Matthew 10 and 11 gives us a similar perspective of Jesus' role in the world but places the matter in the context of the sending of the twelve disciples on their first missionary venture and John the Baptist's question as to whether Jesus was the Messiah. Jesus answered John with a summary of his role in the world: "Go and tell John what you hear and see: the blind recover their sight, the lame walk, the lepers are made clean, the deaf hear, the dead are raised to life, the poor are hearing the good news—and happy is the man who does not find me a stumbling-block" (Matt.11:4–6; compare with Luke 7: 18–35).

In this chapter we will look at the work and role of Jesus Christ as a pattern for the Church in the world. Jesus told his disciples, "As the Father sent me, so I send you" (John 20:21; cf. John 13:20). The Church exercises its commission as the body of Christ by living out the role Jesus assigned to it in the world. A review of the gifts of the Spirit in the Church, for example, would immediately impress us with the fact that these gifts are ministries to be exercised in the world. And as they take shape through the Church in the world, they fulfil a role similar to Jesus Christ's. In fact, in his farewell to his disciples Jesus clearly transfers this aspect of his earthly presence to the disciples who will continue his ministry in the world, saying, "he who has faith in Me will do what I am doing; and he will do greater things still because I am going to the Father. Indeed, anything you ask in my name I will do, so that the Father may be glorified in the Son. If you ask anything in my name I will do it. If you love me, you will obey my commands" (John 14:12–15; cf. John 1:50–51).

The Church's transferred apostolate was assumed by the disciples after Pentecost. In his first sermon Peter alluded to the prophecies of Joel 2:28–32 and spoke of "signs and wonders" which were now happening in their midst through the outpouring of the Holy Spirit, just as Jesus had performed them prior to Pentecost (Acts 2:22–33). The disciples proclaimed this truth in word and demonstrated it in deed, doing the same kinds of works which Jesus had done. The lame walked, the dead were raised, and the gospel was preached to the poor.

In Acts 13:2–3, 46–47 Paul articulates the same sort of description of his own mission. Paul seemed to consider it entirely appropriate to apply to himself and his companions the language that up until then had been reserved for the mission of the Messiah. "For this is what the Lord has commanded us: 'I have made you a light for the Gentiles, that you may bring salvation to the ends of the earth'" (Acts 13:47; see Isa. 49:6; Luke 2:32, and Acts 26:23). In Romans 15:15–19 Paul emphasized this transferred mission, speaking of God's grace which had made him a minister to the Gentiles. Paul saw himself as one of those who would continue the ministry of Jesus. Paul's ministry was founded, grounded, and defined by the prior ministry of Jesus. Later Peter would emphasize a similar missional viewpoint of the Church's role in the world in 1 Peter 2:4–12.

## Prophet, Priest, and King

When the Church perceives itself as continuing Christ's ministry in the world, it will do so in relation to Christ's threefold office.[1] Lloyd M. Perry and Norman Shawchuck directly link Christ's offices with the Church's ministry:

> The Old Testament presents three major kinds of ministry: prophet, priest and king. Each of those ministries, although very different, were nonetheless ministries to people. The priest ministered to the private and spiritual needs. The prophet ministered to the public, social, and religious needs. The king ministered to organizational and political needs. The king's ministry was to manage wisely and effectively the human organizational resources put under his care by God. . . .
>
> In the New Testament God laid upon Christ all three of these ministries. He became prophet, priest, and king. Not only did Christ

1. For a detailed discussion of the "munus triplex," the threefold offices of Christ, see Karl Barth (*Church Dogmatics*, 4.3.1ff.) and Hendrikus Berkhof (*Christian Faith: An Introduction to the Study of the Faith*, S. Woudstra, trans. [Grand Rapids: Eerdmans, 1979], 294–95). The idea traces to Eusebius of Caesarea, who based it on Luke 4:18. John Calvin elaborated the concept (*Institutes of the Christian Religion*. [Philadelphia: Westminster, 1960], 494–503), and it is in the Heidelberg Catechism (questions 31, 32). Emil Brunner says,

> It is no accident that it was Reformed theology which, in its doctrine of the "offices" of Christ, re-emphasized this original Biblical stress on saving history. . . . The work of Jesus is the fulfillment of the Old Covenant. . . . The fact that the Reformed theologians speak of the threefold "office" or work of Christ, is due to the fact that under the Old Covenant there were three theocratic figures, the Prophet, the Priest, and the King; in Jesus all that these three represented was fulfilled, since they all merged into a complete unity in His person. . . . It is only Jesus the Messiah, whose Kingship is totally different in kind from that of the Davidic dynasty, and whose Priesthood is so entirely different from that of the Jerusalem priesthood, and, still more, who was not a Prophet of the Old Testament kind at all, who can eliminate these tensions and contradictions [between the three offices] because He gathers up these three "offices" in His own Person. In His Word He is both Reconciler and King; in His sovereignty, He is both Revealer and the Sacrificial Lamb; in His Priesthood, He is both the One who proclaims the Name of God, and asserts God's glory and God's Sovereignty (*The Christian Doctrine of Creation and Redemption* [Philadelphia Westminster, 1952], 272–74). See also John F. Jansen, *Calvin's "Doctrine of the Work of Christ"* (Greenwood, S.C.: Attic, 1956); Wolfhart Pannenberg, *Jesus, God and Man*, L. L. Wilkins and D. A. Priebe, trans. (Philadelphia: Westminster, 1977), and G. C. Berkouwer, *Studies in Dogmatics*, 14 vols. (Grand Rapids: Eerdmans, 1952), vol. 9: *The Work of Christ*.

accept those three ministries as one, but He provided for the continuation of this three-in-one ministry by calling pastors and laying upon them the charge to minister in His stead to whatever local church they were called. . . . Pastors who teach the people to follow Christ's example should do likewise, not only in his priestly and prophetic role, but also regarding his ministry as manager and leader.

Each local church is uniquely chosen by God to be His body in that place. His is an active body, with every member assigned a specific ministry to perform. In order to carry on those many ministries the church must organize itself for action in such a way that every member becomes active in ministry. It must pray for the Spirit of God to fill every minister and anoint every ministry—then the church of the twentieth century will be revitalized, and not until then.[2]

Missionary congregations minister through these three offices, as well as in other ways clearly related to Christ's role in ministry in the world (see figure 7).

Karl Barth showed how the threefold office of Christ gives us clear orders for the Church's ministry in the world when he explained how the ministry of the Church is definite, "because it consists quite simply in the fact that as the community of Jesus Christ it has to exist actively for the world. . . . In the service of God and serving men, there strides Jesus Christ in His prophetic office and work." Barth goes on to relate that the community of believers must be oriented by the ministry of Christ: "It continually orientates itself by it. And inasmuch as it does so, its service of God and man is distinguished by its recognizable and basic unity from all other true or pretended service."[3]

Barth goes on to define this witness as "declaration, exposition, and address" (or "the proclamation, the explication, and the application of the gospel as the Word of God entrusted to [the church]").[4] Barth's treatment of the Church's ministry is arranged around Christ's offices as Lord who humbled himself as a servant to do the work of atonement (priestly office); as royal Man in whom humanity is exalted and adopted to fellowship with God (kingly office), and as God-Man who is the Mediator and Guarantor of reconciliation (prophetic office).[5]

Colin Williams also called attention to this threefold content of the Church's ministry in the world, saying that in Mark 10:45 Jesus interprets his ministry in terms of Isaiah's image of the suffering Servant. If this was

2. Lloyd M. Perry and Norman Shawchuck. *Revitalizing the Twentieth Century Church* (Chicago: Moody, 1982), 143.

3. Karl Barth, *Church Dogmatics*, 4.3.2.

4. Ibid.

5. Ibid.

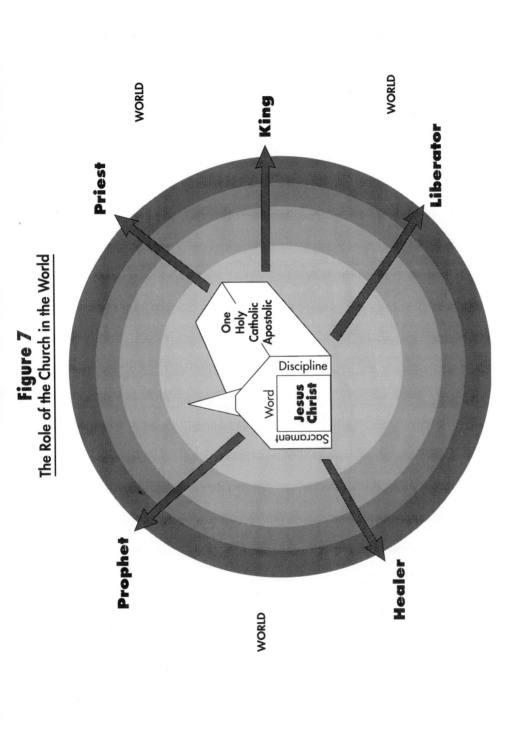

**Figure 7**

The Role of the Church in the World

what Jesus meant by ministry then the ministry of the Church is an extension of it, under the three offices. "It can be quickly seen," Williams remarks, "that these three offices are closely related to the marks of the church in the Reformation tradition. The church is, [the Reformers] said, where the Word is truly preached (prophet), Sacraments duly administered (priest), and godly discipline maintained (king)."[6]

Because the Church is the community of disciples of Jesus, the servant community, and the community of ministry, it therefore must be understood to be the prophetic-priestly-kingly people sent out into the world by Christ.[7] Geoffrey Wainwright points out that Christians are identified as kings and priests in Revelation 1:6 and 5:10, as a priestly community in 1 Peter 2:9, and as a prophetic community in Acts 2. They are these things because they are Christ's people. "Jesus is the eschatological prophet, and more: the Word of God incarnate. Jesus is the high priest, who offered himself and secured an eternal redemption for humanity. Being the divine kingdom in person, . . . Jesus 'reigned from a tree' and God the Father has exalted him and bestowed on him the supreme name of Lord (Phil. 2). Baptism is the sacrament of entry into participation in the prophetic, priestly, and royal dignity of Christ."[8]

The missiological implications of this threefold role of the Church in the world are exciting and staggering. At the very least its *prophetic role* involves the Church in calling for and working toward justice, toward *shalom*, toward righteousness and peace in human relationships and in social structures. The Church's *priestly role* must, by the same token, involve its sacramental presence, its call for reconciliation of people with God, each other, and themselves (2 Corinthians 5), and an offering of the redemption found in Jesus Christ to all who will come. The Church's *kingly role* calls the Church to take seriously its role in nation building, in bringing harmony to chaos, in calling for government which cares for its people, and in organizing itself for the proclamation of the gospel of freedom and grace in Jesus Christ. Church historian Kenneth Scott Latourette often pointed out in his major works on the history of the Church in mission that there is a reciprocal impact between the local congregations and their surrounding environment.

How a local congregation exercises these roles depends very much on the church's context. Such contextualization involves more than the form and shape of the gospel message itself and more than the choice of the kinds of activities to be carried out. Contextualization involves the shape, style, way-of-life, and organization of the local congregation in

6. Colin W. Williams, *The Church* (Philadelphia: Westminster, 1968), 101.

7. Edmund Schlink, *The Coming Christ and the Coming Church* (Philadelphia: Fortress, 1968), chapter 2.

8. Geoffrey Wainwright, *The Ecumenical Moment: Crisis and Opportunity for the Church* (Grand Rapids: Eerdmans, 1983), 103–4.

relation to its own unique setting, as it seeks to be prophetic, priestly, and kingly in that context. The Church itself must become fully and completely contextualized as prophet, priest, and king for the sake of, in dynamic interaction with, and in the midst of its culture.

The congregation's threefold role in the world will need to be modeled by those in leadership. Alvin J. Lindgren and Norman Shawchuck applied the concept of the threefold office to the pastor's role in mobilizing the local congregation in ministry in the world, summarizing the three functions this way.

*Prophetic*—Calling the church to human love and justice; challenging, discomforting, warning; most clearly seen in the activity of preaching.

*Priestly*—Calling the church to its highest possible spiritual state; consoling, comforting, accepting, forgiving; most clearly seen in pastoral-sacramental activities (administering the sacraments, counseling, and similar ministerial work).

*Kingly*—Administering wisely and effectively the resources God has given the church; most clearly seen in organizational activities (management, planning, and training activities).[9]

## Healer and Liberator

In addition to the three traditional offices of Christ as models of the Church's role in ministry in the world, there may be other aspects of Christ's ministry which should also be highlighted. If we take another look at Christ's ministry in the world as expressed in Luke 4:16–20, we will see a picture of the ministry of Jesus (described, for example, in Luke 6, Matthew 12, and Isaiah 42) which would add at least "healer" and "liberator" to the concepts describing Jesus' self-perception and ministry. These last two might in some senses be included in the first three. However, if we look at them from the point of view of the *practice* of ministry, they appear to have validity in their own right. These additional concepts seem also to have been transferred to the disciples of Jesus as appropriate to their role in the world as the body of Christ.

The *healer* dimension was a strong element in the ministry of Jesus and prominent in the early Church, and it is one of the most important functions which the Church can exercise in the world.[10] Be it healing of body, of mind, of psychological stress, or of spiritual illness, the Church

---

9. Alvin J. Lindgren and Norman Shawchuck, *Management for Your Church: How to Realize Your Church Potential Through a Systems Approach* (Nashville: Abingdon, 1977), chapter 13.

10. J. E. Lesslie Newbigin, *The Good Shepherd* (Grand Rapids: Eerdmans, 1977), chapter 13.

has fulfilled the function of healer as an integral part of its being the reconciled and redeemed community of those who beseech humanity, "Be ye reconciled with God" (2 Cor. 5:20, KJV).

The notion of *liberation* is one which many have stressed of late, particularly in relation to various liberation theologies. Christ's activity of liberating from the penalty of sin, from the consequences of sin, from oppression of spirits, from the penalty of the law, and from broken relationships was a major feature of his ministry. So spiritual, emotional, personal, political, economic, and social liberation is being understood more and more as an essential part of the Church's role in the world as the liberated people of God ministering to a world in bondage.

However we interpret the exact content of these additional words, they serve to point us to something basic about the missionary nature of the Church. Whether it be the Church's attributes, the "new words," the Church's ministries of *koinonia*, *kerygma*, *diakonia*, and *martyria*, or the Church's relation to the kingdom of God—all of these must ultimately translate into the Church's *doing something* in the world. Of course this is a highly contextual matter, strongly affected by the internal culture of the missionary congregation, as well as by the surrounding culture in which it ministers. But the complexity of critical contextualization of the Church's ministries in the world must not cause us to minimize the importance of such ministries. The Church cannot be fully the body of Christ, the people of God, unless it ministers in the world. Clergy and laity alike, fellowship and institution together, must give concrete expression to the nature of the Church specifically and specially through the ministries described in the three offices, and other possible words, such as *healer* and *liberator*.

The activities of prophet, priest, king, healer, and liberator are extremely important. They give local congregations and their leaders a view of the areas in which the Church's goals and objectives should fall, translating what the Church is into what the Church does as the body of Jesus Christ. They drive the missionary Church into the world by way of its ministries, ever calling the Church to become in fact and in action what it is in faith and confession. Through its ministries in the world the Church finds its essential nature. This seems to have been the issue when Jesus pointed out, "If you have done it unto the least of these my brethren, you have done it to me" (Matt. 25:45). In the midst of ministering to the world, the Church discovers its character as ambassador, witness, and representative of its Lord.

A vision of the Church's Christlike role impresses upon us that just as the world needs the Church, so the Church needs the world. The missionary Church cannot emerge toward its deepest essence unless it lives out its missionary role in ministry in the world of humanity and creation. It is both a spiritual fellowship and a physical communion of saints placed in the world. As such the Church works out its salvation with fear and trembling, in the midst of a perverse generation among whom the Church shines as light (Phil. 2:12–15).

Although we have little space to pursue this here, there is another way of looking at the role of missionary congregations in the world. The ripple-effect of dropping the people of God into the pool of God's world includes another group of perspectives. These highly relational concepts describe both the indicative and the imperative of the life of missionary congregations in the world. After some reflection we could easily develop a typology of relationships between the community of the King and the world in which the community is sent. As can be seen in figure 8 below, we might highlight the following types of missional relationships: covenanters, illustrations, family, pilgrims, foreigners, witnesses, enfolder-gatherers, providers, lovers, and ambassadors. These are but a few examples of the richness of the biblical images revealing the way in which God's missionary people may relate to their surrounding context. These images allow us to stand in the middle ground between Church and world and ask about the way in which the Church may open its arms in ministry to those for whom Jesus died. In terms of their missiological impact, we need to give these images more thought.

## New Forms of the Church Centered in Ministry in the World

During the last several decades a significant number of new models of missionary congregations have arisen. Although we do not have space here to describe them in detail, we could mention the Circle Church in Chicago, the Church of the Saviour in Washington, D.C.; Bear Valley Baptist Church in Denver, Colorado; Willow Creek Community Church, Chicago, Illinois; New Hope Community Church, Portland, Oregon; Crenshaw Christian Center, Los Angeles; the base ecclesial communities in Latin America; Servant's Community Reformed Church of Grand Rapids, Michigan; the Boston (Mass.) Church of Christ; the house churches in China, and the Yoido Full-Gospel Church in Seoul, Korea, as illustrations of distinctively new attempts to be the Church in ministry in the world. In addition, the phenomenal rise during the 1980s around the globe of very large independent, charismatic congregations numbering in the tens of thousands and hundreds of thousands has stimulated further reflection on the nature, purpose, role, and shape of the church. We seem to be at the threshold of a new era which may involve surprising new contextualized forms of missionary congregations organized primarily with regard to their role in ministry in the world.

In part 3 we will examine some of the organizational, and structural matters involved when we intentionally build the kind of missionary congregations we have envisioned in parts 1 and 2.

# Figure 8
## Relationships Between Church and World

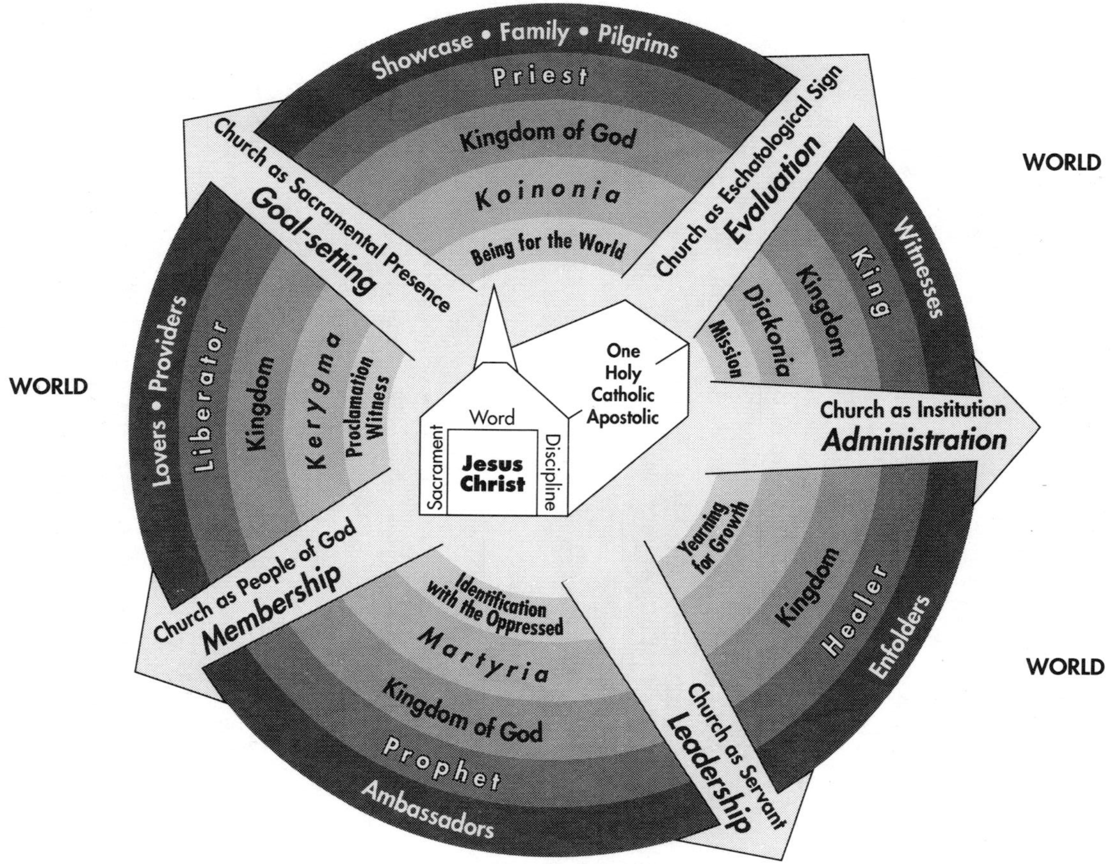

WORLD

WORLD

WORLD

Church as Institution **Administration**

Witnesses

King

Kingdom

Diakonia

Mission

Kingdom

Healer

Enfolders

Yearning for Growth

Church as Servant *Leadership*

Church as Eschatological Sign **Evaluation**

Showcase • Family • Pilgrims

Priest

Kingdom of God

Koinonia

Being for the World

One
Holy
Catholic
Apostolic

Discipline

Word

**Jesus Christ**

Sacrament

Identification with the Oppressed

Martyria

Kingdom of God

Prophet

Ambassadors

Church as People of God **Membership**

Church as Sacramental Presence **Goal-setting**

Kerygma

Proclamation Witness

Kingdom

Liberator

Lovers • Providers

## Further Study

Banks, Robert, and Julia Banks. *The Church Comes Home: A New Base for Community and Mission*. Sutherland, Australia: Albatross, 1989.

Barth, Karl. *Church Dogmatics*, 4.3.1; 4.3.2.

Berkhof, Hendrikus. *Christian Faith: An Introduction to the Study of the Faith*, Sierd Woudstra, trans. Grand Rapids: Eerdmans, 1979. See 294–95.

Boff, Leonardo. *Ecclesiogenesis: The Base Communities Reinvent the Church*, R. Barr, trans. Maryknoll, N.Y.: Orbis, 1986.

————. *Church, Charism, and Power: Liberation Theology and the Institutional Church*, J. Dierksmeyer, trans. New York: Crossroad, 1986.

Bonhoeffer, Dietrich. *The Communion of Saints: A Dogmatic Inquiry into the Sociology of the Church*. E.T., New York: Harper and Row, 1964.

Brueggemann, Walter. *In Man We Trust: The Neglected Side of Biblical Faith*. Richmond: John Knox, 1972.

Brunner, Emil. *The Christian Doctrine of Creation and Redemption*. Philadelphia: Westminster, 1952. See 272ff.

Callahan, Kennon L. *Twelve Keys to an Effective Church*. New York: Harper and Row, 1983.

————. *Effective Church Leadership: Building on the Twelve Keys*. San Francisco: Harper and Row, 1990.

Collum, Danny. "A. J. Muste, The Prophet Pilgrim." *Sojourners*, 13.11 (Dec. 1984): 12–17.

Costas, Orlando E. *Christ Outside the Gate: Mission Beyond Christendom*. Maryknoll: Orbis, 1978.

————. *Liberating News: A Theology of Contextual Evangelization*. Grand Rapids: Eerdmans, 1987.

Dulles, Avery. *A Church to Believe In: Discipleship and the Dynamics of Freedom*. New York: Crossroad, 1982. See chapter 2.

Durnbough, Donald F. *The Believers' Church: The History and Character of Radical Protestantism*. Scottdale, Pa.: Herald, 1985.

Gibbs, Eddie. *I Believe in Church Growth*. Grand Rapids, Eerdmans, 1982. See chapter 2.

Gilliland, Dean. *Pauline Theology and Mission Practice*. Grand Rapids: Baker, 1983. See chapter 4.

Grabowski, Stanislaus J. *The Church: An Introduction to the Theology of St. Augustine*. St. Louis: Herder, 1957. See chapter 3.

Hadaway, C. Kirk, Stuart A. Wright, and Francis M. Dubose. *Home Cell Groups and House Churches*. Nashville: Broadman, 1987.

Haight, Roger S. *An Alternative Vision: An Interpretation of Liberation Theology*. Mahwah, N.J.: Paulist, 1985.

Hesselgrave, David J. *Planting Churches Cross-Culturally*. Grand Rapids: Baker, 1980.

Hodges, Melvin. *The Indigenous Church and the Missionary: A Sequel to The Indigenous Church*. Pasadena, Calif.: William Carey Library, 1978.

Lindgren, Alvin J., and Norman Shawchuck. *Management for Your Church: How to Realize Your Church Potential Through a Systems Approach*. Nashville: Abingdon, 1977. See chapters 1, 2.

"Missionary Structures of the Congregation," in *The Church for Others and the Church for the World: A Quest for the Missionary Structures of Congregations*. Geneva: World Council of Churches, 1968.

Neighbour, Ralph W., Jr. *Where Do We Go From Here? A Guidebook for the Cell Group Church*. Houston: Touch, 1990.

Newbigin, J. E. Lesslie. *The Good Shepherd*. Grand Rapids: Eerdmans, 1977. See chapter 13.

Perry, Lloyd M., and Norman Shawchuck. *Revitalizing the Twentieth Century Church*. Chicago: Moody, 1982.

Sample, Tex. *Blue Collar Ministry*. Valley Forge, Pa.: Judson, 1985.

Schmemann, Alexander. *Church, World, Mission*. Crestwood, N.Y.: St. Vladimir's Seminary Press, 1979. See chapter 11.

Shelp, Earl, and Ronald H. Sunderland. *The Pastor as Prophet*. New York: Pilgrim, 1985.

Smith, Donald P. *Congregations Alive*. Philadelphia: Westminster, 1981.

Snyder, Howard A. *Liberating the Church: The Ecology of Church and Kingdom*. Downers Grove, Ill.: Inter-Varsity, 1982.

Torres, Sergio, and John Eagleson. *The Challenge of Basic Christian Communities*, J. Drury, trans. Maryknoll, N.Y.: Orbis, 1981.

Welsh, John R. "Comunidades Eclesiais de Base: A New Way to Be Church" in *America*, 154.5 (8 Feb. 1986), 85–88.

Williams, Colin W. *The Church*. Philadelphia: Westminster, 1968. See chapters 6, 7.

# PART 3

# Local Churches

## *Becoming God's Missionary People*

# 9

## *Missional Goals in the Local Church*

ach person can play a strategic role in building missionary churches. We have already seen how the scope of the nature of the church keeps expanding in relation to the kingdom of God and the world until we find ourselves pushed all the way out into the world. Now we need to explore the process by which missionary congregations get a vision of their mission in their various contexts. The Church becomes missionary because of the powerful presence of the Holy Spirit who creates, sustains, directs, and propels. *Emerging* is an adjective, a quality of the Church's missionary nature.

But *build* is a verb, and leaders and followers alike are called to actively and intentionally build missionary churches. Obviously this does not ignore the presence of sin, impurity, and the fact that the larger Church is never fully what it is called to be. Neither does building churches mean that we ignore the power and presence of the Spirit in forming this mysterious creation of God. Yet we know that each Christian is empowered by the Spirit and called upon by Scripture to participate in building the Church.

133

## Bridging the Gap

When the People of God set goals with vision, by faith, and with serious consideration for achieving those goals, they translate the statements of faith about the Church into statements of purpose which point toward the Church's becoming what it is confessed to be. Goal-setting bridges the gap between the "from below" and "from above" perspectives of the Church, and we begin to express the vision, desire, and purpose of being a missionary church. Goal-setting places us in the middle ground between confession and action, between the uniqueness of the Church as people chosen, gathered, maintained, and sent by God and the ordinariness of the church as a group of humans who gather in love around a common faith and shared hope.

Goals of an emerging church take on the incarnational perspective in the Sermon on the Mount (Matthew 5–7). The special role, calling, sacrifice, and lifestyle of the disciples is described by their Lord; yet Jesus continually reminds his hearers that discipleship will be lived out in the midst of the surrounding cultural and socio-political environment. To illustrate this Jesus combined the ideas of "salt" and "light" (Matt. 5:13–16). Both these elements must be dispersed to be effective. Light cannot be kept under a basket, but must be placed on a hill to shine through the surrounding darkness. Salt in Jesus' day was both for purifying and for preserving. Jesus spoke, then, of a saltshaker Church, a communion of disciples who are the salt of the earth. But the salt must be shaken out of the saltshaker, and then rubbed into the food so it may purify and preserve it. The salt itself will disappear in the food, *but the salt must not lose its saltiness*, even when it has been completely absorbed. Salt is of no value unless it be *dispersed* into the world. Yet once dispersed, every grain must preserve its peculiar quality.

This picture should stir some practical ideas about needs and be helpful as we reflect on what each individual ministry of the church should accomplish in the world. In this image the saints are very distinctive in their allegiance and composition. But the image of "salt" reminds us that an important aim must be to scatter or launch the saints. Unless they are the *missionary* people of God, they cannot be the salt *of the earth.* Goal-setting becomes the primary arena where the unique saltiness and the scattering of the saints is intentionally built into the life of missionary congregations. Specifically, as they aim to be the salt of the earth, congregations will shape their life so that they bring purification and preservation to God's world. The Lord commands his own special fellowship of disciples to *go* as witnesses in Jerusalem, Judea, Samaria, and the farthest corners of the earth (Acts 1:8). Each aspect of congregational life must be evaluated. Does it keep people in the "saltshaker" as an introverted, ingrown, self-centered fellowship, negating the very reason for the existence of the fellowship? Or does it equip people and disperse the fellowship to maintain its uniqueness. If the fellowship of disciples becomes just like the world, it loses its saltiness, and is good for nothing but fodder and road-fill, but the very existence of this special communion of saints depends on its world-directed life.

Therefore the congregation sets priorities, builds goals, creates plans, and carries out actions by which it lives in the world, for the sake of the world, but in distinction from the world. Leaders continually evaluate to see if they are seeking to emerge as a missionary church whose very nature is itself a call to action in the world. Goals recognize how the church's gift is its task and how its faith and hope are its command and course of action.[1] Missionary congregations open to their environment will intentionally create those perspectives, attitudes, priorities, goals, plans, and activities which will aid them in interacting with their context in purification and preservation of truth, justice, equality, faith, hope, and love.

At this point the dialectical paradigm of modern ecclesiology contributes to bring the "from above" and "from below" perspectives together, so that the local church emerges as it is being built. Beginning with Dietrich Bonhoeffer's ecclesiological emphasis on the *communio sanctorum*, Karl Barth developed the idea that the Church grows of its own inherent nature, yet through the efforts of Christians in building the Church. Barth explained this dialectical reality of the Church:

> If we are to use it in interpretation of the concept of "upbuilding" the term communion must be given the strict sense of the Latin communio and the Greek κοινωνια. Communion is an action in which on the basis of an existing union (unio) many (people) are engaged in a common movement towards the same union. This takes place in the power and operation of the Holy Spirit, and the corresponding action of those who are assembled and quickened by Him. . . . The secret of the communion of saints is that it is capable of this expansion and engaged in it. That human planning and speech and faith and love and decision and action are also involved according to the divine will and order is also true. This is not compromised by the reference to the secret of the growth of the community. But in itself this is no explanation of the secret, nor can it call in question the reference to it. That the community as the communion of saints grows like a seed to a plant, or a sapling to a tree, or a human embryo to a child and then to a man, is the presupposition of the divine as well as the human action by which it is built. It grows—we may venture to say—in its own sovereign power and manner, and it is only as it does this that it is built and builds itself.[2]

1. Robert Worley, *A Gathering of Strangers: Understanding the Life of Your Church* (Philadelphia: Westminster, 1976), 68.
2. Karl Barth, *Church Dogmatics* 4.2.

As members obey Christ's purpose, summons, call, and command they naturally join to build the Church's inherent dynamic of mission. There is no choice but to set goals and objectives, since the Church's nature already assumes goals for which the community of saints is accountable. That which has been given as a gift is in reality to be perceived as a task.[3] In figure 8 we modified our concentric circles to show that, just as the words about the Church's nature are concepts which force the local church outward in an emerging pattern toward the world, so also goal-setting, member activities, leadership, and administration enable the communion of saints to build itself in mission in the world. In *Congregations Alive* Donald Smith stresses planning, leadership, and administration for the creation of congregations which share ministry.[4]

This process of translating the Church's nature into defined goals, objectives, plans, and tasks makes a church relevant and powerful. This process unites the concepts of Church and mission in such a close connection that churches find themselves becoming missionary congregations. Here the Church as both organism and organization participates in Spirit-led missional action arising out of its missionary nature.[5] The interaction between the Church's nature and its place in the world has also been emphasized by consultants in church management, primarily with regard to the systems approach.

## Responding to the System

Since the late 1970s a number of professionals have suggested a systems approach to managing the local church. Such a program views a congregation as a *system*, comprised of a number of *subsystems*. All of the parts together form the whole, and each subsystem relates to every other subsystem within the congregation and to the larger social system of the cultural context.

3. G. C. Berkouwer (*Studies in Dogmatics: The Church* [Grand Rapids: Eerdmans, 1976]) and Hans Küng (*The Church* [London: Search, 1971]) are among the foremost proponents of this perspective. Avery R. Dulles, Gregory Baum, Howard A. Snyder, Gene A. Getz, John R. W. Stott, and Hendrikus Berkhof have followed their lead.

4. Philadelphia: Westminster, 1981, 154. A helpful process for congregational planning and goal-setting is outlined in Jackson W. Carroll, Carl Dudley, and William McKinney, eds., *Handbook for Congregational Studies* (Nashville: Abingdon, 1986).

5. Abraham Kuyper reflected deeply on the fact that the Church is simultaneously organism and organization—and that it is in the intimate intertwining of the two that the Church's full being occurs. See Abraham Kuyper, *Tractaat van de Reformatie der Kerken* (Amsterdam: Hoveker, 1884); G. C. Berkouwer, *The Church* (Grand Rapids: Eerdmans, 1976); Henry Zwaantra, "Abraham Kuyper's Conception of the Church," in *Calvin Theological Journal*, 9 (April–Nov. 1974): 159–64; George Peters, *A Theology of Church Growth* (Grand Rapids: Zondervan, 1981), 134 ff., and Roland Allen, *The Spontaneous Expansion of the Church and the Causes Which Hinder It* (Grand Rapids: Eerdmans, 1962), chapter 7.

Quite a variety of relating elements may be found in even a small congregation: leaders; various ministry groups; organizational structures; communication channels; educational networks, and webs of interpersonal and interfamily relationships are but a few examples of the various subsystems within the larger system of the congregation. In day-to-day life the mutual impact of various subsystems on one another can be productive or counterproductive. Churches, like families, may be functional or dysfunctional systems. Two church analysts who have popularized the impact of systems theory in relation to congregations are Lyle E. Schaller[6] and Kennon L. Callahan.[7]

Alvin Lindgren and Norman Shawchuck also lead in this movement. Their picture of a local congregation viewed as a system can be seen in figure 9. There are normally two kinds of boundaries that differentiate a local congregation from its surrounding environment. There are physical boundaries to buildings, neighborhoods, and the like. Another kind of boundary includes how the congregation perceives itself and its context and how people outside the church perceive the congregation. These boundaries mark off arenas in which the internal subsystems of the congregation work. The sum of all these complex interactions will determine the overall impact a congregation may have. Goal-setting defines the subsystems and orients them toward more positive impact within the congregation and in the surrounding society.[8]

Lindgren and Shawchuck have demonstrated that, although a number of organizational theories (the traditional, the charismatic leader, the human relations, and the classical) are viable, there are some distinct advantages to the systems approach.

1. The systems approach offers diagnostic tools for identifying problems, and helps to get a handle on the dynamics that cause the Church to behave as it does.

2. A systems view will greatly increase the effectiveness of any planning process by identifying all the components of the

6. I am thinking here especially of Schaller's *Looking in the Mirror: Self-Appraisal in the Local Church* (Nashville: Abingdon, 1984), in which he describes the way a congregational system is affected by the size of its membership. Schaller shows how congregations operate differently if they are small like a cat, slightly larger like a collie, larger still like a garden, awkwardly large like a house, even larger like a ranch, and very large indeed like a nation.

7. See his earlier *Twelve Keys to an Effective Church* (New York: Harper and Row, 1983) and his more recent *Effective Church Leadership: Building on the Twelve Keys* (San Francisco: Harper and Row, 1990).

8. Carl George of the Charles E. Fuller Institute has been developing a systems analysis of "mega churches" (churches with membership in the thousands) and of "meta churches" (with membership in the tens of thousands) to assist the pastors in leading these new types of congregations.

# Figure 9

## Interacting Systems Between Church and World

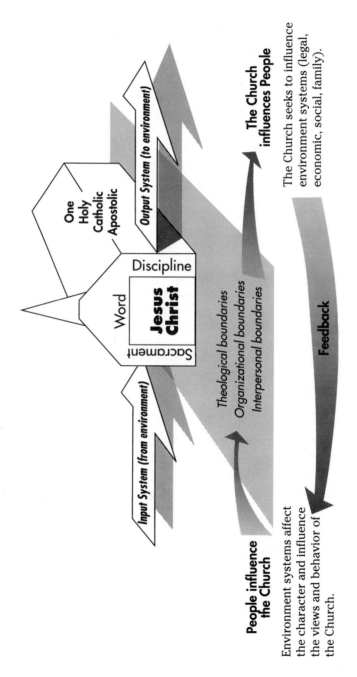

One
Holy
Catholic
Apostolic

Output System (to environment)

Discipline

Word

**Jesus Christ**

Sacrament

*Theological boundaries*
*Organizational boundaries*
*Interpersonal boundaries*

Input System (from environment)

**The Church influences People**

The Church seeks to influence environment systems (legal, economic, social, family).

**Feedback**

**People influence the Church**

Environment systems affect the character and influence the views and behavior of the Church.

Adapted from Alvin J. Lindgren and Norman Shawchuck, *Management for Your Church: How to Realize Your Church Potential Through a Systems Approach* (Nashville: Abingdon, 1977), 34.

church and its environment that will act as resources or constraints upon the plan.

3. Systems thinking offers a perspective of wholeness, a gestalt view of the entire church that is often easily overlooked because of one's involvement in a particular organization within the church.

4. The systems approach enables a leader or group to predict more accurately the effects and implications of alternative courses of action.

5. A systems view requires the church to see itself in relationship to other systems in its environment. Such perspective keeps the church from becoming introvertedly focused upon itself.

6. Systems theory elicits flexible leadership behavior contingent upon conditions in the environment, the goals, and characteristics of the church.[9]

The systemic approach was clearly the background to another of Lindgren and Shawchuck's works, *Let My People Go: Empowering the Laity for Ministry*.[10] They prefaced that work by saying,

> A major concern of both clergy and laity must be the discovery of how laity can be enlisted and equipped to increase the church's ability to enact the gospel in all areas of personal and contemporary society's complex concerns. Today's needs and concerns are such that only team work of lay persons and clergy can affect social structure and personal life-styles. If the church is to make a corporate witness and impact today, increased lay involvement in every area of the church's life is essential.[11]

As can be seen from figure 9, the real strength of the systems approach is that it takes into account the dynamic interrelationship of the Church with its environment. Charles Kraft called for a similar perspective with regard to the concept of "dynamic-equivalence churchness." Kraft stressed that the Church is and must be in dynamic interrelatedness with its cultural matrix. The cultural system affects and is affected by the Church within it.[12]

9. Alvin J. Lindgren and Norman Shawchuck, *Management for Your Church: How to Realize Your Church Potential Through a Systems Approach* (Nashville: Abingdon, 1977), 25.

10. Nashville: Abingdon, 1980, 10.

11. See also Arthur Adams, *Effective Leadership for Today's Church* (Philadelphia: Westminster, 1978), 76–82.

12. Charles H. Kraft, *Christianity in Culture: A Study in Dynamic Biblical Theologizing in Cross-Cultural Perspective* (Maryknoll, N.Y.: Orbis, 1979), 315 ff.

In his analysis of why churches have been declining in membership in the United States, Carl Dudley finds both internal reasons and external cultural shifts in the 1960s and 1970s that churches failed to understand. In dealing with Dean M. Kelley's work, *Why Conservative Churches Are Growing*,[13] and Dean R. Hoge and David Roozen's *Understanding Church Growth and Decline*,[14] Dudley attempted to give some insight into the interrelationships of environment and Church.[15] People like David Moberg, Peter Berger, Charles Glock, Robert Bellah, and others have helped the Church begin to understand the importance of a broad view of itself which sees not only the Church and not only the world, but Church-and-world in dynamic and fruitful interaction.[16]

Schaller pointed to this creative interrelation as it affected new church development. In this case, says Schaller, it is extremely important to understand just who the church serves, answering Schaller's question, "Who is the client?"[17]

From the systems perspective, mission becomes integral to development of a dynamic ecclesiology. The people of God focus their attention in mission by interacting with their environment in the world. This is precisely what Roozen, William McKinney, and Jackson W. Carroll found empirically when they studied twelve different congregations in Hartford, Connecticut. The interaction of each of these congregations with the same environment gave rise to four major "mission orientations": activist, citizen, sanctuary, and evangelist.[18] Priorities, goals and plans take into account more than the nature of the Church or what the pastor or people want. When goal-setting is pro-active and missiological, it will carefully consider the missionary congregation within its contex-

---

13. Dean M. Kelley, *Why Conservative Churches Are Growing: A Study in the Sociology of Religion*. 2d ed. (New York: Harper and Row, 1977).

14. Dean R. Hoge and David A. Roozen, *Understanding Church Growth and Decline* (New York: Pilgrim, 1979). See also Benton Johnson, "Is There Hope for Liberal Protestantism?" in Dorothy Bass, Benton Johnson, and Wade Clark Roof, eds., *Mainstream Protestantism in the Twentieth Century: Its Problems and Prospects* (Louisville: Committee on Theological Education, Presbyterian Church, USA, 1986), 13–26.

15. Carl S. Dudley, *Where Have All Our People Gone? New Choices for Old Churches* (New York: Pilgrim, 1979).

16. See, for example, David Roozen, William McKinney, and Jackson W. Carroll, *Varieties of Religious Presence: Mission in Public Life* (New York: Pilgrim, 1984); David Moberg, *The Church as a Social Institution: The Sociology of American Religion* (Grand Rapids: Baker, 1984); Robert Bellah, et al., *Habits of the Heart* (New York: Harper and Row, 1985); Wade Clark Roof and William McKinney, *American Mainline Religion: Its Changing Shape and Future* (New Brunswick: Rutgers, 1987); Peter Berger, *The Sacred Canopy* (Garden City, N.Y.: Doubleday, 1967), and Peter Berger, Brigette Berger, and Hansfried Kellner, *The Homeless Mind: Modernization and Consciousness* (New York: Random House, 1973).

17. Lyle E. Schaller, *Growing Plans* (Nashville: Abingdon, 1983), chapter 4. Some of the systemic interaction of congregations with their environment is also brought out by Schaller in *It's a Different World* (Nashville: Abingdon, 1987).

18. Roozen, McKinney, and Carroll, *Varieties of Religious Presence*, 247–65.

tual environment as part of a unique system, impacted by and acting upon that system.

Figure 9 shows how missional interaction occurs. We could illustrate this by thinking about a week in the life of a congregation. On Sunday the people of God gather for worship, and all the various internal systems operate at a maximum. Theological-missional matters of vision, perspective, and self-identity are formed through the education, worship, music, preaching, liturgy, and sacraments. The organizational issues are brought to the fore by the leaders. And the intrapersonal and interpersonal relationships are heightened as people gather to present themselves as one before God.

But where is the congregation on Monday morning? It has now been scattered. Because the Church is *people* the congregation has now entered the various subsystems of its context. There it is involved in mission—sent to influence its environment. If it is too much like its environment, the impact is minimal. If it is too countercultural, the influence may be rejected. At the same time there is a two-way interaction between people of God and world. The Church is sent to influence the subsystems of its culture, but the congregation also may be strongly influenced by the subsystems.

The sum of these influences, then, gathers with the congregation the next Sunday. Consciously or unconsciously, "input" from the social context is carried back into the life of the congregation by its members. If the church has strongly influenced its environment in a positive way, that input may include more members for the body. A variety of concerns and issues important to those within that environment also invade the body as it gathers. These issues may or may not be overtly addressed during worship. If they are not, people may go away with a feeling that the experience lacks relevance for their everyday lives.

Obviously, then, the *transforming* nature of the congregation is not just a theoretical concern. It is through all the various subsystems of the congregation that the people of God preserve their saltiness so they may contribute missionally to the transformation of the world in which they have been placed and for which Christ died. Being "in the world" but not "of the world" (John 17:11–16), the Church is continually interacting with the world so that the world may believe (John 17:21). Goal-setting gives concrete shape to the missional relationship of church and context.

## Setting Priorities

Many missiologists have spoken of priority setting in relation to the mission of the Church. Donald McGavran, for example, set as highest priority church growth and "harvest," but he was not the first. Gisbertus

Voetius spoke of a threefold goal of mission: conversion of the heathen; planting the church, and glorification and manifestation of divine grace.[19] Johannes Verkuyl outlined several possible long-range priorities to be sought as results of particular mission endeavors and seen as the ultimate reasons for the Church's outreach in the world. Verkuyl mentioned the following possible priority areas of the life of the Church in the world:

1. The pietistic goal of saving individual souls
2. *Plantatio ecclesiae* (church planting)
3. The three-self formula
4. Numerical church growth
5. A Christian society
6. The social gospel
7. Improving macrostructures
8. Establishing the kingdom of God[20]

It is important to notice that the priorities for the life and mission of the Church must be appropriate to the nature of the missionary congregation, the nature of the congregation's cultural and human environment, and the changing patterns of the interrelation of the congregation to its environment. Dean Gilliland has referred to this as the "contextuality of the Church."[21]

Priorities for the life and ministry of the Church in any given place and time constantly change. Any mission priority must be set in relation to the nature of the surrounding environment and culture. But those priorities must be reevaluated and reassigned time and again as the culture and the community of Christians in that culture change. A ministry which is given top priority in the first year or two of outreach in a given context may not be so important three or four years later.

But this readjustment process does not mean falling into relativity or subjectivity in mission and ministry. *We can only set priorities for the mission of the Church which are natural, missional aspects of the life of the one, holy, catholic, and apostolic community of Jesus Christ, the Word*

19. J. H. Bavinck, *An Introduction to the Science of Missions* (Philadelphia: Presbyterian and Reformed, 1960), 155.

20. Johannes Verkuyl, *Contemporary Missiology* (Grand Rapids: Eerdmans, 1978), 176–97. See also David Watson, *I Believe in the Church* (London: Hodder and Stoughton, 1978), 301, and Harvey Conn, *Evangelism: Doing Justice and Preaching Grace* (Grand Rapids: Zondervan, 1982).

21. Dean Gilliland, *Pauline Theology and Mission Practice* (Grand Rapids: Baker, 1983), 209.

*made flesh.* We must know what the Church is and where the Church lives, so that in relation to both we may see what the Church *must become* as it emerges in ministry in the world. James Anderson and Ezra E. Jones say that what is needed in pastoral leadership is "trained people who can assist a congregation to think about its life, its faith commitments, its relations to the community, its care of its own members— help them think about . . . those commitments, and create the means whereby they can act upon them."[22]

## Building Goals

The missionary Church begins to take place in ministry in the world when its nature is translated into priorities which lead to intentional mission goals. There is a wealth of literature on how to set goals. Our interest is to show how goal-setting is the intentional step whereby the missionary congregation takes upon itself the task of building itself up toward becoming what it is. Edward R. Dayton and Theodore Engstrom call a goal "a future event toward which we can measure progress" and remind us of "the awesome power of goals" for the life of the Church in the world.[23]

Goals must be purposeful. Lindgren suggested five possible goals of purposeful church administration in *Foundations of Purposeful Church Administration*:

1. To secure understanding of and commitment to the Christian faith.

2. To coordinate all experiences and activities so that they mutually support one another and the common mission of the church.

3. To see every aspect of church life as an opportunity to minister to persons.

4. To understand the surrounding culture and to communicate effectively to it.

5. To involve all members of the church in the work of a ministering community.[24]

A church's goals must incorporate the personal and corporate goals of the members. There is one body, but that body is made up of many

22. James D. Anderson and Ezra E. Jones, *The Management of Ministry* (New York: Harper and Row, 1978), 17–18.
23. Edward R. Dayton and Theodore Engstrom, *Strategy for Leadership* (Old Tappan, N.J.: Fleming H. Revell, 1979), 53–54.
24. Nashville: Abingdon, 1980, 84–85.

members. Robert Worley stresses the need to distinguish between, but coordinate among, the personal goals of the congregation as a "gathering of strangers" and the organic and corporate goals of the congregation as the communion of believers.[25]

A missionary congregation's goals also must not be set exclusively by the leadership. Everything we have seen about the nature of the Church shows that all the members of the body, through their gifts, are to be instruments of ministry in the world. Thus the church's goals must involve the participation, support, and calling of each one of the people of God. Ministry belongs to the whole people of God, not just to a select few.

## Creating Plans

Finally, church planning which takes into account the missionary nature of the Church must also translate into actual ministry. Based on his study of various ministering congregations in the United Presbyterian Church in the USA (before its 1983 merger with the Presbyterian Church in the U.S.), Smith called for the ministry of all God's people:

> Ministry is carrying out Christ's work in the world. In Jesus of Nazareth, the Creator of the universe became a human being. Although Jesus was the Messiah, the promised one of God, he became the Suffering Servant. He healed the sick, opened the eyes of the blind, and set captives free. Through his life, death, and resurrection, God reconciled the world to Himself. So Jesus Christ is both our model for ministry and the source of energizing power which calls our ministries into being.
>
> Ministry is the work of the church among its own members and in the world. It is carried out both corporately and individually and is not the exclusive responsibility of ordained ministers of the Word. In fact, it is the work of all the people of God.[26]

W. Harold Fuller provided us with an excellent discussion of priorities, goals, and plans of action in *Mission-Church Dynamics*. Fuller attempted to bring out the distinction between a church-centric perspective as contrasted with a mission-centric perspective on the mission of the Church. Fuller shows the strengths and weaknesses of each viewpoint, observing that "actually, there should be no polarization into church-centric and mission-centric extremes."[27] This is particularly so

25. Worley, *Gathering of Strangers*, 22–26.

26. Donald P. Smith, *Congregations Alive* (Philadelphia: Westminster, 1981), 15–16. See also Donald Metz, *New Congregations* (Philadelphia: Westminster, 1967), 41–50.

27. W. Harold Fuller, *Mission-Church Dynamics: How to Change Bicultural Tensions into Dynamic Missionary Outreach* (South Pasadena, Calif.: William Carey Library, 1980).

within the new paradigm of the missionary congregation. The Church needs to set priorities in the midst of the Church-kingdom-world interaction, and follow them with a series of goals, translated into plans of action for all the people of God. Then the Church *as mission* will begin to reach out to the world to find there that what it does in the world it in fact does "unto Me," unto its Saviour and Lord.

As the Church translates its nature into priorities and goal-statements, it must go one step further and convert that knowledge and faith into action in the world through its members. It must create concrete, workable, time-lined, and prayerful plans of action whereby the people of God can become truly the "salt of the earth" in our world and in our generation. Without such careful and intentional planning, missionary congregations never emerge and are never built up to become God's people in mission in the world. The chapters which follow will discuss some of the dynamics involved in fulfilling such plans of action as they relate to the membership, leadership, and administrative structures necessary for the Church to be the Church-in-mission.

## Further Study

### Setting Priorities

Anderson, James D., and Ezra E. Jones. *The Management of Ministry*. New York: Harper and Row, 1978. See chapter 3.

Costas, Orlando. *Christ Outside the Gate: Mission Beyond Christendom*. Maryknoll, N.Y.: Orbis, 1982.

Dulles, Avery. *The Resilient Church: The Necessity and Limits of Adaptation*. New York: Doubleday, 1977.

Getz, Gene A. *Sharpening the Focus of the Church*. Chicago: Moody, 1974.

Gilliland, Dean. *Pauline Theology and Mission Practice*. Grand Rapids: Baker, 1983. See 209ff.

McGavran, Donald A. *Understanding Church Growth*, rev. eds. Grand Rapids: Eerdmans, 1980, 1990. See chapter 2.

McGavran, Donald W., and Winfield Arn. *Back to Basics in Church Growth*. Wheaton, Ill.: Tyndale, 1981. See chapter 6.

————. *Ten Steps for Church Growth*. New York: Harper and Row, 1977. See chapter 4.

Padilla, C. René. *Mission Between the Times: Essays by C. René Padilla*. Grand Rapids: Eerdmans, 1985.

Savage, Peter. "The Church and Evangelism" in C. René Padilla, ed., *The New Face of Evangelicalism: An International Symposium on the Lausanne Covenant*. Downers Grove, Ill.: Inter-Varsity, 1976.

Schaller, Lyle E. *The Pastor and the People: Building a New Partnership for Effective Ministry*. Nashville: Abingdon, 1973. See chapter 3.

_____. *Activating the Passive Church*. Nashville: Abingdon, 1981.

Shenk, Wilbert, ed. *The Challenge of Church Growth*. Scottdale, Pa.: Herald, 1973. See chapter 3.

Stott, John, and Robert T. Coote, eds. *Down to Earth: Studies in Christianity and Culture*. Grand Rapids: Eerdmans, 1980.

Verkuyl, Johannes. *Contemporary Missiology: An Introduction*, D. Cooper, trans. Grand Rapids: Eerdmans, 1978. See 176 ff.

Wagner, C. Peter. *Church Growth and the Whole Gospel: A Biblical Mandate*. San Francisco: Harper and Row, 1981. See chapter 6.

_____. *Your Church Can Grow*, rev. ed. Glendale, Calif.: Regal, 1984. See chapter 11.

Watson, David. *I Believe in the Church*, 1st American ed. Grand Rapids: Eerdmans, 1979. See chapter 17.

## Building Goals

Bavinck, J. H. *An Introduction to the Science of Missions*, D. Freeman, trans. Philadelphia: Presbyterian and Reformed, 1960. See chapter 9.

Beyerhaus, Peter. "The Three Selves Formula," *International Review of Missions* 53 (1964): 393–407.

Hodges, Melvin L. *The Indigenous Church and the Missionary: A Sequel to "The Indigenous Church."* South Pasadena, Calif.: William Carey Library, 1977. See chapter 10.

Hoge, Dean R., et al. *Converts, Dropouts, Returnees: A Study of Religious Change among Catholics*. New York: Pilgrim, 1981. See pages 166–83.

Hogue, C. B. *I Want My Church to Grow*. Nashville: Broadman, 1977. See chapter 4.

Hull, Bill. *Jesus Christ, Disciple-Maker: Rediscovering Jesus' Strategy for Building His Church*. Colorado Springs, Colo.: NavPress, 1989.

Kane, J. Herbert. *Understanding Christian Missions*. Grand Rapids: Baker, 1974. See chapter 8.

MacNair, Donald J. *The Growing Local Church*. Grand Rapids: Baker, 1975. See chapter 10.

McGavran, Donald A. *Understanding Church Growth*, rev. ed. Grand Rapids: Eerdmans, 1980. See chapter 21.

McGavran, Donald A., and Winfield Arn. *How to Grow a Church*. Glendale, Calif.: Regal, 1973.

Mayers, Marvin K. *Christianity Confronts Culture: A Strategy for Cross-Cultural Evangelism*. Grand Rapids: Zondervan, 1974. See pages 249 ff.

Metz, Donald L. *New Congregations: Security and Mission in Conflict*. Philadelphia: Westminster, 1967. See chapter 3.

Nelson, C. Ellis. *Congregations: Their Power to Form and Transform*. Atlanta: John Knox, 1988.

Ott, E. Stanley. *The Vibrant Church: A People-Building Plan for Congregational*

*Health*. Ventura: Regal, 1989.

Schuller, Robert. *Your Church Has Real Possibilities*. Glendale, Calif.: Regal, 1974. See chapter 8.

Towns, Elmer L., John Vaughan, and David Seifert, *The Complete Book of Church Growth*. Wheaton, Ill.: Tyndale, 1981. See part 4.

*Leadership*, 8.4 (Fall 1987) 12–115.

## Creating Plans

Arias, Mortimer. *Announcing the Reign of God: Evangelization and the Subversive Memory of Jesus*. Philadelphia: Fortress, 1984.

Barrett, Lois. *Building the House Church*. Scottdale, Pa.: Herald, 1986.

Belew, M. Wendell. *Churches and How They Grow*. Nashville: Broadman, 1971.

Du Bose, Francis M. *How Churches Grow in an Urban World*. Nashville: Broadman, 1978.

Fuller, W. Harold. *Mission-Church Dynamics: How to Change Bicultural Tensions into Dynamic Missionary Outreach*. South Pasadena, Calif.: William Carey Library, 1980. See chapters 1–4, 6.

Hodges, Melvin L. *A Theology of the Church and Its Mission: A Pentecostal Perspective*. Springfield, Mo.: Gospel, 1977. See chapter 5.

Hunter, George G., III. *To Spread the Power: Church Growth in the Wesleyan Spirit*. Nashville: Abingdon, 1987.

Pendorf, James G., and Helmer C. Lundquist. *Church Organization: A Manual for Effective Local Church Administration*. Wilton, Conn.: Morehouse-Barlow, 1977. See chapter 2.

Rose, Larry L., and C. Kirk Hadaway, eds. *An Urban World: Churches Face the Future*. Nashville: Broadman, 1984.

Schaller, Lyle E. *Planning for Protestantism in Urban America*. New York: Abingdon, 1965. See chapter 5.

Shenk, Wilbert, ed. *Exploring Church Growth*. Grand Rapids: Eerdmans, 1983. See 171–302.

# 10

# *Missionary Members in the Local Church*

In the mid-1960s Wesley Baker offered a provocative analysis of the role of individual members in today's Church. In *The Split-Level Fellowship*,[1] Baker gave a new name to a phenomenon with which church leaders have long been familiar—the disturbing difference between the committed few and the uninvolved many. Baker calls this phenomenon "factor Beta."

This factor is the simple, plain fact that within the recognized corpus of the church there are two quite different kinds of people—or at least two different sets of motive patterns. It would be inaccurate to separate them into "leaders" and "followers," yet that has a small amount of accuracy. . . .

Look at the parish today. Made up, usually, of a small inner core of believers who assume the necessary posts of leadership with gratitude and devotion (albeit frequently naive), and surrounded by a cloud of uninvolved and mildly approving witnesses, it can move in no prophetic direction "as the church" without doing greater interior battle with the forces of inertia, practically sealed in by the religiously immobile whose grasp of the meaning of the church is some-

1. Philadelphia: Westminster, 1965.

149

thing less than courageous. No local parish is free to be a church, in the sense of a community holding unspoken, deeply valid affirmations to action, because of the sheer tons of dead weight. This is not so much a problem of Christian education, or evangelism, but rather, a definition of the Church.[2]

After a brief historical analysis of the requirements for someone to be considered a church member, Baker made a case that "factor Beta" be erased through a two-pronged approach: First, more stringent requirements must be set for actual membership. Second, the distinction between "clergy" and "laity" must be attacked through liturgy, Christian nurture, evangelism, and Christian ethics. We may not agree with some of Baker's solutions to the problem, but let us look carefully at the matter he highlighted, because the twenty-five years since Baker's work appeared has not brought us any closer to dealing with the central issue. It is still true that a church is composed of 10 percent active, core, dedicated people—and 90 percent inactive, peripheral, semi-interested people. Though the percentages may vary, the general pattern holds true in too many congregations. Moreover, the situation is evident in all six continents, although Europe and North America suffer the most from "factor Beta." In the early stages of work in establishing a mission congregation the ratio of inactive to active is at least is as high as Baker's 90–10.

How, then, can we speak of the Church emerging to be the people of God? Does the people of God include the 90 percent or do we limit ourselves to the 10 percent? Is it realistic to expect the inactive majority to reflect the unity, holiness, catholicity, and apostolicity of the body of Christ? Is it possible for the 90 percent to be involved in *koinonia*, *kerygma*, *diakonia*, and *martyria*? Must we settle for only 10 percent of the Church exercising a priestly, prophetic, kingly, liberating, and healing role in the world? Maybe we must admit that all along we were really only talking about a select few and not about the entire membership: the "ordained," the "clergy," the "nuns and monks," the "priests and religious" of the Church!

The Protestant Reformation attributed great importance to the "priesthood of all believers" and the fact that every Christian is called to intercession, prayer, justification, sanctification, and service. At stake in factor Beta is the question of whether Protestant Christianity retains any meaning. As Hendrik Kraemer wrote in *A Theology of the Laity*,[3] it is biblically indefensible to say that only a few should participate in the ministry of Christ in the world. Congregations can become missionary branch offices of the kingdom of God only through the lives of the members—that 90 percent, guided, trained, assisted, and encouraged by the

2. Ibid., 34–42, 60ff.
3. Philadelphia: Westminster, 1958.

10 percent. Missionary congregations will emerge when leaders equip all the members to realize their greatest potential for growth, maturity and service in a relationship of shared ministry and cooperative outreach of the whole gospel by the whole Church to the whole world.[4]

## A Biblical Perspective of the "Laity"

So much has been written on the laity that we will limit ourselves to relating the idea to missionary congregations. Here David Watson is of great help. He devoted over fifty pages of *I Believe in the Church* to a discussion of ministry, membership, and leadership, pointing out that the idea of a two-class church structure cannot be justified through the New Testament: "In the biblical sense all Christians are priests and clergy, and this is a crucial starting-point if we are to re-discover the true concept of ministry and leadership within the church."[5]

The term *laity*, if used, must be given its biblical sense of the "people (Gk. *laos*) of God," with distinction in gift, function, and ministration—but not distinction in holiness, prestige, power, commitment, or activity. Today we often use the term "layperson" in contra-distinction from the word "professional," and we mean that the layperson in a certain discipline is one who dabbles, muddles, tries hard, but certainly does not have expertise. The professional is "in the know," the expert, the person dedicated to competence in the discipline. There is no biblical basis for such a distinction in the Church, and the unbiblical practice has only served to place "professional" clergy on a pedestal as being "close to God," removing the vast majority further from holiness and the activity of the Spirit in their lives. The rise of a clergy-laity distinction from the third century on continues in the Protestant denominations since the Reformation as one of the main sources of decline, secularization, and sinfulness of the Church.

In the New Testament it is the *whole people of God* together who are called to be the Church. All the members are joined to grow up into maturity, to the stature of the fulness of Christ (Eph. 4:15). Such fulness is not possible if only 10 percent or fewer exercise their place and calling. Fulness will be found when the other 90 percent join in ministry. The real meaning of *laity* is that everyone who is in Christ is a new creature. Old things (including gender, professional, racial, cultural, and economic distinctions) have passed away, the walls of partition having been broken (2 Cor. 5:17). All those who believe in their heart and confess with their mouth that Jesus is Lord are in fact the *laos* of God. Vatican

4. When those involved in the Lausanne Movement met in Manila in 1989, they gathered under this theme.

5. David Watson, *I Believe in the Church*, 1st American ed. (Grand Rapids: Eerdmans, 1979), 248–50.

Council II strongly affirmed this view of the Church, a view which has since had a profound impact on the entire Christian Church.[6]

## Implications of the "People-of-God" Concept

The biblical perspective of the Church as the people of God has far-reaching implications for missionary congregations. We can here enumerate only a sample.

### Conversion

When a person becomes part of the "people of God" much more is involved than going forward at an altar call, burning old fetishes, or beginning to attend corporate worship. Our understanding of conversion must be broadened. Conversion in this sense is the change of those who were "not a people" to become the ministering people of God, the active, involved, serving body of Christ (1 Pet. 2:10). This is a conversion out of selfishness, out of self-centeredness, out of serving the rulers of darkness and into agape love, discipleship, and serving Jesus Christ. This conversion moves from decision through a process of discipleship, with the disciple seeking to minister in Christ's name as a follower of Jesus. In fact a case could be made that full and complete conversion in the biblical sense is a three-part process involving (1) conversion to God in Jesus Christ; (2) conversion to the Church, the body of Christ, and (3) conversion to ministry in the world for whom Christ died.[7]

### Literacy and Theological Education

If we come to believe that the Church is the whole people of God, we will take seriously the task of literacy and theological education. In many countries this means new converts must immediately be enrolled in classes to teach them how to read, how to read the Scriptures, and how to understand what they read. It means also that theological education, whether in residence or through extension systems cannot be the property of a select few. Theological training must belong to, be open for, and actively involve the whole people of God.[8]

---

6. See, for example, Austin P. Flannery, ed., *Documents of Vatican II* (Grand Rapids: Eerdmans, 1975); and idem, ed., *Vatican II: More Postconciliar Documents* (Grand Rapids: Eerdmans, 1982).

7. See, for example, James E. L. Newbigin, *The Open Secret* (Grand Rapids: Eerdmans, 1978).

8. There is an extensive literature on the development of nonformal, informal, and formal theological education in the churches around the world. See, for example, Ralph D. Winter, *Theological Education by Extension* (South Pasadena, Calif.: William Carey Library, 1969); F. Ross Kinsler, *Ministry by the People: Theological Education by Extension* (Geneva: World Council of Churches, 1983), and Ray Anderson, *The Praxis of Pentecost: Revisioning the Church's Life and Mission* (Pasadena, Calif.: Fuller Theological Seminary, 1991).

Our educational programs in the Church must be understood to be the equipping of the people of God for a dynamically missional discipleship in service to the world. Thus theological training cannot be aimed at making a great many laypersons into professionals. It no longer will be the pursuit of some mysterious academic discipline open only to a few initiates. Rather, theological education must teach the essentials of biblical faith in order to mobilize all the people of God to live out in day-to-day existence the implications of their radical discipleship. This type of theological education must be "inside out," directed toward the world and expressing the meaning of discipleship in the here-and-now of ministry in the world. This is precisely why we must further the development of our teaching elders and free their time so they can do theological education in their local congregations for the sake of all the people of God.

### Avoiding the "Santa's-Helpers" Syndrome

One of the most common errors in the popular shared-ministry movement is a tendency to equip the 10 percent by teaching them techniques for doing ministry *in the church*—such as visiting the sick, calling on people, leading prayer or Bible study groups, and teaching a Sunday school class. So much of our training of the people of God amounts to making a few willing members into a cadre of second-class professionals who can relieve the "ministers" of some of their work load. These "lay ministers" then function like little elves in Santa's toy shop, scurrying around doing and making goodies which Santa (the "minister") will dispense.

Too often we see the same thing happening in cross-cultural church-planting. The pioneer missionary learns the language, translates the Scripture, and forms a small group of converts. There is not enough time or energy for the missionaries to evangelize the entire people-group, so they quickly train a few others to do what they would like to be doing but don't have enough time and energy to do. They may then move on to do the same in another place, or they may move "up" into administration, supervision and training. Finally the day comes when the national church separates from the missionary leadership so that top native clergy can become the primary administrative heads. This pattern has been fostered in part by the "three-self formula," but more profoundly it is brought about by an unbiblical perspective of the people of God.

What should instead happen within the people of God is that the pioneer missionary equips those early converts *for ministry* (prophetic, priestly, kingly, healing and liberating *koinonia*, *diakonia*, *kerygma*, and *martyria*) in their culture and among their people. They should be trained, with the missionaries themselves setting the example, in serving rather than being served. Those early believers could be taught to teach others to serve. The longer the missionaries remain, the greater should be their role of "giving their lives a ransom for many."

Out of this more Christlike and incarnational pattern, the spiritual gifts and abilities of the people of God would surface. Ephesians 4:11–13 would begin to happen. Some would be called to be prophets, some to be evangelists, and some to be pastors and teachers, to prepare God's people for works of service, so that the body of Christ might be built up until all would reach unity in the faith in the knowledge of the Son of God, becoming mature and attaining to the whole measure of the fulness of Christ.

This is the missionary Church where the people of God are taught, trained, encouraged, and mobilized to find their missionary nature. They grow numerically, corporately, spiritually, and missionally as they minister in their contexts. Cultural forms are then filled with Christian meanings for Christian ministry. Cultural leadership patterns are defined and related to mission and ministry. The here-and-now of the Church is given a new eschatological and missional reality through serving the King in the world. Based on this ecclesiology, the Church will be as interested in the broad development of the whole people of God as in the training of individual leaders.

## The Missionary Church as the Body of Christ

There is outstanding agreement among theologians of different traditions that the relationship between spiritual gifts and life and ministry of the Church needs to be reaffirmed. This has strong implications within our view of missionary churches.

### The Church Is Not a Dictatorship

Led by Christ as Head, the Church is made up of many diverse persons, each exercising a personal uniqueness and functioning through an individual set of particular spiritual gifts. A partial list of such gifts may be constructed by looking at Romans 12, 1 Corinthians 12, Ephesians 4, and 1 Peter 4. Each church might make its own list to reflect the time and place to which it belongs and how the local church perceives the Spirit enabling the body to function in ministry. The variety of gifts shows us that there is no way in which one person, the "minister," can possibly be the only one designated to carry out the "ministry" of the body of Christ. Neither is one person called upon to put everyone else to work. Rather, the leaders equip, organize, assist, and serve the bearers and executors of the Spirit's gifts, but do not control, determine, or assign such gifts. Management-by-objective and organizational-development techniques are called into question here, because they do not belong to the essence of the Church as the body of Christ.

## The Church Is Neither a Democracy Nor a Tribe

The people-of-God perspective also calls us to reexamine our usual democratic methods of governing our congregational and denominational structures. The democratic system of government and decision-making is certainly effective, especially to control the abuse of power and to create equality among the members. But in the Church *Jesus Christ rules* through the operation of the Holy Spirit who distributes gifts for ministry as, when, and how he wills. Here is a completely different model of organization, with no room for rugged Western individualism. Instead, the members of the body gain their identity, their function, their reason-for-being, and their place in ministry as they participate in the body. The Church is more than a composite of individuals. A bodiless arm, an armless hand, or a legless foot would be impossible to use. Only through intimate correlation with the body as the communion of saints can individual members realize their own spiritual nature as disciples of Jesus Christ.[9]

But neither is the body superior to the individual. In Marxism and in tribalism the individual is seen to exist for the sake of the group. This too must be eliminated from our conception of the Church. The Church as the body is incomplete if it is missing one of its members. The Church functions at its ideal when the full spiritual life of each person is in action. Paul says that when any member hurts, the whole body hurts. The individuals do not exist for the sake of the body. Rather, they derive their unique function as the bearers of the gifts of the Spirit in the Church. The loss of any one of these means a loss of vitality for the body of Christ.

## The Church Is Not a Club

A third affirmation related to the view of the Church as the people of God has to do with its nature as a voluntary association. All over the world voluntary associations and organizations have sprung up because likeminded individuals with a common interest have thought it advantageous to cooperate. It is easy to consider the Church to be the same sort of social organization, yet the opposite is true.

The Church is presented as a body, of which Jesus Christ is Lord and Head. He is the one who calls the individuals to allegiance and obedience. His Spirit convicts, converts, transforms, and enables the members to be what they are as members. They are joined to each other, not

9. Robert Wuthnow points this out in "Evangelicals, Liberals, and the Perils of Individualism," *Perspectives*, 6.5 (May 1991): 10–13. Wuthnow demonstrates that the probability of individuals being involved in activities of social transformation seems to correlate closely with their active participation in a local church, regardless of whether they categorize themselves as "liberal" or "conservative."

so much because they are "like-minded individuals," but because the Head of the Church, the one in whom "all things hold together" (Col. 1:17), has joined them to each other. They did not choose him; neither did they choose each other (Eph. 2:14–16).

In a social club the members choose those they like to associate with, and reject those they would rather avoid. Jesus Christ, through his Spirit, constitutes the Church, gathers the individual members, unites them, and commands and sends them for ministry into the world. It is not for us to accept or reject each other; it is for us to demonstrate to the world that we love one another and so fulfil the law of God.

## A Biblical View of the Clergy

When missionary congregations see themselves as the whole people of God, they may have to change their definition of *ordination*. As disciples of Jesus are confirmed as members of the body of Christ, they must recognize that in that confirmation there is a mandate for ministry in the Church and in the world. Ordination becomes the setting apart by the whole people of those who will equip, motivate, and mobilize the members for ministry and mission. In some ways ordination, then, will set aside those who will assist the members to confirm their calling as God's missionary people. This view of ordination challenges our thinking at several points:

1. The ordained person has no higher status, no more important role, no increased sanctity, no more power than other members.

2. The ordained person is intentionally and consciously assigned by the people to hold increased power, respect, and prestige in order to enable and equip the congregation. This role is a gift from the people of God to the leaders for the sake of God's mission in the world.

3. The success or failure of the ordained person's work and ministry will be judged only according to the degree to which the Church becomes the missionary people of God.

4. The ordained person is the servant of all. This is borne out in the injunction Jesus gives to his disciples. Though they have a special calling in the Church, nevertheless they must understand that "the greatest among you should be like the youngest, and the one who rules like the one who serves" (Luke 22:26, NIV). Jesus confers on the disciples a kingdom, yet they will participate in that kingdom as foot-washing servants.

5. The ordained person is designated to exercise a very special prophetic, priestly, kingly, and healing ministry in the Church

and through the Church in the world, in order to facilitate the exercise of the people's spiritual gifts in ministry.

6. The ordained servant is the one who constantly strives to bring Church and world into dynamic interrelation so that all the people of God may emerge in ministry.

7. Ordained persons are recognized because of their function in the body and through their unique calling as disciples of Jesus Christ.

Notice that there is no mention here of professionalism, careers, or financial remuneration. Although all these aspects of ordination are important, they are not essential to the nature of the Church. They are not on the same plane with such concepts as unity, holiness, catholicity, and apostolicity. Nor are they essential activities like the pure preaching of the Word and the right administration of the sacraments. Yet ordination is very important. Its importance derives from the fact that the ordained persons, through personal piety, faith, hope, love, and sacrificial discipleship, are called by God to dedicate themselves to equipping God's missionary people for ministry in the world.

The ordained person, in this view, is not called to ministry any more than is anyone else; rather, the ordained person is designated to enable each member in ministry. At the same time, we must understand that such leaders cannot enable if they do not have authority over willing followers. This authority is given to them to enable them to be dedicated disciples and obedient servants in the tasks they fulfil.

The relationship between leaders and followers can be illustrated by the use of three diagrams (see figure 10). The structuring of the relationships between leaders and led influences the freedom with which the Church is allowed to emerge. Each of the three models involves both positive and negative elements that show the *impact* the structures have in facilitating emergence as a missionary congregation. If we compare the three structures with the seven observations made earlier concerning ordination, we begin to see that each structure defines the role of the leaders among the people in a slightly different way.

Whether ordination should be seen in purely functional terms or in personal terms of the call of an individual should make no difference if our ecclesiology is missiologically oriented. Clearly the ordained person cannot function properly unless that person has been called, transformed, and brought near to God. The ordained person's primary function, however, will be to build up the body of Christ so it will emerge to become God's missionary people.

Figure 11 illustrates two other possible models. The "satellite structure" is based on the National Presbyterian Church of Mexico's work in the state of Chiapas. There an organized church with either one or no

# Figure 10
## Models of Church Structure for Ministry

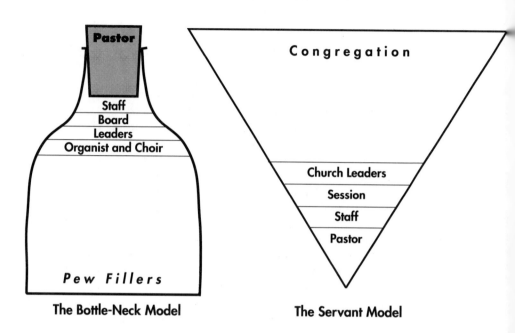

The Bottle-Neck Model

The Servant Model

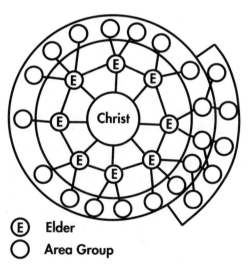

Ⓔ  Elder

Ⓞ  Area Group

The Shared-Ministry Model

# Figure 11
## The "Satellite" and "House Church" Models

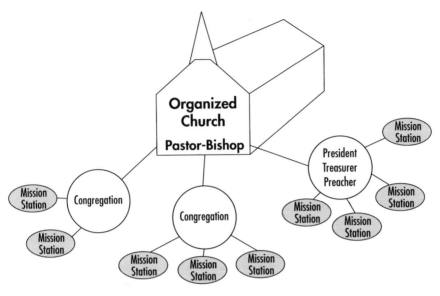

**Satellite Model**

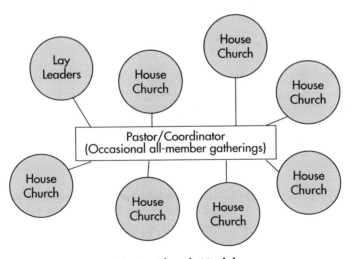

**House Church Model**

Adapted from David Watson, *I Believe in the Church*, 1st American ed. (Grand Rapids: Eerdmans, 1979), 246, 293.

ordained person consists of a network of smaller "congregations," each with its own executive committee (president, treasurer, and preacher) elected annually from among the members. Each congregation in turn is a mother to several smaller missions or preaching stations which are evangelistic outposts served by the members of the "congregation." The involvement of the membership and the results in church growth are impressive. In discipling and equipping, everyone who is taught teaches, building a network of relationships. Supervision and accountability are provided within the network, where all members are related structurally to the larger governing body and ordained pastor. There are some close similarities between this structure and the "house church structure" which is gaining more attention and credibility. Paul Yonggi Cho of the Yoido Full-Gospel Church of Seoul, Korea, for example, has used the model to develop his church of more than 500,000 members.[10]

The reader might compare the model here presented with views arising from ecumenical issues. A good source may be found in *Baptism, Eucharist, and Ministry*, which provides information on recent Consultation on Church Union (COCU) discussions in the United States and the ongoing Anglican-Roman Catholic dialogue. These various discussions seem to have a common characteristic: They look only inward. All that matters are mutual recognition of one another's professional ministry and mutual acceptance of differences in the practice of the sacraments. The relationship of churches to the world and the corresponding mission of the people of God in the world are essentially ignored; instead, the churches become islands in an undefined sea.

The perspective we have been considering represents a dynamic, purposeful, world-directed ecclesiology that would redirect these ecumenical discussions. Rather than ask if one denomination may recognize the professional clergy of another, missionary churches would ask to what extent the "clergy" facilitated, transformed, and impelled the people of God in mission. Recognition would be in missional terms. Translated into language of evangelism and church growth, for example, this would mean that an individual's ordination would be validated on the basis of the numerical growth of the congregation! For older churches in Europe and North America that would be quite revolutionary.

---

10. Cf. Paul Yonggi Cho, *Successful Home Cell Groups* (Plainfield, N.J.: Logos, 1981); idem, *More Than Numbers* (Waco, Tex.: Word, 1984), and Lois Barrett, *Building the House Church* (Scottdale, Pa.: Herald, 1986). C. Kirk Hadaway, Stuart A. Wright, and Francis M. Dubose have given us what appears to be the best treatment of this subject in *Home Cell Groups and House Churches* (Nashville: Broadman, 1987). See chapters 3, 8 for relevant discussion on this point.

## Further Study

Adams, Arthur M. *Effective Leadership for Today's Church*. Philadelphia: Westminster, 1978. See 62–82.

Allen, Roland. *The Spontaneous Expansion of the Church and the Causes Which Hinder It*. Grand Rapids: Eerdmans, 1962. See chapters 7–9.

Anderson, Andy. *Where Action Is*. Nashville: Broadman, 1976.

Anderson, James D., and Ezra E. Jones. *Ministry of the Laity*. New York: Harper and Row, 1985.

Banks, Robert J. *Paul's Idea of Community: The Early House Churches in Their Historical Setting*. Grand Rapids: Eerdmans, 1980.

Bassham, Rodger C. *Mission Theology, 1948–1975: Years of Creative Tension—Ecumenical, Evangelical and Roman Catholic*. South Pasadena, Calif.: William Carey Library, 1980. See pages 69ff.

Boff, Leonardo. *Ecclesiogenesis: The Base Communities Reinvent the Church*, J. Dierksmeyer, trans. Maryknoll, N.Y.: Orbis, 1986.

_____. *Church, Charism and Power: Liberation Theology and the Institutional Church*, J. Dierksmeyer, trans. New York: Crossroad, 1985.

Braun, Neill. *Laity Mobilized*. Grand Rapids: Eerdmans, 1971. See chapter 6.

Chaney, Charles. *Design for Church Growth*. Nashville: Broadman, 1977. See pages 53ff.

Conners, Kenneth W. *Stranger in the Pew*. Valley Forge, Pa.: Judson, 1970.

Dietterich, Paul M. "New Ways of Thinking About Supervision." *The Center Letter*, 13.4 (April 1983).

Dudley, Carl. *Building Effective Ministry*. New York: Harper and Row, 1983.

Dunn, James. "Ministry and the Ministry: The Charismatic Renewal's Challenge to Traditional Ecclesiology," in: Cecil M. Robeck, ed. *Charismatic Experience in History*. Peabody, Mass.: Hendrickson, 1985.

Hanson, Paul D. *The People Called: The Growth of Community in the Bible*. New York: Harper and Row, 1986.

Hogue, C. B. *I Want My Church to Grow*. Nashville: Broadman, 1977. See chapters 2–6.

Kraemer, Hendrick. *A Theology of the Laity*. Philadelphia: Westminster, 1958.

Kraft, Charles H., and Tom N. Wisley, eds. *Readings in Dynamic Indigeneity*. Pasadena: William Carey Library, 1979.

Küng, Hans. *Structures of the Church*, S. Attanasio, trans. New York: Nelson, 1964. See chapters 4, 5.

McGavran, Donald A., and G. G. Hunter. *Church Growth Strategies That Work*. Nashville: Abingdon, 1980.

MacNair, Donald J. *The Growing Local Church*. Grand Rapids: Baker, 1975.

Mickey, Paul A., and Robert L. Wilson. *What New Creation?* Nashville: Abingdon, 1977. See chapter 2.

Moltmann, Jürgen, and Hans Küng. *Who Has the Say in the Church?* New York: Harper and Row, 1981. See chapter 2.

Peck, George, and John Hoffman, eds. *The Laity in Ministry.* Valley Forge, Pa.: Judson, 1984.

Quin, Bernard, et al. *Churches and Church Membership in the United States, 1980.* Atlanta, Glenmary Research Center, 1982.

Richards, Lawrence O., and Clyde Hoeldtke. *A Theology of Church Leadership.* Grand Rapids: Zondervan, 1980. See chapter 3.

Richards, Lawrence O., and Gilbert Martin. *Lay Ministry: Empowering the People of God.* Grand Rapids: Zondervan, 1981.

Richardson, William, ed. *The Church as Sign.* Maryknoll, N. Y.: Orbis, 1968.

Schaller, Lyle E. *Getting Things Done*, Nashville: Abingdon, 1987.

————. *The Decision-Makers.* Nashville: Abingdon, 1974. See chapters 1–2.

Schuller, Robert. *Your Church Has Real Possibilities.* Glendale, Calif.: Regal, 1974. See chapter 7.

Segundo, Juan Luis. *The Community Called Church,* J. Drury, trans. Maryknoll, N.Y.: Orbis, 1973.

Shannon, Foster H. *The Growth Crisis in the American Church.* Pasadena: William Carey Library, 1977. See chapter 10.

Shenk, Wilbert. *The Challenge of Church Growth.* Scottdale, Pa.: Herald, 1973. See chapters 2–3.

Sobrino, Jon. *The True Church and the Poor.* Maryknoll, N.Y.: 1984.

Southard, Samuel. *Training Church Members for Pastoral Care.* Valley Forge, Pa.: Judson, 1982.

Van den Heuvel, Albert H. *The Humiliation of the Church.* Philadelphia: Westminster, 1966. See chapter 3.

Wagner, C. Peter. *Your Church Can Grow.* Glendale, Calif.: Regal, 1984. See chapter 5.

————. *Your Spiritual Gifts Can Help Your Church Grow.* Glendale, Calif.: Regal, 1974.

Wakatama, Pius. *Independence for the Third World Church.* Downers Grove, Ill: Inter-Varsity, 1976. See chapters 1–4.

Watson, David. *I Believe in the Church*, 1st American ed. Grand Rapids: Eerdmans, 1979.

Weeden, Larry K., ed. *The Magnetic Fellowship: Reaching and Keeping People.* Waco, Tex.: Word, 1988.

Werning, Waldo. *Vision and Strategy for Church Growth.* Chicago: Moody, 1977. See chapters 2–3.

# 11

## *Missionary Leaders in the Local Church*

The fact that church members are the people of God in ministry in the world has far-reaching implications for the understanding and development of leadership. We follow Peter's viewpoint here. After Peter described the Church as "a chosen race, a royal priesthood, a holy nation, a people for God's own possession" (1 Peter 2:9, NASB), he went on to apply this description to government, family, life in the midst of persecution, and individual faith in Christ (1 Peter 2–4). Then Peter turned to the matter of leadership in the Church.

> Therefore, I exhort the elders among you (*presbyterous oun en hymin parakalō*), as your fellow-elder and witness (*ho sympresbyteros kai martys*) of the sufferings of Christ, and a partaker also of the glory that is to be revealed, shepherd the flock of God among you, not under compulsion, but voluntarily, according to the will of God; and not for sordid gain, but with eagerness; nor yet as lording it over those allotted to your charge, but proving to be examples to the flock (1 Pet. 5:1–3, NASB).

Peter's line of thought was followed by Lawrence O. Richards and Clyde Hoeldtke, who stressed the spiritual nature of leadership in the Church when they noted that the Church "is a living body of the living Jesus. Since we are part of a body, not part of an institution, the task of body leaders must be distinctively different from the management tasks of institutional leaders."[1]

As we build missionary congregations, then, it is extremely important to understand what is involved in leading them. At every level of congregational life missionary churches require dynamic, forceful, optimistic, and organized leaders who can direct the potential abilities and resources of the members as they emerge in ministry in the world.

## Defining Leadership

Theodore W. Engstrom once offered a candid definition of leadership: "Well, what is leadership? Everyone knows what it is. Or do they? No one seems really to be sure. We are able to define what managers do, but the closest we seem able to come to a broadly acceptable definition of leadership is, it is what leaders do. Then when we try to define leaders, about all the agreement we get is that leaders lead."[2]

Engstrom went on to explain that leaders possess at least three qualities: (1) They make things happen; (2) they are never passive puppets, and (3) they perform.[3]

> Leadership is a quality; management is a science and an art. Leadership provides vision; management supplies realistic perspectives. Leadership deals with concepts; management relates to functions. Leadership exercises faith; management has to do with fact. Leadership seeks for effectiveness; management strives for efficiency. Leadership is an influence for good among potential resources; management is the coordination of available resources organized for maximum accomplishment. Leadership provides direction; management is concerned about control. Leadership thrives on finding opportunity; management succeeds on accomplishment.[4]

From the standpoint of organizational dynamics, Paul Hersey, Kenneth N. Blanchard, and Walter E. Natemeyer suggested defining leadership as,

---

1. Lawrence O. Richards and Clyde Hoeldtke, *A Theology of Church Leadership* (Grand Rapids: Zondervan, 1980), 6.

2. Theodore W. Engstrom, *The Making of a Christian Leader* (Grand Rapids: Zondervan, 1976), 19.

3. Ibid., 20–23.

4. Ibid., 22–23. See also Robert Schuller, *Your Church Has Real Possibilities* (Glendale, Calif.: Regal, 1974), 48–49; Richards and Hoeldtke, *Theology,* 90–92; and James D. Anderson and Ezra E. Jones, *The Management of Ministry* (New York: Harper and Row, 1978), 78–89.

"the process of influencing the activities of an individual or a group in efforts toward goal accomplishment."[5]

Church leadership is very difficult to define with precision. Much depends on the personality of the leader; the skills and abilities of the leader; the roles, functions and power of the leader as perceived by both leader and followers, and the personal perceptions of the followers.

None of the above definitions is adequate for this work. We are interested in how leaders act as catalysts for mobilizing the people of God in mission in the world. A more directly missiological definition of leadership in missionary congregations might go something like this:

> Leadership is a corporate event. The people of God move forward in mission in the world as they live out their vision of God's call and will for them, stimulated by a number of leader-catalysts, and mobilized by the Holy Spirit in response to what God is doing in their midst and in their context of mission in the world.

This definition differs markedly from those which look at leadership from an introverted perspective, examining the relationship of leaders and followers. Such conceptions lack an emphasis on leadership within the purpose and role of the church. We have defined leadership, not as structure or interpersonal dynamic, but primarily as a missiological *event*. Our attention is less on the internal relationship between leaders and followers than on a conscious mobilization of the *whole* people of God in *mission* in the world. Here leadership as an *event* is the product of the empowering activities of the Holy Spirit, the catalytic enabling of the leaders, and the serving work of the members. Leadership, as seen here, emanates in mission in the world.

Leadership happens as a corporate event when the believing community allows certain members to act as its leader-catalysts, inspiring it toward greater exercise of a whole range of spiritual gifts distributed throughout the members. Leaders, then, become the creative, motivational, visionary, enthusiastic, positive, and forward-looking catalysts to mobilize the people of God in mission in the world.

This definition of leadership calls for leader-catalysts who are more than care-givers, more than counselors, more than preachers, more than managers, more than organizers, and more than supervisors. Merely delegating authority—only telling people what they should do and devising programs to do it—will not be enough to mobilize the people of God.

5. Paul Hersey, Kenneth H. Blanchard, and Walter E. Natemeyer, "Situational Leadership, Perception, and the Impact of Power" (Escondido, Calif.: Center for Leadership Studies, 1979), 142–47; cf. Paul Hersey and Kenneth H. Blanchard, *Management of Organizational Behavior: Utilizing Human Resources* (Englewood Cliffs, N.J.: Prentice Hall, 1988), 202; J. Robert Clinton, *The Making of a Leader* (Colorado Springs: NavPress, 1988), 127.

The people must be shown a model that presses them to want to achieve those intentionally missionary goals of the congregation.

The spiritual, emotional, and mental personhood of their leaders provides the *heart* of missionary congregations, their managerial acumen provides the *structure* for missional outreach, and the members provide the *hands*, *feet*, and *spiritual gifts* necessary to carry out the congregation's missional intentions.

## Identifying Missionary Leaders

Just who are these leader-catalysts whom the Spirit uses to mobilize the people of God for mission in the world? An initial answer may be identified in the historical development of the Church. The past twenty centuries of the Church's life have seen a number of ways whereby leaders were differentiated from followers. In Acts 1 and 2 some were set apart because they were witnesses who walked with Jesus during his earthly ministry and after the resurrection (Acts 1:21–22). By the time of Constantine, however, a class structure differentiated among bishops, members, and catechumens. The gulf became wider as the "*ecclesia docens*" was seen as something qualitatively different from the "*ecclesia audiens*." By the later Medieval period bishops, priests, and monks were considered the essence of the Church, radically distinct from the faithful. This difference has continued to this day, as James Dunn has demonstrated.[6]

But another theme threads its way through the story. Ever since Pentecost some have stood to remind the church that all Christians are called to ministry, and leaders are called for the sake of all the people, not as a separate class. From Pentecost through the Protestant Reformation to early Pentecostalism, the Charismatic Movement, and the emphasis on body-life and the gifts of the Spirit—always there has been a call for a broad range of gifted leaders to facilitate and mobilize people in mission. This does not mean total anarchy, complete democracy, or homogeneous uniformity. When we look at a local congregation we need to see great variety among those who can influence the people of God in mission. As suggested in figure 12, there is a whole range of different types of leaders influencing the direction of the local congregation.

Parents and grandparents in extended families are some of the most influential leaders in a congregation. This is especially true in two-thirds-world settings, where age and maturity are associated with wisdom and power. Cell group leaders, teachers and youth sponsors can bring sur-

6. James Dunn, "Ministry and the Ministry: The Charismatic Renewal's Challenge to Traditional Ecclesiology" in Cecil M. Robeck, Jr, ed., *Charismatic Experience in History* (Peabody, Mass.: Hendrickson, 1985), 81–101.

# Figure 12
## Typology of Congregational Leaders

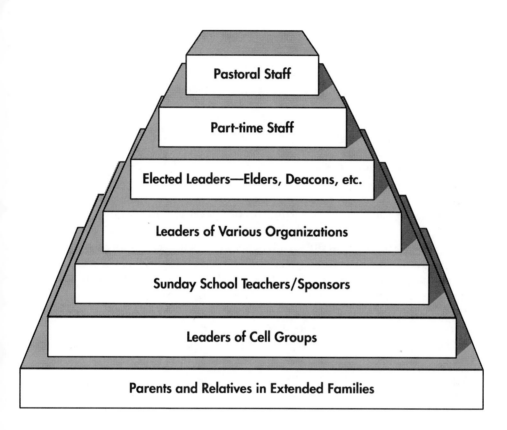

Pastoral Staff

Part-time Staff

Elected Leaders—Elders, Deacons, etc.

Leaders of Various Organizations

Sunday School Teachers/Sponsors

Leaders of Cell Groups

Parents and Relatives in Extended Families

prising changes. The leaders of all the various organizations of a congregation are potential mobilizers. Elected office holders need to see their role as one of servant-leadership rather than one of control.[7]

Each type of leader will exercise a different kind of influence. Yet the differences do not obscure the fact that each type has the potential to move onward a part of the congregation. Dynamic, forceful, visionary senior pastors will recruit leaders of every type. It is the responsibility of the various leaders to develop in their followers a sense of God's presence, calling, and commission into the world. Local congregations will be mobilized for mission when their senior administrative pastors

7. Peter Wagner speaks of this type of thorough-going organization for growth by using the concepts of cell, congregation, and celebration.

begin to let this catalytic missionary vision permeate all corners of their congregation's life through the influence of every type of leader-catalyst.

Once we have identified the types of leader-catalysts, we need to carefully analyze the manner in which they lead. And Scripture is quite clear at this point. In the Church, leaders lead through servanthood.

## Recognizing Servant Leaders

Luke records Jesus' words of rebuke and exhortation that provide a very distinctive view of how leaders are to lead.

> The kings of the Gentiles lord it over them; and those who have authority over them are called "Benefactors." But not so with you, but let him who is the greatest among you become the youngest, and the leader as the servant (Luke 22:25–26, NASB—cf. Matt. 20:25–28).

Luke sets this teaching within the Eucharistic context, and Matthew in anticipation of the triumphal entry. Yet both understand the saying to be Jesus' response to a power-struggle between the disciples as to who would be the leaders. Luke gives the pictorial response in terms of foot-washing and table-setting. Matthew illustrates the servant principle in the blind men who cry out "Son of David," and the entry of the king who rides a donkey and receives flowers from the multitudes. In both the concern is to define apostolic servant leadership.

The difference between the "rulers of the Gentiles" and the disciples is shown in figure 13. Notice that in the traditional hierarchical concept the authority is from top down, the commands coming from leader to led, and the ideas originating with the leader. The world is below the membership. The most important person is the one who gives the orders, and the members are those who carry out the orders.

But Jesus inverts reality. The servant concept makes modeling, illustrating, and doing a part of leadership itself. The leader serves other leaders to help them serve the membership, in order that they in turn may be able to serve the world. The world is at the top. The most important people are those in the world, and the members are stimulated to serve the world because they are served by the leader.

In the first two pyramids we begin to realize that the model Jesus left his disciples actually includes both perspectives. Jesus is the *King* who rides on a donkey, the *King* of the Jews who hangs on the cross, the *Lord* who demands obedience from his disciples. Jesus is the suffering Servant *Messiah*, the *Alpha* and *Omega* who embodies both sacrifice and kingly rule. He rules the universe through sacrifice. Is this not the essence of what Paul is trying to tell us in Philippians 2? This is the Son

## Figure 13
### Three Concepts of Leadership

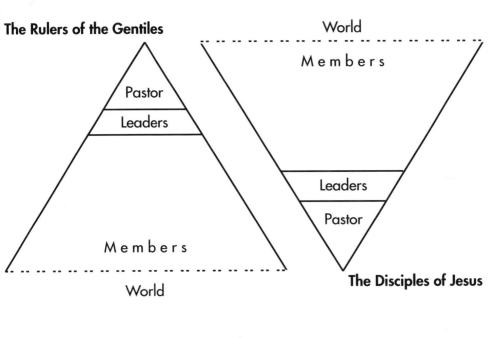

The Rulers of the Gentiles

Pastor

Leaders

Members

World

World

Members

Leaders

Pastor

The Disciples of Jesus

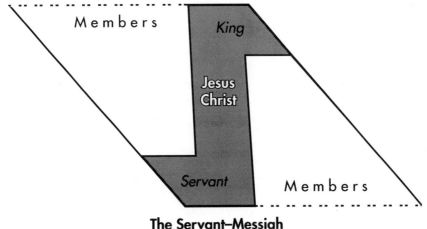

Members

King

Jesus Christ

Servant

Members

The Servant–Messiah

of God who left his throne to take the human life of a servant in death for humanity—so that at the name of Jesus every knee shall bow, and he shall be exalted above every name. This is all one process in which *diakonia* becomes, in and of itself, a kingly ministry. Jesus Christ is both at the top of the pyramid and at the base of the pyramid. He is "at the right hand" of power, yet immanently "emmanuel," God with us.[8]

This perspective of kingly service to others helps us understand the nature of the authority which servant-leaders exercise in the Church. Arthur Adams reminds us that "authority in the church is defined by the Lord. Jesus deliberately turned his back on all the ideas of power held in the world and proposed something new: 'servanthood.' 'Servant' and 'slave' are strange words for leaders, but the early Christians took Jesus seriously."[9]

If in both congregational pastorates and cross-cultural missionary situations the pastors and missionaries of the last several decades had remembered this biblical mode of leading, we might have avoided some severe problems. To some extent the domineering, hierarchical style of leading has produced many inactive, unconcerned, and sometimes angry church members who find themselves faced with the choice of either doing what they are told or doing nothing at all. Since the late 1960s churches in Africa, Asia, and Latin America have sometimes voiced a strong sentiment against the presence of expatriate missionaries. "Missionary, go home!" often has been heard, with a significant number of native leaders calling for a "moratorium." Often this meant a call for the complete nationalization of missionary enterprises, and the removal of expatriate missionaries from major administrative control over church matters in the two-thirds world. Many cases of missionary paternalism and domination, which too often fed the flames of the "moratorium" debate, might have been avoided if the missionaries had remembered that they were the ones to set the table, to wash the others' feet, to serve the national Christians, and to demonstrate a model of servant ministry—true ministry—for the national leaders themselves. We have not yet taken to heart or put into practice what we have known for so long—that the leader in the Church must be the servant of all. When leaders rule rather than serve they lose their right to lead. This servant leadership is not passive nor impotent. It still leads, but through a particular kind of leader who empowers and actualizes the led.[10]

8. Stephen C. Neill points this out in *Fulfill Thy Ministry* (New York: Harper, 1952), 95–96.

9. Arthur M. Adams, *Effective Leadership for Today's Church* (Philadelphia: Westminster, 1978), 38–39. In Mark 10:42–45 Jesus speaks about leaders who come "not to be served but to serve." Paul repeatedly calls himself a "slave" of Jesus Christ, as do other New Testament writers. See Rom. 1:1; Gal. 1:10; Phil. 1:1; 2 Tim. 2:24; Titus 1:1; James 1:1, and 2 Peter 1:1.

10. See Eddie Gibbs, *I Believe in Church Growth* (Grand Rapids: Eerdmans, 1982), 379ff; idem, *Followed or Pushed?* (London: MARC Europe, 1987).

Nehemiah is an excellent biblical example of the type of dynamic, visionary, and mobilizing leader we have been describing. We could summarize some of his qualities as a leader.

1. He identifies himself with the problems and the sins of the people in a personal and committed solidarity with them (Neh. 1:3–4).
2. He has vision (1:9).
3. He has courage (1:11; 2:4–5; 6:11).
4. He makes definite plans (2:6–9, 12–16).
5. He demonstrates self-confidence (2:17).
6. He inspires the people toward the goal (2:18).
7. He does not quit in spite of opposition (2:10, 19).
8. He uses the resources of others (3:1).
9. He delegates the work to everyone (3:2–32).
10. He knows how to stand up to opposition (4:9–14, 6:5–8).
11. He inspires a discouraged people (4:14–23).
12. He organizes to cover every aspect of the work (4:16–21).
13. He works alongside all the others (4:21–23, 5:16).
14. He is strong-willed when necessary (5:6–8).
15. He can convince the people to work toward the goal (5:8–12).
16. He can communicate his ideas well in an inspiring way (5:13).
17. He is self-disciplined and sacrifices himself to live with the people, at the level of the people (5:14–15).
18. He is generous with what he has (5:17–18).
19. He is not easily side-tracked from working toward the goal (6:3–4).
20. He achieves the goal (6:15).
21. He organizes the people for a second phase (7:4–5).
22. He organizes a great feast of thanksgiving, and renews the covenant (chapters 8–9; 12:27–43).
23. He stands up against sin and corrects it (chapter 13).

## Determining Appropriate Leadership Styles

It is one thing to know what leadership is in theory but another to be able to model that in one's life, personality, and ministry. Although this is not a "how-to" book, it is necessary to understand the implications for our life and practice in the Church of the missionary perspective we have outlined. We need to look at leadership styles, the pastor's role in building missionary congregations, and the necessity of developing and training new leaders in the Church.

Theodore Engstrom defined style as the way leaders carry out their functions and how they are perceived by those they attempt to lead. In a very helpful chapter concerning "Styles of Leadership," Engstrom saw four main styles of leadership: laissez-faire, democratic-participative, benevolent-autocratic, and autocratic-bureaucratic. Engstrom goes on to ask: "Which style is best?" and answers, "Leaders are different. But so are followers! Which is another way of saying that some situations demand one style of leader, while others demand a different one. . . . At any given time the leadership needs of an organization may vary from another time. The appropriate style depends a great deal on the task of the organization, the phase of life of the organization, and the needs of the moment."[11]

We need to be aware of the kinds of leadership styles which can best be used to mobilize missionary congregations. Here the reader needs to keep in mind how culturally-conditioned and contextually-influenced all our discussion must be. Again, we are involved in the "systems" dynamic which must relate the leader to the led; together they need to consider themselves in relation to the purpose of the Church, the prevailing situation in the world around them, and the type of leader they are called to be.[12]

An excellent source for reflection on leadership styles is Alvin J. Lindgren and Norman Shawchuck's work, *Management for Your Church*. As noted earlier, Lindgren and Shawchuck consider five basic management theories (the traditional, the charismatic, the classical, the human relations, and the systems theory) in their work on church management. They go on to summarize the leadership styles that would be most prevalent in each organizational theory. They differentiate among the five theories by pointing out the function of the leaders in each:

---

11. Theodore W. Engstrom, *The Making of a Christian Leader*, 39–40. Other sources, including Warren Bennis and Burt Nanus, *Leaders: The Strategies for Taking Charge* (Philadelphia: Harper and Row, 1985), and Hersey and Blanchard, *Management of Organizational Behavior* provide a more complete understanding of this complex matter.

12. Charles Chaney summarized Donald A. McGavran's four types of leaders in *Design for Church Growth* (Nashville: Broadman, 1977), 50. See also Donald McGavran and Winfield C. Arn, *How to Grow a Church* (Glendale, Calif.: Regal, 1973), 89–97, and Gibbs, *I Believe*, 361–64. J. Robert Clinton and Edgar Elliston suggest a modified typology of church leaders. See J. Robert Clinton, *Leadership Emergence Theory* (unpublished manuscript, 1989), and Edgar Elliston, *Home Grown Leaders* (unpublished manuscript, 1989). There are also differences related to congregation size and age. See, for example, Lyle E. Schaller, *Looking in the Mirror: Self-Appraisal in the Local Church* (Nashville: Abingdon, 1984), and Martin F. Saarinen, "The Life Cycle of a Congregation" in *Action Information*, 12.3 (May–June, 1986): 9–11.

*Traditional* (paternal-priestly): to maintain the tradition and preserve the status quo.

*Charismatic* (prophetic-inspirational): to lead and motivate through personal appeal.

*Classical* (aggressive-directive): to direct by handing down decisions.

*Human Relations* (sensitive-non-directive): to create an atmosphere conducive to expression and participation.

*Systems* (professional-activator): to clarify goals, interpret environment, and monitor change.[13]

In other words the type of organizational theory one adopts will influence the style of leadership most effective for that situation. We must keep in mind that "organizational theory" really means a portrayal of the way in which the leader relates to the followers. The personality, leadership style, and symbolic presence of the leader strongly influence whether the congregation emerges to become a missionary people of God. The essence, purpose, role in the world, and goals of missionary congregations must be integrated into the life, ministry, and outlook of the leader, who is then able to lead as a servant and motivate the members to emerge toward ministry in the world. It is extremely important, therefore, that missionary leaders embody the emerging explosion they hope to ignite in their congregation, denomination, or mission church. As servant-leaders it is in their life, their enthusiasm, their vision, and their driving concern that the members of the body be propelled ever outward toward ministry in the world.

In relation to cross-cultural mission activity, Max Warren mentioned the great variety of personal leadership qualities which are necessary. He drew a series of pictures of what the missionary looks like in various contexts and summarized them with words that reflect the stages through which missionaries pass in their relationships with the people they are called to serve. It is interesting to compare Warren's words with the seven stages of the development of missionary congregations which we saw in chapter 2. Warren suggested that cross-cultural missionaries need to be "inquirers, learners, listeners, in love with their people, links with other organizations, change-agents, and signs of the end."[14]

Here we have an idea of the qualities we would foster in ourselves and others as leaders of missionary churches. And there are so many

13. Alvin J. Lindgren and Norman Shawchuck, *Management for Your Church* (Nashville: Abingdon, 1977), 26.

14. Max Warren, *I Believe in the Great Commission* (Grand Rapids: Eerdmans, 1976), chapter 10. We could also use such words as "example," "sage," "seer," "student," and "sacrifice" to portray the leader's role in being a catalyst in the development of missionary congregations. See Charles Van Engen, "Pastors as Leaders in the Church" in *Theology News and Notes* (June 1989): 15–19.

activities in the Church which can foster these qualities. Through the musical, educational, relational, liturgical, didactical, and homiletical activities of the Church those qualities may be nurtured which will enable the creativity and spontaneity of leader and led alike to emerge in an explosion of the Church's ministry in the world. Maybe if we had more cross-cultural missionaries and national church leaders who exemplified these qualities we would have less paternalism and more understanding between missions and churches.

Certainly one person cannot be all things to all people. However, it is extremely important that missionaries carefully consider their personality and leadership styles with reference to the people they serve and the environment in which they minister. Through careful analysis of leadership issues missionaries may develop that type of leadership that will most effectively mobilize the Church in that context for ministry in the world.

But styles of leadership are never static. The congregation, the context, the leaders, and the followers are in constant change. This prompted Hersey and Blanchard to call for "situational leadership."

# Figure 14
## Leader-Follower Interaction Within Typical Leadership Styles

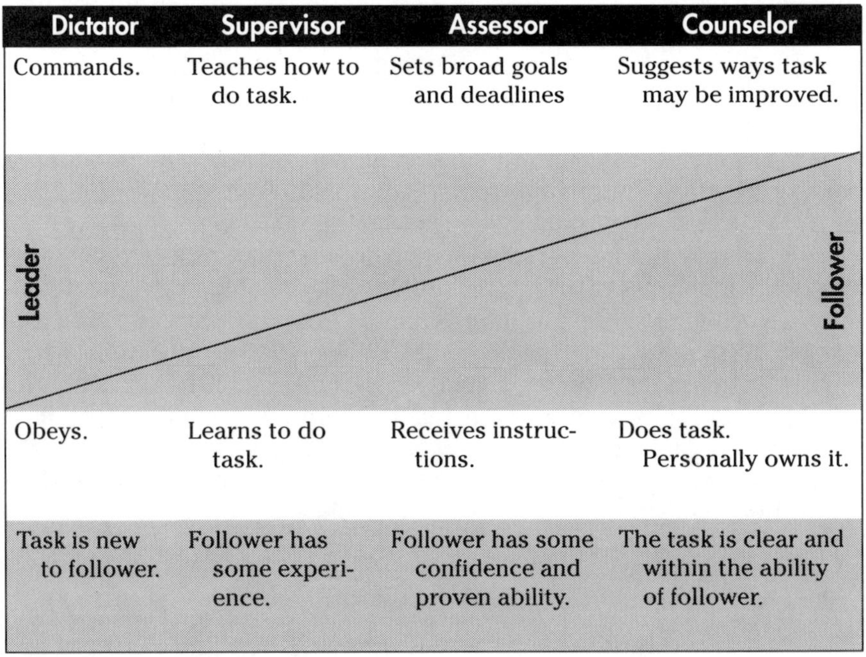

| Dictator | Supervisor | Assessor | Counselor |
|---|---|---|---|
| Commands. | Teaches how to do task. | Sets broad goals and deadlines | Suggests ways task may be improved. |
| *Leader → Follower (diagonal)* | | | |
| Obeys. | Learns to do task. | Receives instructions. | Does task. Personally owns it. |
| Task is new to follower. | Follower has some experience. | Follower has some confidence and proven ability. | The task is clear and within the ability of follower. |

Diagram adapted from Robert Tannenbaum and Warren H. Schmidt, "How to Choose a Leadership Pattern" in *Harvard Business Review* (May–June 1973).

Their point is especially important in developing missionary congregations in cross-cultural and multi-cultural settings. In such contexts we need Hersey and Blanchard's "situational leadership" to maximize our sensitivity to the relationship of leaders and led. Styles of leadership must change to fit the growth of the followers.[15]

There may be situations which demand a certain leadership style, while others call for something different. The style of leadership a particular organization needs at a particular time and place will vary according to the moment, the context, and the goals which need to be achieved. Moreover, the abilities, readiness, and maturity of the followers are also in flux. Some organizations have trouble changing their leaders. In this case the leaders themselves need to modify their leadership styles, depending on the task to be done, the changes going on in the life of the organization, the needs of the moment, the followers involved, and the processes needed to achieve the desired goals. Thus Hersey and Blanchard advocate a situational approach which sensitively monitors the relationship of leader and follower and appropriately modifies the leader's style of leadership in relation to the leader's power bases (see figure 14).[16] We could represent this visually by means of the diagram on page 174.

## Developing New Missionary Leaders

If we know the kind of leaders we need in missionary congregations, why do we so often fail to develop them? Here are some of the reasons:

1. We have trained our laity to be passive because we have made "ministry" a professional role of a few ordained persons.

2. The pastor or missionary assumes no one else could do the job and therefore is reluctant to let anyone try.

3. We make of "leadership" such a large, frightening, demanding affair that no "laypeople" in their right mind would care to "volunteer" for it.

4. We do not know how to be equipping leaders. We are able to do the tasks, but not to teach others to do them.

5. We stress the "Santa's Helper Syndrome," expecting "laypeople" to handle unpleasant internal up-keep jobs in the Church rather than preparing them for real "ministry" in the world.

6. We do not know how to graciously delegate authority and may, in fact, be afraid of losing control if we do so.

7. We delegate responsibility but do not know how to assist the members in performing their tasks, nor do we readily check

15. See Hersey and Blanchard, *Management of Organizational Behavior*, chapters 8, 9.
16. Ibid., 105–26.

back with the members at the right times during the course of their ministerial activity.

8. We are endlessly "preparing" the members for something in ministry, but never get around to planning, organizing, or programming the "ministry" activities themselves. (This is a common problem for those congregations which spend a long time training for evangelism, but never seem to be able to get out into the streets, homes, businesses or schools to actually do evangelism.)

9. As pastors and missionaries we may be afraid of training others who might do "ministry" better than we can, and thus we might lose our own position, prestige, power, or job.

10. We hold a professional perspective of the nature of the Church which leaves room only for full-time, specially-trained, and specially-paid "professionals" to do the work of the Church within itself as well as out in the world.

For missionary churches to emerge through the life and ministry of the people of God in the world, the training of congregational leaders of all types and at all levels is not an option. No longer can we afford to have pastors, missionaries, mission executives, or third-world national bishops, executives, or pastors doing their ministry alone. The New Testament pattern is clear. Every church leader should carry out tasks accompanied by another Christian who in turn is being equipped to become a leader. Only as the whole people of God together develop their gifts, leadership, and ministries can missionary churches emerge.

Thus one criterion of the effectiveness of missionary leadership should be whether the whole membership of the Church is growing in grace and in the knowledge of God toward "mature adulthood." Where this is happening, the leadership is effective. Where "factor Beta" continues to exist the leaders are not leading, but rather are sidetracking the people of God and obstructing their ministry. In missionary churches the effectiveness of the leaders is not measured by what they do or do not accomplish, but by how the people of God are equipped, enabled, organized, and inspired to participate in God's mission in the world.

## Further Study

### Defining Leadership

Anderson, Ray S. *Minding God's Business*. Grand Rapids: Eerdmans, 1986.

Barth, Karl. *Church Dogmatics*, 4.1.

Bennis, Warren, and Burt Nanus. *Leaders: The Strategies for Taking Charge*. Philadelphia: Harper and Row, 1985.

Callahan, Kennon L. *Twelve Keys to an Effective Church*. New York: Harper and

Row, 1983. See pages 35–63.

Clinton, J. Robert. *The Making of a Leader*. Colorado Springs: NavPress, 1988.

Dulles, Avery. *Models of the Church*. Garden City, N.Y.: Doubleday, 1974. See chapter 10.

Greenleaf, Robert K. *Servant Leadership*. New York: Paulist, 1977. See chapters 1, 2, 7.

Harper, Michael. *Let My People Grow! Ministry and Leadership in the Church*. Plainfield, N.J.: Logos International, 1977.

Hersey, Paul, and Kenneth H. Blanchard. *The Situational Leader*. Escondido, Calif.: Center for Leadership Studies, 1985.

Hersey, Paul; Kenneth H. Blanchard, and Walter Natemeyer. "Situational Leadership, Perception, and the Impact of Power." Escondido, Calif.: Center for Leadership Studies, 1979.

Hesselgrave, David J. *Planting Churches Cross-Culturally*. Grand Rapids: Baker, 1980. See pages 355ff.

Myra, Harold, ed. *Leaders: Learning Leadership from Some of Christianity's Best*. Carol Stream, Ill.: Christianity Today, 1986.

Perry, Lloyd M., and Norman Shawchuck. *Revitalizing the 20th Century Church*. Chicago: Moody, 1982. See chapter 4.

Phillips, William. "In Search of a Leader." *Action Information*, 13.3 (May-June 1988): 1–6.

Richards, Lawrence O., and Clyde Hoeldtke. *A Theology of Church Leadership*. Grand Rapids: Zondervan, 1980. See pages 89–150, 209–356.

Schaller, Lyle E. *Getting Things Done: Concepts and Skills for Leaders*. Nashville: Abingdon, 1986. See chapters 4, 5.

Schillebeeckx, Edward. *Ministry*, J. Bowden, trans. New York: Crossroad, 1981. See chapter 1.

Smith, Donald P. *Congregations Alive*. Philadelphia: Westminster, 1981. See pages 116–30.

Southard, Samuel. *Training Church Members for Pastoral Care*. Valley Forge, Pa.: Judson, 1982.

Wofford, Jerry, and Kenneth Kilinski. *Organization and Leadership in the Local Church*. Grand Rapids: Zondervan, 1973.

## Identifying Missionary Leaders

Adams, Arthur M. *Effective Leadership for Today's Church*. Philadelphia: Westminster, 1978. See chapter 3.

Engstrom, Theodore W. *The Making of a Christian Leader*. Grand Rapids: Zondervan, 1976. See pages 39–40.

Getz, Gene A. *Sharpening the Focus of the Church*. Chicago: Moody, 1974. See pages 84–129.

Gibbs, Eddie. *I Believe in Church Growth*, Grand Rapids: Eerdmans, 1982. See chapter 9.

_____. *Followed or Pushed?* London: MARC Europe, 1987.

Greenleaf, Robert K. *Servant Leadership.* New York: Paulist, 1977. See chapters 1, 2, 7.

Kelley, Arleon L. *Your Church: A Dynamic Community.* Philadelphia: Westminster, 1982. See chapters 6, 7.

McGavran, Donald A., and Winfield C. Arn. *How to Grow a Church.* Glendale, Calif.: Regal, 1973. See chapter 5.

MacNair, Donald J. *The Growing Local Church.* Grand Rapids: Baker, 1975. See chapters 1–5.

Osborne, Larry W. *The Unity Factor: Getting Your Church Leaders to Work Together.* Waco, Tex.: Word, 1989.

Powell, Paul. *How to Make Your Church Hum.* Nashville: Broadman, 1977. See chapter 6.

Richards, Lawrence O., and Clyde Hoeldtke. *A Theology of Church Leadership.* Grand Rapids: Zondervan, 1980. See pages 24–28, 106ff.

Schaller, Lyle E. *Getting Things Done: Concepts and Skills for Leaders.* Nashville: Abingdon, 1986. See chapters 4, 5.

Schaller, Lyle E., and C. A. Tidwell. *Creative Church Administration.* Nashville: Abingdon, 1975. See chapter 3.

Silber, Mark B. "Successful Supervisory Secrets: Lessons of Leadership" in *PACE* (Nov. 1985): 89–93.

Smith, Donald P. *Congregations Alive.* Philadelphia: Westminster, 1981. See pages 136ff.

Tollefson, Kenneth. "The Nehemiah Model for Christian Missions" in *Missiology*, 15.1 (Jan. 1987): 31–55.

### Determining Appropriate Leadership Styles

Engstrom. *Making of a Christian Leader.* See chapter 12.

Lindgren, Alvin J. *Foundations for Purposeful Church Administration.* Nashville: Abingdon, 1980. See chapter 8.

Neill, Stephen C. *Fulfill Thy Ministry.* New York: Harper, 1952. See pages 115ff.

Richards, Lawrence O., and Clyde Hoeldtke. *A Theology of Church Leadership.* Grand Rapids: Zondervan, 1980. See pages 127–32.

Schaller, Lyle E., and C. A. Tidwell. *Creative Church Administration.* Nashville: Abingdon, 1975. See pages 82–104.

Smith, Donald P. *Congregations Alive.* Philadelphia: Westminster, 1981. See pages 116ff.

Watson, David. *I Believe in the Church*, 1st American ed. Grand Rapids: Eerdmans, 1979. See pages 264–76.

# 12

# *Missional Administration in the Local Church*

**N**one of what we have seen thus far is possible unless it is given hands and feet through careful and intentional administration. Administrative structures facilitate the actual doing of congregational mission in the world. Here is the most critical step in the process of building missionary congregations, the step which seems to be the most ignored. Time and again, as this author speaks with pastors and missionaries, they are delighted to hear all that he has said up to this point. But when he begins to speak of administration, they seem to have ears but cannot hear. So many missionaries and pastors want their churches to grow and want their congregations to reach out in mission, but they are unwilling to pay the price in careful, intentional, disciplined, and visionary administration. In this chapter we want to create an image of dynamic, living, Spirit-filled administration which aims at equipping ministry.

Dynamic administration would include at least the following activities.

1. Analyzing, studying, understanding the context of the congregation's ministry.
2. Articulating the vision.

179

3. Designing contextually and missiologically appropriate goals.

4. Developing concrete, doable, measurable, and specific plans of action.

5. Recruiting the persons to be involved in carrying out the congregation's missional plans.

6. Structuring ways to strengthen people in their ministries.

7. Delegating, training, demonstrating, and equipping those involved in the various ministries.

8. Supporting the members in their ministry in whatever they need to carry out their ministry, applauding and encouraging them.

9. Holding people accountable to do what they have accepted as their responsibility.

10. Evaluating the over-all missional outreach of the congregation, making necessary changes, and continually doing more of each step.

We need to recognize that dynamic administration must be culturally-appropriate and contextually-equivalent. Thus, for many missionaries and pastors, exercising dynamic administration will necessarily be a matter of trial-and-error, discovering with the people what structures are most effective in their particular context. Nevertheless, we need to make some broad theological and missiological observations concerning dynamic, missionally-creative administration.

## Administration Is a Spiritual Activity

The Bible is relatively silent regarding organizational and administrative patterns. But this is not without design, for nothing becomes obsolete so quickly as structural forms. They are but a means to divine ends. Furthermore, life is made up of so many variables and unpredictable events that creativity in this area must be constant.

But the Bible does speak in this area, and when it does, its examples yield some dynamic and powerful principles. . . . Both in Old Testament and New Testament illustrations of organization and administration the same basic principles surface. This again helps to show that the patterns are not absolute, but the principles are.[1]

With these words Gene A. Getz began his treatment of administration and organization in the Church. Getz reviewed four administrative situations from Scripture: Moses in Exodus 18, Nehemiah in Nehemiah 1–12, the apostles in Acts 6, and the Jerusalem council in Acts 15. In each case,

1. Gene A. Getz, *Sharpening the Focus of the Church* (Chicago: Moody, 1974), 131.

# Figure 15

## Organizing God's People in Exodus and Acts

| Leading Israel in the Wilderness | Caring for Neglected Widows |
|---|---|
| **Problem:** | **Problem:** |
| **Exodus 18:13–18** The people stood about Moses from morning until evening. Moses tried to lead by himself. Moses was attempting to resolve the problems of the people. He served as judge and taught the people the laws of God. This labor caused stress for Moses and for all the people. | **Acts 6:1–2** The number of disciples was increasingly rapidly, placing the communal system under stress. Certain Hellenistic Jews were being overlooked in the daily serving of food. Consequently the Hellenists complained. The twelve became involved in these administrative details, causing them to neglect their primary responsibility to teach God's Word. |
| **Solution:** | **Solution:** |
| **Exodus 18:19–22** Moses' father-in-law, Jethro, served as his consultant. Jethro advised Moses to establish priorities. His own work was to mediate between the people and God and to teach the people as a group God's statutes. A group of leaders were to handle interpersonal problems of everyday life. These leaders were to be qualified by administrative ability, fear of God, love of truth, and honesty. Only major problems were to be judged by Moses. | **Acts 6:2–4** The Twelve called a meeting of the body. They informed the people that their own ministry was prayer and teaching. |
| **Deuteronomy 1:9–18** Moses communicated his problem to the people. He instructed each tribe to choose wise, discerning, experienced men. Moses appointed those chosen to be leaders. He then carefully instructed them concerning everything they were to do. | **Acts 6:3–6** The apostles instructed the body to select seven qualified leaders to care for the need, wise men of good reputation, full of the Holy Spirit. The congregation wisely chose leaders who were Hellenists (as indicated by their Greek names). The apostles confirmed the choices through prayer and the laying on of hands. |
| **Results:** | **Results:** |
| **Exodus 18:22–23** Moses was assisted and so was able to endure the demands of his leadership role. The people's needs were met, so they were satisfied. | **Acts 6:7** Evidently the needs were met, for unity was restored. The apostles were able to fulfil their primary work so the Word of God continued to spread. The number of believers kept on increasing. |

Adapted from Gene A. Getz, *Sharpening the Focus of the Church* (Chicago: Moody, 1974), 131–32.

he observed, there was a problem to be faced, a solution to be found, and results to be sought. We could compare the situation Moses faced organizing the descendents of Abraham at Sinai (Exod. 18:13–26; Deut. 1:9–18) with the situation faced by the disciples when they began to organize the new believers in Jerusalem (Acts 6). In figure 15 we see that organization is very much a part of Scripture's view of the life and nature of the people of God. God was concerned even with the way the Israelites encamped around the Tabernacle (Num. 2:1–31; 10:11–28). What if we were as intentional about organizing our congregations? What if we made sure no member of our churches was left without direct, personal pastoral care offered to them by another member? What surprises might be in store for us to see the Church emerge in unexpected and exciting ways if we carefully structured our congregations in this way?[2]

Other biblical figures who maximized their ministry through administration would include Joseph and Daniel. In these two cases the administrative gifts were not so much focused within the people of God as outside, among the nations. Administration as a divine gift brings harmony and wisdom to those who as yet do not worship God. We should not forget that Paul placed the gift of administration alongside gifts of apostle, prophet, teacher, worker of miracles, healing, helps, and speaking in tongues (see 1 Cor. 12:27–29).

Based on the biblical data in Exodus 18, Deut. 1:9–18, Nehemiah, and Acts 6 and 15, Getz suggested some principles of administration and organization which might be helpful to the church leader.

### Principles of Administration

1. Face the reality of problems.
2. Develop a proper perspective on each problem.
3. Establish priorities.
4. Delegate responsibility to qualified people.
5. Maintain a balance between divine and human factors.
6. Approach problem solving and decision making with consideration for the attitudes and feelings of everyone.

2. In 1989 the author had the opportunity of visiting the Yoido Full-Gospel Church (Paul Yonggi Cho, pastor) in Seoul, South Korea. Although the church leadership attributes the phenomenal growth of the church (to more than 500,000 members) to the work of the Holy Spirit, their organization is impressive. From cell groups of ten to the hundreds of pastors on staff, the administrative structures are geared for growth. Carl George of the Charles E..Fuller Institute has been working on models for mega- and metachurch administration and is developing revolutionary ideas. An impressive home-cell system also is being developed by Dale Galloway at New Hope Community Church in Portland, Ore.

7. Solve every problem creatively under the leadership of the Holy Spirit.

### Principles of Organization

1. Organize to apply New Testament principles and to reach New Testament purposes.
2. Organize to meet needs.
3. Keep organization simple.
4. Keep organization flexible.[3]

Although the precise methods and forms of administration may vary, the need for thoughtful administration and organization is always great. Unfortunately, many missionaries and church leaders view administration and organization as a necessary evil at best, and something to escape at worst. But leaders, pastors, and missionaries involved in a congregation must realize that, just as Moses, Nehemiah, and the apostles found it essential to administrate and organize, so today's leaders must become actively, joyfully, and intentionally involved in the administration and organization of missionary congregations. If we are to reject the alternatives of total, autocratic control; leader burnout; endless divisions, or untold members limping along because of unmet needs, then loving, intentional administration is a must. Especially in times of growth and heightened enthusiasm and lay participation, the leaders must keep abreast of their burgeoning needs by administration and organization. To fail to do so is to lose great opportunities for growth, maturation, and development of the whole people of God.[4]

### Administration Focuses the Church's Ministry

Alvin J. Lindgren gave us a fine description of what is entailed in effective church administration, which he defines as "the task of discovering and clarifying the goals and purposes of the field it serves and of moving in a coherent, comprehensive manner toward their realization."[5] Lindgren sees important implications in the concept of administration. The admin-

3. Getz, *Sharpening*, 148–63. See also E. Stanley Ott, *The Vibrant Church: A People-Building Plan for Congregational Health* (Ventura, Calif.: Regal, 1989), 87ff, and Lloyd M. Perry and Norman Shawchuck, *Revitalizing the Twentieth-Century Church* (Chicago: Moody, 1982), 47ff.

4. Cf. David Leuke and Samuel Southard, *Pastoral Administration: Integrating Ministry and Management in the Church* (Waco, Tex.: Word, 1986), 11–25.

5. Alvin J. Lindgren, *Foundations for Purposeful Church Administration* (Nashville: Abingdon, 1965), 22–25.

istrator must share the group's common understanding of its purposes; the administrator must understand the field well enough to determine what means are needed to achieve the objectives and be able to work with others, understanding that their contributions are also essential. "Administration properly understood simply provides the means through which a group can fulfill its purpose," according to Lindgren.[6]

Administration is essential because knowing what we ought to do does not necessarily lead to doing it. The proper understanding of the Church's missionary nature does not automatically issue in appropriate action. This can be done only through intentional and careful administration.

In *Management for Your Church*[7] Lindgren and Norman Shawchuck devote a chapter to "The Pastor as Church Manager." They stress that management and organization in the Church must not only vary according to the environment but also must be adapting constantly to changes in the lives of the people involved. Noting that the Church has always adopted management and organizational structure from its secular environment, Lindgren and Shawchuck warn that secular practices often do not fit religious organizations. "The Church has a totally unique mission to perform, and persons join its ranks for unique and special reasons. This uniqueness of mission and membership requires the Church critically to examine secular organization design and procedure before adapting it for its purposes. When and if adapted, such procedures need to be made subservient to the mission they are intended to facilitate."[8]

They recommend keeping in mind three tasks of management set forth by Peter F. Drucker.[9] The first task is to clarify the specific purpose and mission of the institution. The second is to make work productive, and the worker achieving. The third task is to manage social impacts and social responsibilities. Say Lindgren and Shawchuck, "the most valuable resource of any church is its human resources. Therefore, as a second responsibility the pastor-as-manager must see persons as such, and seek to have their involvement be fruitful not only in accomplishing the church's mission but in contributing to their personal growth and achievement."[10]

Here we have one of the clearest pictures of the administrative task of leadership in the Church, and we see that all the subjects covered to this point have involved us in administrative thinking. *It is in administra-*

6. Ibid.

7. Nashville: Abingdon, 1977.

8. Ibid., 135; see Peter F. Drucker, *Management: Tasks, Responsibilities, Practices* (New York: Harper and Row, 1974).

9. Drucker, *Management*, 135–40.

10. Alvin J. Lindgren and Norman Shawchuck, *Management for Your Church: How to Realize Your Church Potential Through a Systems Approach*, 135. Guidelines for the day-to-day operations of doing this can be found in literature on church management. We are in need of contextually-appropriate manuals for just this kind of help to be offered pastors in many two-thirds-world situations.

# Figure 16
## Linking the Church's Programs to Its Actions in the World

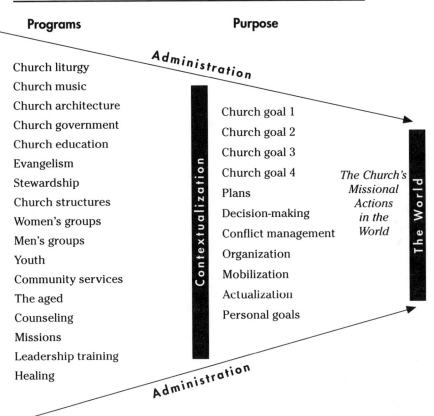

| Programs | Purpose |
|---|---|
| | Administration |
| Church liturgy | |
| Church music | |
| Church architecture | Church goal 1 |
| Church government | Church goal 2 |
| Church education | Church goal 3 |
| Evangelism | Church goal 4 |
| Stewardship | Plans |
| Church structures | Decision-making |
| Women's groups | Conflict management |
| Men's groups | Organization |
| Youth | Mobilization |
| Community services | Actualization |
| The aged | Personal goals |
| Counseling | |
| Missions | |
| Leadership training | |
| Healing | |

*The Members of the Church* — *Contextualization* — *The Church's Missional Actions in the World* — *The World* — Administration

*tion that missionary congregations are given their concrete, practical, livable form.* It is in administration that the "from above" perspective of the Church is joined with the "from below" viewpoint. In administration the organism is welded to the institution.

Pastors and missionaries serve the Church best administratively when they know exactly the purposes, goals, objectives, and strategies of their congregation, denomination, or mission organization and then organize and involve people in the pursuit of those purposes. The purposive and intentional administrator will best serve the Church by keeping the large picture in mind, continually emphasizing it to the members and tirelessly calling the institution to reflect in program and activity the mission and purpose of the organism.

Furthermore, the missionally intentional administrator will move the congregation to create plans, make decisions, and resolve internal conflicts always with the objective of mobilizing God's missionary people.[11] It is the task of the administrator to continually check performance and program against purpose and goal in order to keep the ship of the gospel on its true course in ministry. We might illustrate the function of administration in the Church by way of figure 16.

The administrative leaders of a congregation are called to provide the necessary context in which the members, individually and corporately, may act out their nature as the people of God called to mission in the world.[12] James D. Anderson and Ezra E. Jones have said it this way:

> A major test of the structure of any church (and therefore also of its administration) is the degree to which each individual is enabled to freely join and participate in an association of other Christians. What happens to the new member who has not joined or who has not yet found a family home in the congregation is a crucial test of church structure. The extent to which the membership can be placed in a church family group and the extent to which all groups coexist in some harmony is an indication of the extent to which fellowship (*koinonia*) is present in the congregation.[13]

This principle applies to small or large congregations, though structure will vary according to size.[14] This principle applies equally well to European, North-American, and two-thirds-world churches. Everywhere men and women want to belong. They want to feel a part of the family of God, and they want to have a reason for belonging which will inspire, direct, and unify them around a common goal. This should help us to understand the Church's integral growth as an emerging process by which the members corporately grow toward the full stature of Christ, and are transformed for ministry.[15] This is the radically outward-directed, exploding function of a missionary administration that focuses

11. It is beyond the scope of this work to provide guidelines for the day-to-day operations of doing this mobilizing. The reader can consult literature on church management.

12. James D. Anderson and Ezra E. Jones, *The Management of Ministry* (New York: Harper and Row, 1978), 63.

13. Ibid., 67.

14. See, for example, Carl S. Dudley, *Making the Small Church Effective* (Nashville: Abingdon, 1978), chapter 4; Thomas C. Campbell and Gary B. Reierson, *The Gift of Administration* (Philadelphia: Westminster, 1981), 127ff; Lyle E. Schaller, *Growing Plans: Strategies to Increase Your Church's Membership* (Nashville: Abingdon, 1983), and idem, *Looking in the Mirror: Self-Appraisal in the Local Church* (Nashville: Abingdon, 1984).

15. Orlando Costas dealt extensively with the concept of "integral church growth." He spoke of "numerical expansion, organic expansion, conceptual expansion, and incarnational growth" in *The Church and Its Mission: A Shattering Critique from the Third World* (Wheaton, Ill.: Tyndale, 1974), 90. See also idem, *The Integrity of Mission: The Inner Life and Outreach of the Church* (New York: Harper and Row, 1979).

the fantastic personal and corporate power of the Church toward ministry in the world.

## Administration Seeks Contextualization

The church administrator should be concerned with fitting the congregation's life to its context. An administrative duty of the leaders is to constantly check the shape, form, and lifestyle of their missionary congregations against the matrix of the culture they wish to reach. In the perspective of "systems theory" the role of the administrator becomes clear. Decisions should in some way contribute to developing a more indigenous, dynamically-equivalent church.[16] Good administrative leaders are conscious of how the environment influences the congregation, in what positive and negative ways those influences are changing the body, and whether the church is a transforming influence in its world. The "feedback loop" thus becomes an important administrative tool, since it measures how fruitful the church is performing its role of system-transformation. Anderson and Jones wrote that the most important factor in shaping congregational structure should be the nature of the surrounding community.

> Church leaders are conditioned to assume that any and all changes in the environment can be accommodated by adjustments within the existing organization. This is manifestly untrue, and yet countless clergy [and we might add, missionaries] feel guilty and depressed about the state of the congregation they serve because they assume that if the preaching were better, the program more exciting, and the congregation more friendly, then the dilemmas posed by a changing community and neighborhood could be resolved by the existing congregation. . . . A truly missionary model of the congregation would focus on the degree to which the parish is alien to or indigenous to the culture and community in which it finds itself. . . . Effective ministry calls for indigenous structure.[17]

We have found that the most effective missionary congregations are incarnational—that is, they reflect the presence of Jesus Christ and embody the Holy Spirit within their communities. Therefore, Spirit-led administration is an absolute requirement at all levels— sending church, mission agency, and receiving congregation. Only with the Holy Spirit's

---

16. One of the strongest voices calling for "dynamic equivalence churchness" has been Charles Kraft. The world church has yet to open itself to viable ways of building this matter into its consciousness and its structures. See Charles H. Kraft, *Christianity in Culture: A Study in Dynamic Biblical Theologizing in Cross-Cultural Perspective* (Maryknoll, N.Y.: Orbis, 1979), 315–27.

17. Quoted in Kraft, *Christianity in Culture*, 54–56.

understanding can a church balance the tasks of contextualizing the church's witness to the culture and also calling the culture to repent and conform to the unchanging demands of Scripture. No missions strategist can make a sweeping generalization to define how the gospel must be addressed to a people. The vast variety of cultural settings demands that each congregation very specifically apply the Church's essence and purpose as it develops members, leaders, and administrative structures.

## Administration Helps Us Avoid Manipulation

Another reason administration is essential for missionary churches is that it aids us in avoiding the manipulative activities that plague missionary endeavors.[18] Some years ago Methodist ministers Maxie Dunnam and Gary Herbertson and psychologist Everett Shostrom, the author of *Man, the Manipulator*, teamed to provide some positive suggestions for creating an "actualizing" administration that would prevent manipulation. Saying that almost everyone, consciously or subconsciously, contributes to the society's "sickness of manipulation," they define a *manipulator* as "a person who exploits, uses, or controls himself and others as 'things' in self-defeating ways."[19]

The alternative to being a manipulator is to be an actualizer who (1) integrates leadership and empathy; (2) integrates respect and appreciation; (3) integrates assertiveness and caring, and (4) integrates expression and guidance.[20]

Out of this concern to be nonmanipulative, North American churches developed passive or soft forms of "enabling" leadership in the late 1960s and 1970s. This is not the kind of enabling we have in mind. That style of leadership was so nondirective and unassuming it did not lead. Predominantly it was reactive, waiting for the members of churches to decide what they might want to do, then joining them rather passively to encourage them in their vision. It was a disaster. It did not really avoid manipulation; in fact, the "enabler" mentality was often itself manipulative, laying the responsibility for leadership totally on the members, with pastors abdicating their role.[21]

Missionary congregations must embody the "actualizing" type of personal and interpersonal environment which calls out of both leaders

18. Juan Isais effectively demonstrated this problem in *The Other Side of the Coin*, E. F. Isais, trans. (Grand Rapids: Eerdmans, 1966).

19. Maxie D. Dunnam, Gary J. Herbertson, and Everett L. Shostrom, *The Manipulator and the Church* (Nashville: Abingdon, 1968), 83.

20. Ibid., 83–87.

21. C. Peter Wagner has highlighted this issue in several of his works, but states it particularly strongly in *Leading Your Church to Growth: The Secret of Pastor-People Partnership in Dynamic Church Growth* (Ventura, Calif.: Regal, 1984).

and members an externalized faith, hope, and love which Christ brings to the Church. The actualizer type of leader can be instrumental in building missionary churches through freely equipping and facilitating the people of God for ministry.

Lyle E. Schaller and Charles A. Tidwell described some of the factors which motivate the Church toward participation and actualization in mission. They distinguished between *motivator* factors and *demotivator* (manipulative) factors of human relationships in the Church. Motivating factors impel work because the individual feels the worthiness of the cause; the individual feels needed; there is a cooperative, mutually-supportive environment, and motivating information is dispensed. Demotivation occurs when the leader calls on the people for the leader's own advantage; the leader lacks integrity; the "You suggest ideas and I'll tell you how stupid you are" game is played, and there are too many responsibilities for too few people.[22]

We need to stress the vital importance of an actualizing administration for the life and ministry of missionary congregations. Administration that actualizes is biblical. It focuses the purpose for which the Church exists, and it helps us to avoid manipulation. Creative administration builds organizational infrastructures that provide opportunities for service not otherwise available. This has been stressed by many authors, and the reader can consult the literature cited at the end of this chapter.

In spite of all that has been said and shown by others, why is it that, in church and para-church situations alike, we are so slow to create structures that encourage people in ministry? There are many Bible institutes and seminaries in the third world, for example, but few of them teach leaders how to organize, set up boards, develop strategies, and build organizational structures. We are often preoccupied with the personal, spiritual, and liturgical aspects of new churches and denominations we plant, but we do not seem to get around to teaching them contextualized administration, accounting, stewardship, organization and the building of church structures. In Europe and North America we have thousands of very qualified church members serving on church boards and yet we seldom teach them the uniqueness of the Church, the purpose of the Church, the way the Church builds its structures, and how the Church allows the best resources in people, time, talents, and money to surface. In both older and younger churches we seem to allow our traditional ecclesiastical polity to determine our administration, rather than being creative administrators who build dynamically emerging churches in new and uncharted ways.

Here is one of the most demanding, critical, and needed tools of creative churchmanship—one which awaits new and forceful thinking

22. Lyle E. Schaller and Charles A. Tidwell, *Creative Church Administration* (Nashville: Abingdon, 1975), 66–81.

among pastors, church executives, mission executives, missionaries, and third-world pastors and missionaries. Together we need to explore, through the building of new and effective structures, what it means for the Church to become what it claims to be in faith and hope.

With the fields white with harvest let us pray the Lord of the harvest to give us administrative leaders who can direct the laborers in an efficient, strong, and fruitful way. If there is one great pressing need in the church today, it is for people with the gift of administration. As we train church planters and pastors we must dedicate a major share of attention to training visionary, compassionate administrators to direct missionary congregations, denominations, and mission agencies in effective ministry.

## Administration Facilitates Evaluation

So many voices advocate ways to evaluate the life and practice of the Church: Some emphasize the social implications of the gospel; others stress the evangelistic task; still others, such as Donald McGavran and C. Peter Wagner, have called for measuring the Church's effectiveness by the number of people who are gathered and incorporated.

The emerging Church will recognize that its basis for evaluation can be none other than the Church's own nature as contextualized in the midst of a particular culture. Evaluation in missionary congregations should be a process by which we compare what we actually see with what we confess. The evaluation of our goals, our strategies, our leadership, our membership, and our administration should cause us to ask: How close are we to the one, holy, catholic and apostolic community of Word and sacrament, gathered around Jesus Christ? And the amazing discovery is that the nearer we get, the more we find ourselves exploded outward to give our lives for the world, because Jesus did not come to condemn the world, but that the world might be saved through himself (John 3:17).

Missionary congregations can only evaluate themselves on the basis of who they are. It is not possible to expect the Church to be other than what it is. Pastors and missionaries can create nothing other than what is already in the flock of God. Otherwise they create human institutions—their own little kingdoms, but not the Church of Jesus Christ. Missionaries who build missionary churches can do nothing but stimulate the transformation whereby the seed that is already there may become the tree that is promised. Evaluation forces pastor and missionary alike to look again at the essence of the Church, for it is there that the criteria of evaluation will be found. This involves continually progressing through the issues raised in this book, ever seeking to become who we already are.

But there is a further dimension in this evaluation. Missionary churches must evaluate their life and effectiveness as an eschatological, emerging reality. There need be no fear of failure here, for evaluation measures progress toward becoming—not arrival. It is a pressing on to the mark of the high calling of God in Jesus Christ (Phil. 3:12–14). In the evaluation of emerging missionary congregations there is always hope, eschatology, a becoming more completely who we are. Thus even in our evaluative processes we allow our future to break in upon our present so that our evaluative questions themselves deal not only with our proximity to the center but also with our movement toward the future.

One major implication of this eschatological perspective on the Church's missionary nature has to do with our definitions of success. Sociologists like Donald Maxam and others have helped us see the importance of analyzing our definitions of success, particularly as those impinge upon urban ministries. Here again we must take a "systems" approach which considers the nature of the Church, the Church's missional movement outward to the world, and the peculiar characteristics of its context. All these must be allowed to influence the way we define success or the bases on which we evaluate our intentions, structures, and activities.

Alvin Lindgren offered the following evaluative questions which, though applied by Lindgren to the evaluation of a specific activity in the congregation, could just as well be aimed at the whole ministry of the whole Church taking the whole gospel to the whole world:

1. What are the goals toward which the activity is supposedly moving?
2. Are these goals in harmony with the nature and mission of the Church?
3. Will the activity actually contribute to achieving the goals?
4. Is the activity in conflict with any other equally valid project of the congregation?
5. Are sufficient personnel and resources available to carry out the activity? Or will the congregation be overburdened by it?
6. Will all the techniques employed bear examination in the light of the gospel?
7. Is there a danger that this activity, as a means to an end, will become an end in itself, thus obscuring the real goal by its very "success"?
8. Are there other basic goals that require prior attention?[23]

23. See Lindgren, *Foundations*, 30–31; Lyle E. Schaller, *Hey! That's Our Church!* (Nashville: Abingdon, 1975), chapter 8; David Watson, *I Believe in Evangelism*, 1st American ed. (Grand Rapids: Eerdmans, 1977), and Gene A. Getz, *The Measure of a Church* (Glendale, Calif.: Regal, 1975).

Evaluation is indispensable for missionary congregations. If we hope to build missionary churches in the world we must be dissatisfied, measuring what we see against what we confess. All the people of God should participate in the process, evaluating as part of their continuing obedience to Jesus Christ. It is through this on-going spiral of reflection on the Church's essence, goals, people, administration, and evaluation that we will experience the way Jesus Christ builds his Church, against which the gates of Hell themselves will not prevail.

Remember that little shrub in my front yard in Tapachula? I never imagined that it would grow to be such an enormous tree! Yet that mystery of growth is also one of the inherent qualities of the Church. Jesus emphasized this mystery of the growth of missionary congregations in the parable of the mustard seed. All three synoptic Gospels mention this parable (Matt. 13:31–32; Mark 4:31–32; Luke 13:19); Matthew and Luke couple it to the parable of the yeast (Matt. 13:33; Luke 13:21). The point seems clear: There is something inherently marvelous, mysterious, and creative in the nature of the kingdom as signified in the Church.

My wife cultivates roses at the entrance to our house. And we enjoy watching the small buds mature, begin to stretch, and then almost overnight explode into full bloom. Is not our hope and joy for the Church of equal measure? Although you and I build the Church—some of us plant, and some of us water—God gives the increase through the mysterious flowering of the Church's vital missionary essence, emerging by the operation of his Spirit in the midst of the people of God. Listen again to the way Jesus explained the dynamic interrelationship of our act of building and the Spirit's dynamic energy causing missionary churches to emerge.

> Then Jesus asked, "What is the kingdom of God like? What shall I compare it to? It is like a mustard seed, which a man took and planted in his garden. It grew and became a tree, and the birds of the air perched in its branches." Again he asked, "What shall I compare the kingdom of God to? It is like yeast that a woman took and mixed into a large amount of flour until it worked all through the dough" (Luke 13:18–21, NIV).

Our commitment to dynamic and visionary administration is like fertilizing, watering, weeding, and pruning those trees and roses. Missionary congregations will only emerge when we actively, prayerfully, and intentionally develop administrative structures which propel the people of God out in ministry in the world.

## Further Study

### *Administration Is a Spiritual Activity*

Anderson, Ray S. *Minding God's Business*. Grand Rapids: Eerdmans, 1986. See chapter 7.

Callahan, Kennon. *Effective Church Leadership: Building on the Twelve Keys*. San Francisco: Harper and Row, 1990.

_____. *Twelve Keys to an Effective Church*. New York: Harper and Row, 1983.

Campbell, Thomas, and G. Reierson. *The Gift of Administration*. Philadelphia: Westminster, 1981. See chapters 16, 19.

Costas, Orlando. *Liberating News: A Theology of Contextual Evangelization*. Grand Rapids: Eerdmans, 1989.

Getz, Gene A. *Sharpening the Focus of the Church*. Chicago: Moody, 1974.

Gray, Robert M. *Managing the Church*. Enid, Okla.: Phillips University Press, 1970. See chapters 3 , 4.

Jones, Ezra Earl, and Robert L. Wilson, eds. *What's Ahead for Old First Church?* New York: Harper and Row, 1974.

Marcum, Elvis. Outreach: *God's Miracle Business*. Nashville: Broadman, 1975.

McGavran, Donald A., and Winfield C. Arn. *Growth: A New Vision for the Sunday School*. Pasadena, Calif.: Church Growth, 1980.

_____. *Ten Steps for Church Growth*. New York: Harper and Row, 1977. See chapter 9.

Perry, Lloyd M., and Norman Shawchuck. *Revitalizing the 20th Century Church*. Chicago: Moody, 1982.

Peters, George L. A Biblical *Theology of Missions*. Chicago: Moody, 1972. See pages 231–41.

_____. *Saturation Evangelism*. Grand Rapids: Zondervan, 1970. See especially pages 92–93.

Powell, Paul. *How to Make Your Church Hum*. Nashville: Broadman, 1977. See chapter 6.

Reeves, R. Daniel, and Ronald Jenson. *Always Advancing: Modern Strategies for Church Growth*. San Bernardino, Calif.: Here's Life, 1984.

Richards, Lawrence O., and Clyde Hoeldtke. *A Theology of Church Leadership*. *Grand Rapids*: Zondervan, 1980. See chapters 2, 6, 8–10, 14.

Schaller, Lyle E. *Activating the Passive Church*. Nashville: Abingdon, 1981.

_____. *Growing Plans: Strategies to Increase Your Church's Membership*. Nashville: Abingdon, 1983.

_____. *Looking in the Mirror: Self-Appraisal for the Local Church*. Nashville: Abingdon, 1984.

_____. *The Change Agent: The Strategy of Innovative Leadership*. Nashville: Abingdon, 1972.

Sundkler, Bengt. *The World of Mission*. London: Lutterworth, 1963. See chapter 2.

Tillapaugh, Frank. *The Church Unleashed: Getting God's People Out Where the Needs Are.*Ventura, Calif.: Regal, 1982.

Voelkel, Jack. *Student Evangelism in a World of Revolution.* Grand Rapids: Zondervan, 1974.

C. Peter Wagner. *Church Growth and the Whole Gospel: A Biblical Mandate.* San Francisco: Harper and Row, 1981. See chapters 8–10.

Walrath, Douglas A. *Leading Churches Through Change.* Nashville: Abingdon, 1979.

_____. *Planning for Your Church.* Philadelphia: Westminster, 1984.

## Administration Facilitates Evaluation

Anderson, Ray. *The Praxis of Pentecost: Revisioning the Church's Life and Mission.* Pasadena, Calif.: Fuller Theological Seminary, 1991.

Costas, Orlando. *"Churches in Evangelistic Partnership,"* in C. Rene; Padilla, ed., *The New Face of Evangelicalism: An International Symposium on the Lausanne Covenant.* Downers Grove, Ill.: Inter-Varsity, 1976.

Dietterich, Paul M., ed. *"Managing Clergy Transition." The Center Letter,* 13.5 (May 1983).

Gatu, John. *"The Urgency of the Evangelistic Task,"* in Padilla, ed., *The New Face of Evangelicalism.*

Isais, Juan M. *The Other Side of the Coin,* E. F. Isais, trans. Grand Rapids: Eerdmans, 1966.

Latourette, Kenneth Scott. *The Emergence of a World Christian Community.* New Haven: Yale University Press, 1949. See chapter 3.

Lindgren, Alvin J. *Foundations for Purposeful Church Administration.* Nashville: Abingdon, 1965. See chapter 2.

McGavran, Donald A. *Understanding Church Growth,* rev. ed. Grand Rapids: Eerdmans, 1980. See chapter 19.

_____. *Ethnic Realities and the Church: Lessons from India.* South Pasadena, Calif.: William Carey Library, 1978. See chapter 9.

McGavran, Donald A., and Winfield C. Arn. *How to Grow a Church.* Glendale, Calif.: Regal, 1973. See chapter 1.

Neill, Stephen C. *Colonialism and Christian Mission.* New York: McGraw-Hill, 1966. See "Conclusion."

Schaller, Lyle E. *Hey! That's Our Church!* Nashville: Abingdon, 1975. See chapter 8.

Wagner, C. Peter. *Your Church and Church Growth,* packaged set of materials. Pasadena, Calif.: Fuller Evangelistic Association, 1976. See handbook.

Watson, David. *I Believe in Evangelism,* 1st American ed. Grand Rapids: Eerdmans, 1977.

# Bibliography

A. J. Muste. "Of Holy Disobedience." *Sojourners*, 13.11 (Dec. 1984): 21–22.

Adams, Arthur M. *Effective Leadership for Today's Church*. Philadelphia: Westminster, 1978.

Allen, Roland. *The Spontaneous Expansion of the Church and the Causes Which Hinder It*. Grand Rapids: Eerdmans, 1962.

Alston, Wallace M., Jr. *The Church*. Atlanta: John Knox, 1984.

Anderson, James D., and Ezra E. Jones. *The Management of Ministry*. New York: Harper and Row, 1978.

————. *Ministry of the Laity*. New York: Harper and Row, 1985.

Anderson, Andy. *Where Action Is*. Nashville: Broadman, 1976.

Anderson, Gerald H., ed. *The Theology of the Christian Mission*. Nashville: Abingdon, 1961.

————., ed. *Witnessing to the Kingdom: Melbourne and Beyond*. Maryknoll, N.Y.: Orbis, 1982.

Anderson, Gerald H., and Thomas F. Stransky, eds. *Mission Trends No. 2: Evangelization*. Grand Rapids: Eerdmans, 1975.

Anderson, Ray S. *Minding God's Business*. Grand Rapids: Eerdmans, 1986.

————. *Mission Theology and Church Theology: An Integrative Approach*. Unpublished manuscript, 1989.

————. *The Praxis of Pentecost: Revisioning the Church's Life and Mission*. Pasadena, Calif.: Fuller Theological Seminary, 1991.

Arias, Esther, and Mortimer Arias. *The Cry of My People: Out of Captivity in Latin America*. New York: Friendship, 1980.

Arias, Mortimer. *Announcing the Reign of God: Evangelization and the Subversive Memory of Jesus*. Philadelphia: Fortress, 1984.

_____. *Salvación es Liberación*. Buenos Aires: Aurora, 1973.

Arn, Winfield C., ed. *The Pastor's Church Growth Handbook*. Pasadena, Calif.: Church Growth, 1982.

Arn, Winfield C., and Charles Arn. *Who Cares About Love?* Pasadena, Calif.: Church Growth, 1986.

Avis, Paul D. L. *The Church in the Theology of the Reformers*, P. Toon, R. Martin, eds. Atlanta: John Knox, 1980.

Baker, Wesley C. *The Split-Level Fellowship*. Philadelphia: Westminster, 1965.

Banks, Robert J. *Paul's Idea of Community: The Early House Churches in Their Historical Setting*. Grand Rapids: Eerdmans, 1980.

_____. "A Biblical Vision of the People of God." *Theology News and Notes* (June 1990): 4–7.

Banks, Robert J., and Julia Banks. *The Church Comes Home: A New Base for Community and Mission*. Sutherland, Australia: Albatross, 1989.

Barbour, Ian G. *Religion in an Age of Science*. San Francisco: Harper and Row, 1990.

"Barnabas: The Ministry of Encouragement." *Christian Leadership Letter* (July 1987): 1–3.

Barrett, David B. *World Christian Encyclopedia*. Oxford: Oxford University Press, 1982.

_____. "Five Statistical Eras of Global Mission." *Missiology*, 12.1 (Jan. 1984): 21–39.

_____. "Silver and Gold Have I None: Church of the Poor or Church of the Rich?" *International Bulletin of Missionary Research*, 7.4 (Oct. 1983): 146–51.

Barrett, Lois. *Building the House Church*. Scottdale, Pa.: Herald, 1986.

Barth, Karl. *Church Dogmatics*, vol. 4, G. T. Thomson, trans. Edinburgh: T and T Clark, 1958.

_____. *The Church and the Churches*. Grand Rapids: Eerdmans, 1936.

_____. *Theology and Church: Shorter Writings 1920–1928*, L. P. Smith, trans., 1st American ed. New York: Harper and Row, 1962.

Bassham, Rodger C. "Willingen: Seeking a Deeper Theological Basis for Mission." *International Review of Mission*, 67.267 (July 1978): 329–37.

_____. *Mission Theology, 1948–1975: Years of Creative Tension—Ecumenical, Evangelical and Roman Catholic*. South Pasadena, Calif.: William Carey Library, 1980.

Baum, Gregory. *The Credibility of the Church Today: A Reply to Charles Davis*. New York: Herder and Herder, 1968.

_____. "Commentary," in Edward H. Peters, ed.: *De Ecclesia, The Constitution on the Church of Vatican Council II Proclaimed by Pope Paul VI on November 21, 1964*. Glen Rock, N.J.: Paulist, 1965.

_____. "Introduction" in *The Teachings of the Second Vatican Council: Complete Texts of the Constitutions, Decrees, and Declarations*. Westminster,

Md.: Newman, 1966.

————. *Man Becoming: God in Secular Language*. New York: Herder and Herder, 1970.

Bavinck, Herman. *Our Reasonable Faith: A Survey of Christian Doctrine*, H. Zylstra, trans. Grand Rapids: Eerdmans, 1956; repr. ed., Grand Rapids: Baker, 1986.

Bavinck, J. H. *An Introduction to the Science of Missions*, David Freeman, trans. Philadelphia: Presbyterian and Reformed, 1960.

————. *The Impact of Christianity on the Non-Christian World*. Grand Rapids: Eerdmans, 1948.

Bennis, Warren, and Burt Nanus. *Leaders: The Strategies of Taking Charge*. New York: Harper and Row, 1985.

Belew, M. Wendell. *Churches and How They Grow*. Nashville: Broadman, 1971.

Bellah, Robert N., et al. *Habits of the Heart: Individualism and Commitment in American Life*. Berkeley, Calif.: University of California Press, 1985.

Berkhof, Hendrikus. *Christian Faith: An Introduction to the Study of Faith*, S. Woudstra, trans. Grand Rapids: Eerdmans, 1979.

Berkhof, Hendrikus, and Philip Potter. *Key Words of the Gospel*. London: SCM, 1964.

Berkouwer, G. C. *The Church*, J. E. Davison, trans. Grand Rapids: Eerdmans, 1976.

————. *The Second Vatican Council and the New Catholicism*, L. B. Smedes, trans. Grand Rapids: Eerdmans, 1965.

Berton, Pierre. *The Comfortable Pew: A Critical Look at Christianity and the Religious Establishment in the New Age*. Philadelphia: Lippincott, 1965.

Beyerhaus, Peter, ed. *The Church Crossing Frontiers: Essays on the Nature of Mission in Honour of Bengt Sundkler*. Uppsala: Gleerup, 1969.

————. "The Three Selves Formula." *International Review of Missions*, 53 (1964): 393–407.

Birch, Bruce C. "Sages, Visionaries and Poets." *Sojourners*, 13.11 (Dec. 1984): 25–28.

Bjork, Don. "Foreign Missions: Next Door and Down the Street," *Christianity Today*, 29.13 (12 July 1985): 17–21.

Blauw, Johannes. *The Missionary Nature of the Church: A Survey of the Biblical Theology of Mission*. New York: McGraw-Hill, 1962.

Boer, Harry R. *Pentecost and Missions*. Grand Rapids: Eerdmans, 1961.

————. "Reformed Attitude to the WCC." *Theological Forum*: 10.1–2 (June 1982): 23–29.

Boff, Leonardo. *Ecclesiogenesis: The Base Communities Reinvent the Church*, J. Dierksmeyer, trans. Maryknoll, N.Y.: Orbis, 1986.

————. *Church, Charism and Power: Liberation Theology and the Institutional Church*, J. Dierksmeyer, trans. New York: Crossroad, 1985.

Bonhoeffer, Dietrich. *The Communion of Saints: A Dogmatic Inquiry into the Sociology of the Church*. E.T., New York: Harper, 1963.

Bosch, David J. *Witness to the World: The Christian Mission in Theological Perspective*. Atlanta: John Knox, 1980.

————. "The Scope of Mission." *International Review of Mission*, 73.289 (Jan. 1984): 17–32.

————. "Mission in Jesus' Way: A Perspective from Luke's Gospel." *Missionalia*, 17.1 (April 1989): 3–21.

————. "An Emerging Paradigm for Mission." *Missiology*, 11.4 (Oct. 1983): 485–510.

————. "Evangelism: Theological Currents and Cross-Currents Today." *International Bulletin of Missionary Research*, 11.3 (July 1987): 98–103.

Braun, Neill. *Laity Mobilized: Reflections on Church Growth in Japan and Other Lands*. Grand Rapids: Eerdmans, 1971.

Bright, John. *The Kingdom of God: The Biblical Concept and Its Meaning for the Church*. Nashville: Abingdon-Cokesbury, 1953.

Brueggeman, Walter. *In Man We Trust: The Neglected Side of Biblical Faith*. Atlanta: John Knox, 1972.

Callahan, Kennon L. *Twelve Keys to an Effective Church*. New York: Harper and Row, 1983.

————. *Effective Church Leadership: Building on the Twelve Keys*. San Francisco: Harper and Row, 1990.

"Called and Committed: The Spirituality of Mission." *Today's Ministry*, 2.3 (Spring–Summer 1985): 1, 3–5.

Calvin, John. *Institutes of the Christian Religion*, F. L. Battles, trans. Philadelphia: Westminster, 1960.

Campbell, Thomas C., and Gary B. Reierson. *The Gift of Administration*. Philadelphia: Westminster, 1981.

Cassidy, Richard J. *Jesus, Politics and Society: A Study of Luke's Gospel*. Maryknoll, N.Y.: Orbis, 1978.

Chaney, Charles L. *Design for Church Growth*. Nashville: Broadman, 1977.

Cho, Paul Yonggi. *More Than Numbers*. Waco, Tex.: Word, 1984.

"Christian Unity: Becoming One in Christ," in *Minutes of the General Synod, 1987*. New York: Reformed Church in America, 1987: 53–59.

"Church in Crisis." *Newsweek*, 106 (9 Dec. 1985): 66–76.

Claerbaut, David. *Urban Ministry*. Grand Rapids: Zondervan, 1984.

Clinton, J. Robert. *The Making of a Leader*. Colorado Springs: NavPress, 1988.

Clowney, Edmund P. *Called to the Ministry*. Chicago: Inter-Varsity, 1964.

Coleman, Robert E. *The Master Plan of Evangelism* (Old Tappan, N.J.: Revell, 1963).

Collum, Danny. "A. J. Muste, The Prophet Pilgrim." *Sojourners*, 13.11 (Dec. 1984): 12–17.

Congar, Yves M. J. *The Mystery of the Church*, A. V. Littledale, trans. Baltimore: Helicon, 1960.

Conn, Harvie. *Evangelism: Doing Justice and Preaching Grace*. Grand Rapids: Zondervan, 1982.

Conners, Kenneth W. *Stranger in the Pew*. Valley Forge, Pa.: Judson, 1970.

Cook, Guillermo. "Grassroots Churches and Reformation in Central America." *Latin American Pastoral Issues*, 14.1 (June 1987): 5–23.

_____. *The Expectation of the Poor: Latin American Basic Ecclesial Communities in Protestant Perspective*. Maryknoll, N.Y.: Orbis, 1985.

_____. "The Protestant Predicament: From Base Ecclesial Community to Established Church—A Brazilian Case Study." *International Bulletin of Missionary Research*, 8.3 (July 1984): 98–102.

Costas, Orlando E. *Christ Outside the Gate: Mission Beyond Christendom*. Maryknoll, N.Y.: Orbis, 1982.

_____. "Churches in Evangelistic Partnership," in C. René Padilla, ed. *The New Face of Evangelicalism: An International Symposium on the Lausanne Covenant*. Downers Grove, Ill.: Inter-Varsity, 1976.

_____. *Liberating News: A Theology of Contextual Evangelization*. Grand Rapids: Eerdmans, 1987.

_____. *The Integrity of Mission: The Inner Life and Outreach of the Church*. New York: Harper and Row, 1979.

Cullman, Oscar. *Christ and Time: The Primitive Christian Conception of Time and History*, F. V. Filson, trans. Philadelphia: Westminster, 1964.

Daughdrill, James H., Jr. "A Plea for Laymen's Liberation." *Church Herald*, 30.30 (7 Sept. 1973): 12–13, 22–23.

Davidson, James D. *Mobilizing Social Movement Organizations: The Formation, Institutionalization, and Effectiveness of Ecumenical Urban Ministries*. Storrs, Conn: Society for the Scientific Study of Religion, 1985.

Dayton, Edward R., and Theodore W. Engstrom. *Strategy for Leadership*. Old Tappan, N.J.: Fleming H. Revell, 1979.

De Dietrich, Suzanne. *The Witnessing Community*. Philadelphia: Westminster, 1958.

Dibbert, Michael T. *Spiritual Leadership, Responsible Management: A Guide for Leaders of the Church*. Grand Rapids: Zondervan, 1989.

Dietterich, Paul M., ed. "Managing Clergy Transition." *The Center Letter*, 13.5 (May 1983).

_____. "New Ways of Thinking About Supervision." *The Center Letter*, 13.4 (April 1983).

Dirkswager, Edward J., Jr., comp. *Readings in the Theology of the Church*. Englewood Cliffs, N.J.: Prentice-Hall, 1970.

Dubose, Francis M. *How Churches Grow in an Urban World*. Nashville: Broadman, 1978.

Dudley, Carl S. *Making the Small Church Effective*. Nashville: Abingdon, 1978.

————. *Where Have All Our People Gone? New Choices for Old Churches*. New York: Pilgrim, 1979.

Dulles, Avery R. *A Church to Believe In: Discipleship and the Dynamics of Freedom*. New York: Crossroad, 1982.

————. *Models of the Church: A Critical Assessment of the Church in All Its Aspects*. Garden City, N.Y.: Doubleday, 1974.

————. *The Resilient Church: The Necessity and Limits of Adaptation*. New York: Doubleday, 1977.

Dulles, Avery R., and Patrick Granfield. *The Church: A Bibliography*. Wilmington, Del.: Michael Glazier, 1985.

Dunnam, Maxie D.; Gary J. Herbertson, and Everett L. Shostrom. *The Manipulator and the Church*. Nashville: Abingdon, 1968.

Durnbaugh, Donald F. *The Believers' Church: The History and Character of Radical Protestantism*. Scottdale, Pa.: Herald, 1985.

Ellison, Craig W., ed. *The Urban Mission*. Grand Rapids: Eerdmans, 1974.

Eims, LeRoy. *Be the Leader You Were Meant to Be: What the Bible Says about Leadership*. Wheaton, Ill.: Victor, 1982.

Engstrom, Theodore W. *The Christian Executive: A Practical Reference for Christians in Management Positions*. Waco, Tex.: Word, 1976.

————. *The Making of a Christian Leader*. Grand Rapids: Zondervan, 1976.

Escobar, Samuel. "Base Church Communities: A Historical Perspective." *Latin American Pastoral Issues*, 14.1 (June 1987): 24–33

Flannery, Austin P., ed. *Documents of Vatican II*. Grand Rapids: Eerdmans, 1975.

————. *Vatican II: More Postconciliar Documents*. Grand Rapids: Eerdmans, 1982.

————. *Vatican II on the Church*. 2d ed. Dublin: Scepter, 1967.

Freytag, Walter. "The Meaning and Purpose of the Christian Mission." *International Review of Missions*, 39 (April 1950): 153–61.

Fuller, W. Harold. *Mission Church Dynamics: How to Change Bicultural Tensions into Dynamic Missionary Outreach*. South Pasadena, Calif.: William Carey Library, 1980.

Garvin, G. W. "Marks of Growing Churches." *Action Information*, 11.4 (Aug.–Sept. 1985): 1–4.

Gatu, John. "The Urgency of the Evangelistic Task," in C. René Padilla, ed. *The New Face of Evangelicalism: An International Symposium on the Lausanne Covenant*. Downers Grove, Ill.: Inter-Varsity, 1976.

Getz, Gene A. *Sharpening the Focus of the Church*. Chicago: Moody, 1974.

————. *The Measure of a Church*. Glendale, Calif.: Regal, 1975.

Gibbs, Eddie. *Followed or Pushed?* London: MARC Europe, 1987.

————. *I Believe in Church Growth*. Grand Rapids: Eerdmans, 1982.

Gilliland, Dean. *Pauline Theology and Mission Practice*. Grand Rapids: Baker, 1983.

Good-all, Norman, ed. *Missions Under the Cross: Addresses Delivered at the*

*Enlarged Meeting of the Committee of the International Missionary Council at Willingen, in Germany, 1952.* London: Edinburgh House, 1953.

Grabowski, Stanislaus J. *The Church: An Introduction to the Theology of St. Augustine.* St. Louis: Herder, 1957.

Graham, W. Fred. "Declining Church Membership: Can Anything Be Done?" *Reformed Journal*, 30.1 (Jan. 1980): 7–13.

Granberg-Michaelson, Karin. "Reclaiming the Healing Ministry of the Church." *Perspectives*, 2.7 (Sept. 1987): 4–7.

Gray, Robert M. *Church Business Administration*, 2 vols. Enid, Okla.: Phillips University Press, 1968.

————. *Managing the Church.* Enid, Okla.: Phillips University Press, 1970.

Green, E. Michael B. *Evangelism in the Early Church.* Grand Rapids: Eerdmans, 1970.

Greenleaf, Robert K. *Servant Leadership.* New York: Paulist, 1977.

Greenway, Roger S. *Apostle to the City: Biblical Strategies for Urban Missions.* Grand Rapids: Baker, 1978.

————. *An Urban Strategy for Latin America.* Grand Rapids: Baker, 1973.

Griffiths, Michael C. *God's Forgetful Pilgrims: Recalling the Church to Its Reason for Being.* Grand Rapids: Eerdmans, 1975.

Grimes, Howard. *The Rebirth of the Laity.* New York: Abingdon, 1962.

Guder, Darrell L. *Be My Witnesses: The Church's Mission, Message, and Messengers.* Grand Rapids: Eerdmans, 1985.

Gutiérrez, Gustavo. *A Theology of Liberation*, C. Inda and J. Eagleson, trans. Maryknoll, N.Y.: Orbis, 1973.

————. *We Drink From Our Own Wells: The Spiritual Journey of a People*, M. J. O'Connell, trans. Maryknoll, N.Y.: Orbis, 1984.

Hadaway, C. Kirk, Stuart A. Wright, and Francis M. Dubose. *Home Cell Groups and House Churches.* Nashville: Broadman, 1987.

Hall, Francis J. *The Church and the Sacramental System.* New York: Longman's, Green and Co., 1920.

————. *Dogmatic Theology*, vol. 7: *About the Church.* New York: Longmans, Green and Co. ca. 1910; repr. ed., New York: American Church Union, 1967.

Hale, J. Russell. *Who Are the Unchurched? An Exploratory Study.* Washington, D.C.: Glenmary Research Center, 1977.

Hanson, Paul D. "The Identity and Purpose of the Church." *Theology Today*, 42.3 (Oct. 1985): 342–52.

————. *The People Called: The Growth of Community in the Bible.* New York: Harper and Row, 1986.

Harper, Michael. *Let My People Grow! Ministry and Leadership in the Church.* Plainfield, N.J.: Logos International, 1977.

Hendrix, Olan. *Management for the Christian Worker.* Libertyville, Ill.: Quill, 1976.

Hermelink, J., and H. J. Margull, eds. *Basileia.* Stuttgart: Evang. Missions-Verlag, 1959.

Hersey, Paul, and Kenneth H. Blanchard. *The Situational Leader*. Escondido, Calif.: Center for Leadership Studies, 1985.

————. *Management of Organizational Behavior: Utilizing Human Resources*, 5th ed. Englewood Cliffs, N.J.: Prentice-Hall, 1988.

Hersey, Paul; Kenneth H. Blanchard, and Walter Natemeyer. "Situational Leadership, Perception and the Impact of Power." Escondido, Calif.: Center for Leadership Studies, 1979.

Hesselgrave, David J. *Communicating Christ Cross-Culturally: An Introduction to Missionary Communication*. Grand Rapids: Zondervan, 1978.

————. *Planting Churches Cross-Culturally: A Guide for Home and Foreign Missions*. Grand Rapids: Baker, 1980.

Hesselink, I. John. "Reformed But Ever Reforming." *Church Herald*, 31.21 (18 Oct. 1974): 6–7.

Hill, Bradley N. "An African Ecclesiology in Process: Six Stages of Dynamic Growth." *Missiology*, 16.1 (Jan. 1988): 73–87.

Hodges, Melvin L. *The Indigenous Church and the Missionary: A Sequel to "The Indigenous Church."* South Pasadena, Calif.: William Carey Library, 1977.

————. *A Theology of the Church and Its Mission: A Pentecostal Perspective*. Springfield, Mo.: Gospel, 1977.

Hoekendijk, Johannes C. "The Call to Evangelism." *International Review of Missions*, 39 (Apr. 1950): 162–75.

————. "The Church in Missionary Thinking." *International Review of Missions*, 41 (July 1952): 324–36.

————. *The Church Inside Out*, I. C. Rottenberg, trans. Philadelphia: Westminster, 1966.

Hogue, C. B. *I Want My Church to Grow*. Nashville: Broadman, 1977.

Hoge, Dean R., and David A. Roozen. *Understanding Church Growth and Decline*. New York: Pilgrim, 1979.

Hoge, Dean R., et al. *Converts, Dropouts, Returnees: A Study of Religious Change among Catholics*. New York: Pilgrim, 1981.

Howard, David M. *The Great Commission for Today*. Downers Grove, Ill.: InterVarsity, 1976.

Hull, Bill. *Jesus Christ: Disciple-maker: Rediscovering Jesus' Strategy for Building His Church*. Colorado Springs: NavPress, 1989.

Hunter, George G., III. *To Spread the Power: Church Growth in the Wesleyan Spirit*. Nashville: Abingdon, 1987.

Hunter, Kent R. *Your Church Has Personality*. Nashville: Abingdon, 1985.

Hutcheson, Richard G., Jr. *Mainline Churches and the Evangelicals*. Atlanta: John Knox, 1981.

"Into the Next Century: Trends Facing the Church." *Christianity Today Institute* (17 Jan. 1986).

Isais, Juan M. *The Other Side of the Coin*, E. F. Isais, trans. Grand Rapids: Eerdmans, 1966.

Jenkins, Daniel T. *The Strangeness of the Church*. Garden City, N.Y.: Doubleday, 1955.

Johnson, Benton. "Is There Hope for Liberal Protestantism?" in Dorothy Bass, Benton Johnson, and Wade Clark Roof, eds. *Mainstream Protestantism in the Twentieth Century: Its Problems and Prospects* (Louisville: Committee on Theological Education, Presbyterian Church, USA, 1986): 13–26.

Johnson, Douglas W. *Managing Change in the Church*. New York: Friendship, 1974.

Jones, Ezra Earl, and Robert L. Wilson, eds. *What's Ahead for Old First Church?* New York: Harper and Row, 1974.

Jordan, James B., ed. *The Reconstruction of the Church*. Tyler, Tex.: Geneva Ministries, 1986.

Kane, J. Herbert. *The Christian World Mission*. London: Lutterworth, 1963.

_____. *Understanding Christian Missions*. Grand Rapids: Baker, 1974.

Kelley, Arleon L. *Your Church: A Dynamic Community*. Philadelphia: Westminster, 1982.

Kelley, Dean M. *Why Conservative Churches Are Growing: A Study in the Sociology of Religion*. 2d ed. New York: Harper and Row, 1977.

Kemper, Vicki, with Larry Engel. "Dom Helder Cámara: Pastor of the Poor." *Sojourners*, 16.11 (Dec. 1987): 12–15.

Kgatla, S. T. "The Church for Others: The Relevance of Dietrich Bonhoeffer for the Dutch Reformed Church Today." *Missionalia*, 17.3 (Nov. 1989): 151–61.

Kirk, Andrew J. *The Good News of the Kingdom Coming: The Marriage of Evangelism and Social Responsibility*. Downers Grove, Ill.: Inter-Varsity, 1985.

Kittel, Gerhard, and Gerhard Friedrich, eds. *Theological Dictionary of the New Testament*, G. W. Bromiley, trans., 10 vols. Grand Rapids: Eerdmans, 1964–1976.

Klemme, Huber F. *Your Church and Your Community*. Philadelphia: Co-operative, 1957.

Koster, Edward H. "Leader Relationships: A Key to Congregational Size." *Action Information*, 13.4 (July–Aug. 1987): 1–5.

Kraemer, Hendrik. *A Theology of the Laity*. Philadelphia: Westminster, 1958.

_____. "The Church in Search of Mission." *Christianity Today*, 15.1 (1 Jan. 1971): 10–12.

_____. *The Communication of the Christian Faith*. Philadelphia: Westminster, 1956.

Kraft, Charles H., *Christianity in Culture: A Study in Dynamic Biblical Theologizing in Cross-Cultural Perspective*. Maryknoll, N.Y.: Orbis, 1979.

Kraft, Charles H. and Tom N. Wisley, eds. *Readings in Dynamic Indigeneity*. Pasadena: William Carey Library, 1979.

Krass, Alfred C. *Evangelizing NeoPagan North America: The Word that Frees*. Scottdale, Pa.: Herald, 1982.

_____. *Five Lanterns at Sundown: Evangelism in a Chastened Mood*. Grand Rapids: Eerdmans, 1978.

Küng, Hans. *Structures of the Church*, S. Attanasio, trans. New York: Nelson, 1964.

————. *The Church*, R. Ockenden, trans. New York: Sheed and Ward, 1967.

Küng, Hans, and Jürgen Moltmann, eds. *Who Has the Say in the Church?* New York: Harper and Row, 1981.

Kuyper, Abraham. *Dictaten Dogmatiek*, 5 vols. Kampen, the Netherlands: Kok, 1910: vol. 2: *Locus de Sacra Scriptura*; vol. 4: *Locus de Salute, Ecclesia, Sacramentis*.

————. *Tractaat van de Reformatie der Kerken*. Amsterdam: Hoveker, 1884.

Ladd, George Eldon. *The Gospel of the Kingdom: Scriptural Studies in the Kingdom of God*. Grand Rapids: Eerdmans, 1959.

————. *The Presence of the Future: The Eschatology of Biblical Realism*. Grand Rapids: Eerdmans, 1974.

Langman, Harm Jan. *Kuyper en de Volkskerk*. Kampen, the Netherlands: Kok, 1950.

Larson, Bruce, and Ralph Osborne. *The Emerging Church*. Waco, Tex.: Word, 1970.

Larson, Philip M., Jr. *Vital Church Management*. Atlanta: John Knox, 1977.

Latourette, Kenneth S., et al. *Church and Community*. New York: Willett, Clark and Co., 1938.

————. *The Emergence of a World Christian Community*. New Haven: Yale University Press, 1949.

Lee, Bernard J., and Michael A. Cowan. *Dangerous Memories: House Churches and Our American Story*. Kansas City, Mo.: Sheed and Ward, 1986.

Libanio, J. B. "Base Church Communites (CEBs) in Socio-Cultural Perspective." *Latin American Pastoral Issues*, 14.1 (June 1987): 34–47.

Lindgren, Alvin J. *Foundations for Purposeful Church Administration*. Nashville: Abingdon, 1965.

Lindgren, Alvin J., and Norman Shawchuck. *Management for Your Church: How to Realize Your Church Potential Through a Systems Approach*. Nashville: Abingdon, 1977.

Lingenfelter, Sherwood G., and Marvin K. Mayers. *Ministering Cross-Culturally: An Incarnational Model for Personal Relationships*. Grand Rapids: Baker, 1986.

Linthicum, Robert C. *City of God, City of Satan: A Biblical Theology for the Urban Church*. Grand Rapids: Zondervan, 1991.

————. "Doing Effective Ministry in the City." *Together*, 18 (Apr.–June 1988): 1–2.

————. "Towards a Biblical Urban Theology." *Together*, 18 (Apr.–June, 1988): 4–5.

Löffler, Paul. "The Confessing Community: Evangelism in Ecumenical Perspective." *International Review of Mission*, 66.264 (Oct. 1977): 339–48.

Luzbetak, Louis. *The Church and Cultures: New Perspectives in Missiological Anthropology*. Maryknoll, N.Y.: Orbis, 1989.

McBrien, Richard P. *The Church in the Thought of Bishop John Robinson.* Philadelphia: Westminster, 1966.

McGavran, Donald A. *Ethnic Realities and the Church: Lessons from India.* South Pasadena, Calif.: William Carey Library, 1978.

————. *Understanding Church Growth,* rev. ed. Grand Rapids: Eerdmans, 1990.

McGavran, Donald A., and George G. Hunter III. *Church Growth Strategies That Work.* Nashville: Abingdon, 1980.

McGavran, Donald A., and Winfield C. Arn. *Back to Basics in Church Growth.* Wheaton, Ill.: Tyndale, 1981.

————. *Growth—A New Vision for the Sunday School.* Pasadena, Calif.: Church Growth, 1980.

————. *How to Grow a Church.* Glendale, Calif.: Regal, 1973.

————. *Ten Steps for Church Growth.* New York: Harper and Row, 1977.

Mackay, John. "The Witness of the Reformed Churches in the World Today." *Theology Today,* 11 (Oct. 1954): 373–84.

McKee, Elsie Anne. *Diakonia in the Classical Reformed Tradition and Today.* Grand Rapids: Eerdmans, 1989.

MacNair, Donald J. *The Growing Local Church.* Grand Rapids: Baker, 1975.

Malony, H. Newton. "Organized Disorganization or Disorganized Organization." *Theology, News and Notes* (Oct. 1976): 3–4, 27.

Marcum, Elvis. *Outreach: God's Miracle Business.* Nashville: Broadman, 1975.

Martin, Ralph P. *The Family and the Fellowship: New Testament Images of the Church.* Grand Rapids: Eerdmans, 1979.

Mayers, Marvin K. *Christianity Confronts Culture: A Strategy for Cross-Cultural Evangelism.* Grand Rapids: Zondervan, 1974.

Metz, Donald L. *New Congregations: Security and Mission in Conflict.* Philadelphia: Westminster, 1967.

Metzger, Bruce M. "The New Testament View of the Church." *Theology Today,* 19.3 (Oct. 1962): 369–80.

————. "The Teaching of the New Testament Concerning the Church." *Concordia Theological Monthly,* 34.3 (Mar. 1963): 147–55.

Mickey, Paul A., and Robert L. Wilson. *What New Creation?* Nashville: Abingdon, 1977.

Miguez-Bonino, José. "Fundamental Questions in Ecclesiology," in Sergio Torres and John Eagleson, eds. *The Challenge of Basic Christian Communities: Papers from the International Ecumenical Congress of Theology, February 20–March 2, 1980, São Paulo, Brazil,* J. Drury, trans. Maryknoll, N.Y.: Orbis, 1981: 145–59.

Miller, Donald G. *The Nature and Mission of the Church.* Richmond: John Knox, 1957.

Minear, Paul S. *Images of the Church in the New Testament.* Philadelphia: Westminster, 1960.

————. *Jesus and His People.* New York: Association, 1956.

"Ministry in the Church, Ministry in the World—What's the Connection? A Conversation between James Adams and Celia Hahn." *Action Information*, 12.4 (July–Aug. 1986): 1–5.

"Missionary Structures of the Congregation," in: *The Church for Others and the Church for the World: A Quest of Structures for Missionary Congregations*. Geneva: World Council of Churches, 1968.

Moberg, David O. *The Church as a Social Institution: The Sociology of American Religion*. Englewood Cliffs, N.J.: Prentice-Hall, 1962.

Moltmann, Jürgen, and M. Douglas Meeks. *Hope for the Church: Moltmann in Dialog with Practical Theology*, T. Runyan, ed. and trans. Nashville: Abingdon, 1979.

————. *The Church in the Power of the Spirit*. New York: Harper and Row, 1977.

Myers, David G. "Faith and Action: A Seamless Tapestry." *Christianity Today*, 24.20 (21 Nov. 1980): 16–19.

Myers, Harold, ed. *Leaders*. Waco, Tex.: Word, 1987.

Myra, Harold, ed. *Leaders: Learning Leadership from Some of Christianity's Best*. Carol Stream, Ill.: Christianity Today, 1986.

Neighbor, Ralph W., Jr. *Where Do We Go from Here? A Guidebook for the Cell-Group Church*. Houston: Touch, 1990.

Neill, Stephen C. *Colonialism and Christian Missions*. New York: McGraw-Hill, 1966.

————. *Creative Tension*. New York: Friendship, 1959.

————. *Fulfill Thy Ministry*. New York: Harper, 1952.

————, ed. *Twentieth Century Christianity: A Survey of Modern Religious Trends by Leading Churchmen*, rev. ed. Garden City, N.Y.: Doubleday, 1963.

Nelson, C. Ellis. *Congregations: Their Power to Form and Transform*. Atlanta: John Knox, 1988.

Newbigin, J. E. Lesslie. "Can the West Be Converted?" *Princeton Seminary Bulletin*, n.s. 6.1 (1985): 25–37.

————. *Foolishness to the Greeks: The Gospel and Western Culture*. Grand Rapids: Eerdmans, 1986.

————. *Sign of the Kingdom*. Grand Rapids: Eerdmans, 1981.

————. *The Good Shepherd: Meditations on Christian Ministry in Today's World*. Grand Rapids: Eerdmans, 1977.

————. *The Gospel in a Pluralist Society*. Grand Rapids: Eerdmans, 1989.

————. *The Household of God: Lectures on the Nature of the Church*. New York: Friendship, 1954.

————. *The Life and Mission of the Church*. Bangalore, India: Student Christian Movement, 1958.

————. *The Open Secret: Sketches for a Missionary Theology*. Grand Rapids: Eerdmans, 1978.

Nicholls, Bruce J., and Kenneth Kantzer. *In Word and Deed: Evangelism and Social Responsibility*. Grand Rapids: Eerdmans, 1986.

Niebuhr, H. Richard; Wilhelm Pauck, and Francis P. Miller. *The Church Against the World.* Chicago: Willett, Clark and Co., 1935.

Ogden, Greg. "The Pastor as Change Agent." *Theology News and Notes* (June 1990): 8–10.

Osborne, Larry W. *The Unity Factor: Getting Your Church Leaders to Work Together*, Waco, Tex.: Word, 1989.

Ott, E. Stanley. *The Vibrant Church: A People-Building Plan for Congregational Health.* Ventura, Calif.: Regal, 1989.

Padilla, C. René. "A New Ecclesiology in Latin America." *International Bulletin of Missionary Research*, 11.4 (Oct. 1987): 156–64.

————. *Mission Between the Times: The Essays of C. René Padilla.* Grand Rapids: Eerdmans, 1985.

————, ed. *The New Face of Evangelicalism: An International Symposium on the Lausanne Covenant.* Downers Grove, Ill.: Inter-Varsity, 1976.

Pannenberg, Wolfhart; Avery Dulles, and Carl E. Braaten. *Spirit, Faith, and Church.* Philadelphia: Westminster, 1970.

Payton, James R., Jr. "The Reformed Concept of the Church with Ecumenical Implications." *Reformed Ecumenical Synod Theological Forum*, 10.1, 2 (June 1982): 3–12.

Pederson, Donald R. "Taking Charge as a Pastoral Leader." *Action Information*, 13.1 (Jan.–Feb. 1987): 1–6.

Pendorf, James G., and Helmer C. Lundquist. *Church Organization: A Manual for Effective Local Church Administration.* Wilton, Conn.: Morehouse-Barlow, 1977.

Perry, Lloyd M., and Norman Shawchuck. *Revitalizing the Twentieth-Century Church.* Chicago: Moody, 1982.

Peters, George L. *A Biblical Theology of Missions.* Chicago: Moody, 1972.

————. *A Theology of Church Growth.* Grand Rapids: Zondervan, 1981.

————. *Saturation Evangelism.* Grand Rapids: Zondervan, 1970.

Petersen, J. Randall. "Church Growth: A Limitation of Numbers?" *Christianity Today*, 25.6 (27 March 1981): 18–23.

Phillips, William. "In Search of a Leader." *Action Information*, 13.3 (May-June 1987): 1–6.

————. "Understanding the Congregation: A Systems Approach." *Action Information*, 13.6 (Nov.–Dec. 1987): 18–20.

Piet, John H. *The Road Ahead: A Theology for the Church in Mission.* Grand Rapids: Eerdmans, 1970.

"Planning Concepts." *Christian Leadership Letter* (Sept. 1987): 1–3.

Powell, Paul W. *How to Make Your Church Hum.* Nashville: Broadman, 1977.

Price, Peter. *The Church as the Kingdom: A New Way of Being the Church.* London: Marshal, Morgan, and Scott, 1987.

Raines, Robert A. *The Secular Congregation.* New York: Harper and Row, 1968.

"Redemptive Work of Christ and the Ministry of His Church." *Encounter*, 25.1 (Winter 1964): 105–29.

Reeves, R. Daniel, and Ronald Jenson. *Always Advancing: Modern Strategies for Church Growth*. San Bernardino, Calif.: Here's Life, 1984.

"Report of the Section on Unity," in *New Delhi Report: 3d Assembly, Delhi, 1961*. New York: Association for World Council of Churches, 1962.

Reumann, John, ed. *The Church Emerging: A U.S. Lutheran Case Study*. Philadelphia: Fortress, 1977.

Richards, Lawrence O. *A New Face for the Church*. Grand Rapids: Zondervan, 1970.

————. "The Great American Congregation: An Illusive Ideal?" *Christianity Today*, 24.20 (21 Nov. 1980): 20–23.

Richards, Lawrence O., and Clyde Hoeldtke. *A Theology of Church Leadership*. Grand Rapids: Zondervan, 1980.

Richards, Lawrence O., and Gilbert Martin. *Lay Ministry: Empowering the People of God*. Grand Rapids: Zondervan, 1981.

Richardson, William J., ed. *The Church as Sign*. Maryknoll, N.Y.: Orbis, 1968.

Ridderbos, Herman N. *Church, World, Kingdom*. Potchefstroom, South Africa: Institut vir die Befordering van Calvinisme, 1979.

————. *Paul*, J. R. DeWitt, trans. Grand Rapids: Eerdmans, 1975.

————. *The Coming of the Kingdom*, H. de Jongste, trans. Philadelphia: Presbyterian and Reformed, 1962.

Robinson, Jo Ann D. *Abraham Went Out: A Biography of A. J. Muste*. Philadelphia: Temple University Press, 1982.

Rocker, Dolore, and Kenneth J. Pierre. *Shared Ministry: An Integrated Approach to Leadership and Service*. Minnesota: Saint Mary's, 1984.

Roof, Wade Clark, and William McKinney. *American Mainline Religion: Its Changing Shape and Future*. New Brunswick: Rutgers University Press, 1987.

Roozen, David A.; William McKinney, and Jackson W. Carroll, eds. *Varieties of Religious Presence: Mission in Public Life*. New York: Pilgrim, 1984.

Rose, Larry L., and C. Kirk Hadaway, eds. *An Urban World: Churches Face the Future*. Nashville: Broadman, 1984.

Rouch, Mark A. *Competent Ministry: A Guide to Effective Continuing Education*. Nashville: Abingdon, 1974.

Sample, Tex. *Blue-Collar Ministry: Facing Economic and Social Realities of Working People*. Valley Forge, Pa.: Judson, 1984.

Sauer, James B. *Vision for Tomorrow: Influencing the Future through Planning and Leadership Development*. Presbyterian Church in Canada, 1983.

Savage, John S. "Ministry to Missing Members." *Leadership*, 8.2 (Spring 1987): 116–21.

Sawyer, Dennis. "Torn Between Church and Community." *Leadership*, 7.4 (Fall 1986): 75–77.

Schaeffer, Francis A. *The Mark of the Christian*. Downers Grove, Ill.: Inter-Varsity, 1969.

Schaller, Lyle E. *Activating the Passive Church*. Nashville: Abingdon, 1981.

_____. *Getting Things Done: Concepts and Skills for Leaders*. Nashville: Abingdon, 1986.

_____. *Growing Plans: Strategies to Increase Your Church's Membership*. Nashville: Abingdon, 1983.

_____. *Hey! That's Our Church!* Nashville: Abingdon, 1975.

_____. *It's a Different World: The Challenge for Today's Pastor*. Nashville: Abingdon, 1987.

_____. *Looking in the Mirror: Self-Appraisal in the Local Church*. Nashville: Abingdon, 1984.

_____. "Marks of a Healthy Church." *Parish Paper*. New York: Reformed Church in America, 1983.

_____. *Planning for Protestantism in Urban America*. Nashville: Abingdon, 1965.

_____. *Reflections of a Contrarian: Second Thoughts on the Parish Ministry*. Nashville: Abingdon, 1989.

_____. *The Change Agent: The Strategy of Innovative Leadership*. Nashville: Abingdon, 1972.

_____. *The Decision-Makers: How to Improve the Quality of Decision-Making in the Churches*. Nashville: Abingdon, 1974.

_____. *The Pastor and the People: Building a New Partnership for Effective Ministry*. Nashville: Abingdon, 1973.

Schaller, Lyle E., and Charles A. Tidwell. *Creative Church Administration*. Nashville: Abingdon, 1975.

Schillebeeckx, Edward. *Ministry*, J. Bowden, trans. New York: Crossroad, 1981.

Schlink, Edmund. *The Coming Christ and the Coming Church*. Philadelphia: Fortress, 1968.

Schmemann, Alexander. *Church, World, Mission: Reflections on Orthodoxy in the West*. Crestwood, N.Y.: St. Vladimir's Seminary Press, 1979.

Schuller, Robert. *Your Church Has Real Possibilities*. Glendale, Calif.: Regal, 1974.

Scott, Waldron. *Karl Barth's Theology of Mission*. Downers Grove, Ill.: Inter-Varsity, 1978.

Scouteris, Constantine. "The People of God—Its Unity and Its Glory: A Discussion of John 17:17–24 in the Light of Patristic Thought." *Greek Orthodox Theological Review*, 30.4 (Winter 1985): 399–420.

Segundo, Juan Luis. *The Community Called Church*, J. Drury, trans. Maryknoll, N.Y.: Orbis, 1973.

Sexton, Virgil W. *Listening to the Church: A Realistic Profile of Grass Roots Opinion*. Nashville: Abingdon, 1971.

Shannon, Foster H. *The Growth Crisis in the American Church: A Presbyterian Case Study*. South Pasadena, Calif.: William Carey Library, 1977.

Shelp, Earl E., and Ronald H. Sutherland. *The Pastor as Prophet*. New York: Pilgrim, 1985.

Shenk, Wilbert. *Exploring Church Growth*. Grand Rapids: Eerdmans, 1983.

_____. "Missionary Congregations." *Mission Focus* (March 1978): 13–14.

_____. *The Challenge of Church Growth*. Scottdale, Pa.: Herald, 1973.

Sheppard, David. *Built As a City: God and the Urban World Today*. London: Hodder and Stoughton, 1974.

Sider, Ronald J. *Rich Christians in an Age of Hunger: A Biblical Study*. Downers Grove, Ill.: Inter-Varsity, 1977.

_____, ed. *Cry Justice: The Bible on Hunger and Poverty*. New York: Paulist, 1980.

Silber, Mark B. "Successful Supervisory Secrets: Lessons of Leadership." *PACE* (Nov. 1985): 89–93.

Sine, Tom. *The Mustard Seed Conspiracy: You Can Make a Difference in Tomorrow's Troubled World*. Waco, Tex.: Word, 1981.

Smith, Donald P. *Congregations Alive*. Philadelphia: Westminster, 1981.

Smith, W. Douglas, Jr. *Toward Continuous Mission: Strategizing for the Evangelization of Bolivia*. South Pasadena, Calif.: William Carey Library, 1977.

Snyder, Howard A. *The Community of the King*. Downers Grove, Ill.: Inter-Varsity, 1977.

_____. *The Problem of Wine Skins: Church Renewal in a Technological Age*. Downers Grove, Ill.: Inter-Varsity, 1975.

_____. *Liberating the Church: The Ecology of Church and Kingdom*. Downers Grove, Ill.: Inter-Varsity, 1982.

Sobrino, Jon. *The True Church and the Poor*. Maryknoll, N.Y.: Orbis, 1984.

Southard, Samuel. *Training Church Members for Pastoral Care*. Valley Forge, Pa.: Judson, 1982.

Stapert, John. "What Church Cares About Love?" *Church Herald*, 43.12 (27 June 1986): 4–5.

Stott, John R. W. *Christian Mission in the Modern World*. Downers Grove, Ill.: Inter-Varsity, 1975.

_____. "The Living God Is a Missionary God," in: Ralph D. Winter and Steve Hawthord, eds. *Perspectives on the World Christian Movement: A Reader*. South Pasadena, Calif.: William Carey Library, 1981: 10–18.

Sundkler, Bengt G. *The World of Mission*, E. J. Sharpe, trans. Grand Rapids: Eerdmans, 1963.

Surrey, Peter J. *The Small Town Church*. Nashville: Abingdon, 1981.

Thung, Mady A. "An Alternative Model for a Missionary Church: An Approach of the Sociology of Organizations." *Ecumenical Review*, 30.1 (Jan. 1978): 18–31.

_____. *The Precarious Organization: Sociological Explorations of the Church's Mission and Structure*. The Hague: Mouton, 1976.

Tillapaugh, Frank. *The Church Unleashed: Getting God's People Out Where the Needs Are*. Ventura, Calif.: Regal, 1982.

Tollefson, Kenneth. "The Nehemiah Model for Christian Missions." *Missiology*, 15.1 (Jan. 1987): 31–55.

Torrance, Thomas F. "The Mission of the Church." *Scottish Journal of Theology*, 19.2 (June 1966): 129–43.

Torres, Sergio, and John Eagleson, eds. *The Challenge of Basic Christian Communities*, J. Drury, trans. Maryknoll, N.Y.: Orbis, 1981.

Towns, Elmer L., John N. Vaughan, and David J. Seifert. *The Complete Book of Church Growth*. Wheaton, Ill.: Tyndale, 1981.

Trueblood, D. Elton. *The New Man for Our Time*. New York: Harper and Row, 1970.

Valenzuela, Jose Antonio. "Biblia y Unidad de la Iglesia." *Presencia Ecumenica*, 9 (Apr. 1988): 8–13.

Van den Heuvel, Albert H. *The Humiliation of the Church*. Philadelphia: Westminster, 1966.

Van Engen, Charles. "A Portrait of Our Church." Unpublished congregational self-study form, Holland, Mich., 1985.

————. "Church Growth, Yes! But Which Kind?" *Church Herald*, 34.16 (5 Aug. 1977): 12–13, 28.

————. "Get Behind Me, Satan." *Church Herald*, 37.20 (3 Oct. 1980): 10–12, 29.

————. "Let's Contextualize Kingdom Growth." *Church Herald*, 35.22 (3 Nov. 1978): 10–12.

————. "Pastors as Leaders in the Church." *Theology News and Notes* (June 1989): 15–19.

————. *The Growth of the True Church*. Amsterdam: Rodopi, 1981.

————. "The Kind of Men God Calls." *Church Herald*, 30.33 (5 Oct. 1973): 10, 21.

————. "The Reformed Contribution in Mission in the City Tomorrow." Unpublished lecture, Chicago, 1986.

————. "Who Receives the Vision?" *Church Herald*, 30.22 (1 June 1973): 12–14.

————. "Your Church Cannot Grow—Without the Holy Spirit." *Church Herald*, 35.8 (21 Apr. 1978): 6–8.

Van Klinken, Jaap. *Diakonia: Mutual Helping with Justice and Compassion*. Grand Rapids: Eerdmans, 1989.

Verkuyl, Johannes. *Contemporary Missiology: An Introduction*, D. Cooper, trans. Grand Rapids: Eerdmans, 1978.

————. *Break Down the Walls: A Christian Cry for Racial Justice*. Grand Rapids: Eerdmans, 1973.

Vicedom, Georg F. *The Mission of God: An Introduction to a Theology of Mission*, G. A. Thiele, D. Hilgendorf, trans. St. Louis: Concordia, 1965.

Visser T'Hooft, W. A. *The Pressure of Our Common Calling*. New York: Doubleday, 1959.

Voelkel, Jack. *Student Evangelism in a World of Revolution*. Grand Rapids: Zondervan, 1974.

Vos, Geerhardus. *The Teaching of Jesus Concerning the Kingdom and the Church*. Grand Rapids: Eerdmans, 1958.

Wagner, C. Peter. "Aiming at Church Growth in the Eighties." *Christianity Today* (Nov. 21, 1980): 24–27.

————. *Church Growth and the Whole Gospel: A Biblical Mandate*. San Francisco: Harper and Row, 1981.

————. *Leading Your Church to Growth: The Secret of Pastor-People Partnership in Dynamic Church Growth*. Ventura, Calif.: Regal, 1984.

————. *Our Kind of People: The Ethical Dimensions of Church Growth in America*. Atlanta: John Knox, 1979.

————. *Your Church and Church Growth*, packaged set of materials. Pasadena, Calif.: Fuller Evangelistic Association, 1976.

————. *Your Church Can Be Healthy*. Nashville: Abingdon, 1970.

————. *Your Church Can Grow*. Glendale, Calif.: Regal, 1984.

————. *Your Spiritual Gifts Can Help Your Church Grow*. Glendale, Calif.: Regal, 1979.

Wainwright, Geoffrey. *The Ecumenical Moment: Crisis and Opportunity for the Church*. Grand Rapids: Eerdmans, 1983.

Wakatama, Pius. *Independence for the Third World Church: An African's Perspective on Missionary Work*. Downers Grove, Ill.: Inter-Varsity, 1976.

Wallis, Jim. *Agenda for Biblical People*. New York: Harper and Row, 1976.

Walrath, Douglas A. *Leading Churches Through Change*. Nashville: Abingdon, 1979.

————. *New Possibilities for Small Churches*. New York: Pilgrim, 1983.

————. *Planning for Your Church*. Philadelphia: Westminster, 1984.

Warren, M. A. C. "The Missionary Obligation of the Church in the Present Historical Situation." *International Review of Missions*, 39 (Oct. 1950): 393–408.

————. *I Believe in the Great Commission*. Grand Rapids: Eerdmans, 1976.

Wasdell, David. "The Evolution of Missionary Congregations." *International Review of Mission*, 66 (Oct. 1977): 366–72.

Watson, David C. K. *I Believe in the Church*, 1st American ed. Grand Rapids: Eerdmans, 1979.

————. *I Believe in Evangelism*, 1st American ed. Grand Rapids: Eerdmans, 1976.

Webber, George W. *The Congregation in Mission: Emerging Structures for the Church in an Urban Society*. Nashville: Abingdon, 1964.

Webber, Robert E. *The Church in the World: Opposition, Tension, or Transformation?* Grand Rapids: Zondervan, 1986.

Weeden, Larry K., ed. *The Magnetic Fellowship: Reaching and Keeping People*. Waco, Tex.: Word, 1988.

Wells, David. "Reigniting Some Reformation Fire." *Christianity Today*, 24.18 (24 Oct. 1980): 14–19.

Welsh, John R. "Comunidades Eclesiais de Base: A New Way to Be Church."

*America*, 154.5 (8 Feb. 1986): 85–88.

Werning, Waldo J. *Vision and Strategy for Church Growth*. Chicago: Moody, 1977.

Westerhoff, John H., III. *A Pilgrim People: Learning Through the Church Year*. New York: Harper and Row, 1984.

Wieser, Thomas, ed. *Planning for Mission: Working Papers on the New Quest for Missionary Communities*. New York: U.S. Conference, World Council of Churches, 1966.

Williams, Colin W. *The Church*. Philadelphia: Westminster, 1975.

_____. *Where in the World? Changing Forms of the Church's Witness*. New York: National Council of Churches of Christ, 1963.

Wilson, Frederick, ed. *The San Antonio Report: Your Will Be Done. Mission in Christ's Way*. Geneva: World Council of Churches, 1990.

Wilson, Robert L. "How the Church Takes Shape." *Global Church Growth*, 20.6 (Nov.–Dec. 1983): 325–27.

Woelfel, James W. *Bonhoeffer's Theology: Classical and Revolutionary*. Nashville: Abingdon, 1970.

Wofford, Jerry, and Kenneth Kilinski. *Organization and Leadership in the Local Church*. Grand Rapids: Zondervan, 1973.

Womack, David A. *Breaking the Stained-Glass Barrier*. New York: Harper and Row, 1973.

World Alliance of Reformed Churches. "Diakonia 2000: Who Gives? Who Receives?" *Reformed Press Service*, 254 (Jan. 1987): 1–6.

Worley, Robert. *A Gathering of Strangers: Understanding the Life of Your Church*. Philadelphia: Westminster, 1976.

Wuthnow, Robert. "Evangelicals, Liberals, and the Perils of Individualism." *Perspectives* 6.5 (May 1991): 10–13.

Yancey, Philip. "The Shape of God's Body." *Leadership*, 8.3 (Summer 1987): 88–94.

Yoder, John H. "The Experiential Etiology of Evangelical Dualism." *Missiology*, 11.4 (Oct. 1983): 449–59.

_____. *The Politics of Jesus*. Grand Rapids: Eerdmans, 1972.

*Your Kingdom Come: Mission Perspectives; Report on the World Conference on Mission and Evangelism, Melbourne, Australia, 12–25 May, 1980*. Geneva: World Council of Churches, 1980.

Ziegenhals, Walter E. *Urban Churches in Transition: Reflections on Selected Problems and Approaches to Churches and Communities in Racial Transition Based on the Chicago Experience*. New York: Pilgrim, 1978.

Zikmund, Barbara Brown. *Discovering the Church*. Philadelphia: Westminster, 1983.

Zwaanstra, Henry. "Abraham Kuyper's Conception of the Church." *Calvin Theological Journal*, 9 (Apr.–Nov. 1974): 149–81.

_____. "The Reformed Conception of the Church and Its Ecumenical Implications." *Theological Forum*, 10.1, 2 (June 1982): 13–22.

# Subject Index

# Scripture Index